尊像集成

清康熙北京版藏文《甘珠尔》初印本插图

民族文化宫图书馆　版本提供

杨鸿蛟　魏文　导读

中国藏学出版社

藏传佛教
图像学丛书

本辑选题策划

冯良　先巴　魏文

学术统筹

杨鸿蛟　张荣德

满文、蒙古文题记整理、录文

魏建东　蒋雨航　孙赫阳　梅花

藏文题记整理、录文

索南多杰　先巴　仁青卓玛

英文翻译

HUANG Bo

英文译校

张宁

尊名审校

廖旸

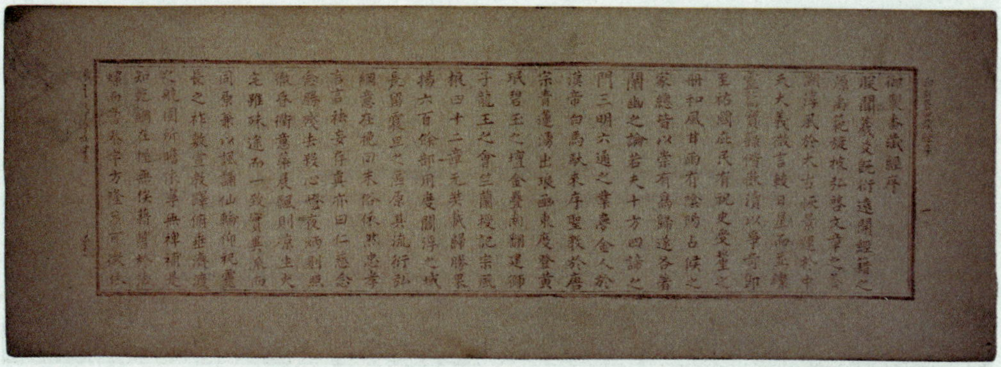

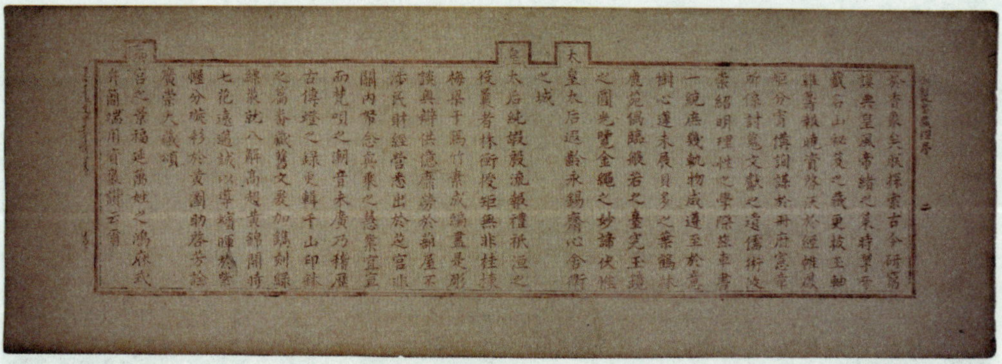

清康熙北京版《甘珠尔》之《御制番藏经序》汉文本

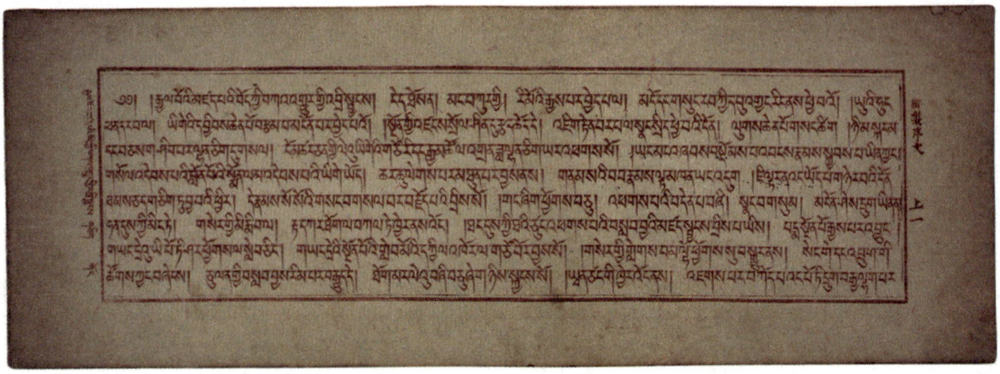

清康熙北京版《甘珠尔》之《御制番藏经序》藏文本首页

清康熙北京版《甘珠尔》之《御制番藏经序》蒙古文本首页

清康熙北京版《甘珠尔》之《御制番藏经序》满文本首页

清康熙北京版《甘珠尔》经墙彩绘

清康熙北京版《甘珠尔》第 20 函（秘密经第十九卷　上一）

清康熙北京版《甘珠尔》第 6 函（秘密经第五卷　上一）扉页

清康熙北京版《甘珠尔》（秘密经第二卷尾）下夹经板插图

清康熙北京版《甘珠尔》（秘密经第七卷）下夹经板插图

【目　录】

六、戒律部　二十六尊

【 Content 】

III. Mahāratnakūṭa Section, 12 icons

IV. Avataṃsaka Section, 12 icons

V. Various Sutras Section, 64 icons

VI. Vinaya Section, 26 icons

导 读

尊像集成：清康熙北京版《甘珠尔》初印本及其经版画

杨鸿蛟 魏文

民族文化宫图书馆（中国民族图书馆）现藏清康熙北京雕印藏文《甘珠尔》朱印本全藏一套（以下简称“康熙北京版”），原为清宫内府旧藏，中华人民共和国成立后由故宫博物院调拨民族文化宫图书馆。该版系康熙二十三年（1684）康熙皇帝为祈愿祖母孝庄文皇后“遐龄永锡”，嫡母孝惠章皇后“纯嘏殷流”特拨内帑虔心雕造，康熙三十一年（1692）已有部分大乘显教经典付梓刷印，至康熙三十九年（1700）全藏方告竣工。刷印装为106函，后又因布顿大师所译“发辫飘举续”（Ral pa gyen brdzes kyi rgyud）占据的经页数量约有一函，因此又增加了一函（Za），形成了107函的总量，宝积部（dKon brtsegs）又增补了两个新文本，同时也通过修补经版的方式进行了千余处订正。[①] 经统计，用梨木经版（尺寸为63×19cm）总共33206块，其所据底本据称为西藏夏鲁寺所藏古写本，实即永乐北京版《甘珠尔》，也就是源自辛岛静志（Seishi Karashima）所谓之《甘珠尔》东部系统蔡巴（Tshal pa）古写本。[②]

康熙北京版全藏共有经典1055部。其中起首为汉、藏、满、蒙古四体对照的数篇序疏，其中包括康熙二十三年八月二十二日康熙皇帝《御制番藏经序》、主持刊刻工作的和硕裕亲王福全（1653—1703）于康熙二十二年

① Bruce C. Hall, *A Descriptive List of the Tibetan (Tib) Collection in the Rare Books Room of the Harvard-Yenching Library*, (Cambridge, MA: 1980), [3]. 民族文化宫图书馆藏康熙北京版《甘珠尔》为完整的一套，共计106函，这是因为目录中记录秘密经为25卷（函），实为24卷（函）。

② 辛岛静志：《论〈甘珠尔〉的系统及其对藏译佛经文献学研究的重要性》，《中国藏学》2014年第3期，第33页；翁连溪：《清代内府刻书图录》，北京出版社，2004年，第23页。

插图一　民族文化宫图书馆藏清康熙北京版《甘珠尔》第 4 函（秘密经第三卷）

（1683）八月十六日所呈《请序疏》、康熙二十二年九月初一日礼部尚书介山等《覆请序疏》及康熙三十九年四月全藏刊成后列出参与编撰的 105 名职官名录。在这以后是经藏正文，内容依次为《秘密部》25 函、《般若部》24 函、《大宝积部》6 函、《华严部》6 函、《诸经部》32 函、《戒律部》13 函，以及康熙三十九年（1700）四月撰写的汉、藏、蒙古、满四种文字对照的《善逝宝经广示目录》（*bDe bar gshegs pavi gsung rab rin po chevi dkar chag bstan pa rgyas pavi nyi vod*）一函，此目为蔡巴 · 贡噶多吉（Tshal pa kun dgav rdo rje，1309—1364）编写，完成于 1323 至 1348 年间。每函由经衣、护经板、经页组成，护经板分上、下两块，长 72 厘米、宽 22 厘米、厚 2.1 厘米，外裱蓝纸，经板内侧正中内凹，作为每函经文首页，两端朱印线刻尊像，其上覆盖黄地暗花如意云纹锦缎经帘，衬里为紫红色绸，[①] 下方护经板印有四尊护法神。经页为双面朱印，四周双栏，栏框左侧刊汉文经名与页码，右侧为藏文经名和页码。经墙绘四角束腰立柱，于四面形成壶门开光，开光内绘制藏传佛教吉祥图案等主题，经墙两侧彩绘缠枝莲托八吉祥纹样，两端分绘三宝珠与拱形背龛，背龛中央书写每函经名。【插图一】

① 外护经板上、下两块，杉木，出脊描金，髹朱漆，长 73.7 厘米、宽 23.3 厘米、厚 2.5 厘米。

民族文化宫图书馆所藏是目前所知仅有的康熙北京版《甘珠尔》初印本全藏，具有十分珍贵的版本学价值，尤其是每部经函扉页朱印线刻的佛教尊像，完整覆刻自永乐版《甘珠尔》的全套尊神图像，共计200余尊。这些图像的内容与风格与永乐版《甘珠尔》别无二致，为我们进一步研究15世纪初宫廷汉藏佛教艺术及其影响提供了全面而典型的图像资料。下文，笔者将从刊刻缘起、版本源流、图像体系、风格来源等几方面予以梳理和介绍。

一、刊刻缘起

据起首的《御制番藏经序》可知，北京版《甘珠尔》的刊刻是由康熙皇帝亲自遴选、和硕裕亲王福全领衔主持，并获颁赐御制序文。最初福全于康熙二十二年八月十六日上疏祈请康熙皇帝为重新刊行番藏御制序文，以昭圣泽：

> 为释藏名经奉命镌梓，恭请御制序文，宣示永久事。窃惟，迦维诞瑞，象法肇开八正五乘，毗邪摩诘授受远矣。自汉帝梦感金仙，遣使天竺，释典诸书之流传于中土者，几二千年，其间虽历唐宋隆盛之朝亦多阐明褒赞，非徒广扬佛教，正欲藉以慈育万有也。恭遇我皇上聪明睿知……，宵衣旰食，勤政爱民，复以万几余闲，研精六经，综览群史，闢图畴未发之渊微，鉴治运相循之理数，以至星官、地志，诸子百家稗乘纬书仙经贝叶，莫不丙夜详探究其旨奥，故能学洞阴阳，博极古今。……重刊番藏名经，用广利益，盖以上凝太皇太后、皇太后万寿无疆之祯，下锡四海臣民亿万载之祉，但四流六度妙理难诠，非得天语发挥，下土尘迷何由共开觉路。昔唐太宗敕名僧，翻译经文六百余部，特制序文；明太祖亲撰佛母像赞；永乐中校刊大藏真经，皆当开国盛时，表章梵典。况我皇上仁敬孝慈，迥非唐明三君所能比拟万一，宸翰所颁，便可烛照诸天，康济率土。伏祈皇上俯念佛果，特赐御制序文，弁诸经首，开示颛蒙，昭垂万禩，庶慧日赖奎章而并焕，慈云同圣泽以长流矣。为此具本谨题请旨。

此请序疏之弘旨在于阐述由帝王亲自为释典刊印作序的意义。一方面，中国古代凡遇盛世明君，尤其是王朝兴始，国运日上时，帝王都会推崇、表彰佛教事业，以期慈悲之力化育群生。另一方面，当时孝庄太皇太后和孝惠章太后在世，以刊印佛经祝厘圣寿绵长，正可借机彰显儒家以孝道治天下的政治观念。由此可见，福全所要表达的是希望通过御制序文宣示皇帝传承中国古代帝王治世的传统，彰显清朝康熙皇帝继承中华正统的合法性。同时，也在暗中称颂清朝为“盛朝”，康熙皇帝为“明君圣主”。

八月十八日，皇帝命礼部详察典例，确议具奏。九月初一日，礼部尚书介山具题本《覆请序疏》称：

> 礼科抄出和硕裕亲王福全等题……臣等，窃惟释典诸书，充牣秘藏，虽教有显、密之分，宗有性、相之异，要其指归，在于利济万品化导群生。历代帝王，往往为之流通宣布，或命翻译，或命镌梓，其教赖以弗替，至于阐物道风恢弘胜果，尤在亲制文辞冠之，简册方足，令神人钦仰，……兹者体天地好生之心，扩圣人止孝之量。上为两宫禔福，下为百姓降祥特命刊刻释藏名经，流通海内。顾释典难诰，梵书乍布，必得天语褒扬，方可炳著日月。允宜俯从，王等所请御制序文冠诸经首，俾琅函宝岌沾被龙光昭示天壤永永无极，诚昌朝之盛事，圣代之旷典也。臣等未敢擅便，谨题旨。

此覆文则以肯定的口吻强化了福全请疏中历代皇帝亲撰序文的意义，进一步申明皇帝亲序可以“上为两宫禔福，下为百姓降祥”，这也是皇家出资刊印佛典的最朴实的初心。九月初四日，康熙皇帝即批复准允恭请御制序事。

翌年，即康熙二十三年八月十三日，康熙皇帝正式颁赐《御制番藏经序》，其文云：

> 朕闻：羲爻既衍，远开经籍之源。禹范旋披，弘启文章之钥。溯淳风于太古，恢景运于中天。大义微言，较日星而并灿。灵篇宝箓，偕岳渎以争奇。既至佑国庇民，有祝史受厘之册。和风甘雨，有阴阳

占候之家。总皆以崇有为归。遂各着阐幽之论。若夫十方四谛之门，三明六通之业。梦金人于汉帝，白马驮来。序圣教于唐宗。青莲涌出，琅函东度，登黄珉碧玉之坛。金迭南翻，建狮子龙王之会。竺兰授记，宗风振四十二章。元奘载归，胜果扬六百余部。用度阎浮之域。长留震旦之区。原其流衍弘网意在挽回末俗。……仰祝灵长之祚。……是知乾纲在握，无俟藉响于法螺。而当泰宇方隆，并可征休于香象矣。朕探索古今，研穷谟典，皇风帝绪之策。……庶几轨物咸遵。至于意树心莲，未展贝多之叶。鹤林鹿苑，偶临般若之台。究玉镜之圆光，览金绳之妙谛。伏惟太皇太后，遐龄永锡，齐心舍卫之城。皇太后，纯嘏殷流。……不涉民财。经营悉出于芝宫，非关内帑。……广崇大藏，颂两宫之景福，延万姓之鸿庥。式弁简端。用资褒讃云尔。

这篇御制序，制以骈文，辞藻华丽，应出自御用文臣之手。而值得我们注意的是，虽是为西番佛教大藏所作序文，却并未将佛教作为文章主旨，亦未见推崇和赞叹佛教的表述。反倒是通篇站在儒家的立场上，从作为“经籍之源”的《周易》起首大加褒扬，又对阴阳占候之家颇为肯定，而后才进一步引入佛教在汉地之历史叙述，显然是将佛教视作阴阳术数之类。且说弘扬佛教无非意在“挽回末俗”，“祝靈長之祚”，而从国家角度看，康熙皇帝“知乾纲在握，无俟藉响于法螺”，对佛教颇有些不屑。文中还进一步描写康熙皇帝孜孜不倦“探索古今”于儒家治世之典，求取“皇风帝续之策”。而对佛教典籍则未曾着意，只是为祈求太皇太后和皇太后“遐齡永錫”“純嘏殷流”才行刊印番经之事，事实上仍是儒家孝道的一种体现。上面这些表述，当与清初儒臣普遍崇尚理学，拒斥佛教，划清儒佛之道有直接关系。突出刊印佛经的孝行因素，以及援引历代帝王崇佛之史事，显然也是刻意营造康熙皇帝中华帝王身份，强调其中华文化正统的一种举措。此外，虽然刊印的是藏文大藏经，但是文中仍以汉地佛教源流作为历史叙述，而未提及任何藏传佛教相关史事，这在某种程度上也反映出儒臣对藏传佛教的一种消极态度。“不涉民财，经营悉出芝官，非关内帑”，也即是指刊经所用一切费资并非民间捐资与国库拨支，而是悉数出自后宫，亦是儒臣所推崇的帝王美德。

根据汉文的职官名录可知，和硕裕亲王福全主要负责领衔总理监造《大藏经》刊刻，监造官员以内阁侍读学士舒辂（šulu）为首，共 30 人；校阅经字喇嘛，以总管京都喇嘛班第查萨克大喇嘛墨尔根绰尔济（jasak da lama mergen corji）为首，番文总教习索诺穆绰尔济（sonom corji）副之。从事具体工作的对读经字喇嘛均为黄寺喇嘛，以根敦达尔扎克龙（gendun darji gelung）为首，共 40 人，对看（总校阅）喇嘛是章嘉胡图克图，下属住持喇嘛王舒（舒的讹字）克津巴格隆（wangšuk jimba gelung）、罗卜藏巴尔柱格隆（lobdzang baljor gelung）等 6 人。监修官以内阁侍读学士食二品俸加四级乌喇代（uladai）为首，共 13 人。校阅序目录官为丹代（dandai）、拜礼（bairi）、翁英（unggin）3 人；翻译番字序目录官为武熙布（usibu）、登德（dengdei）2 人；翻译蒙古字序目录官为喇睦璋（lamjang）、黑钧（hegeo）2 人；满文誊录官为伊巴礼（ibari）、增寿（dzangšeo）、禅布（cambu）3 人；汉文誊录官为曹占吉（tsoo jan gi）、王启沃（wang ki o）2 人。番文誊录喇嘛为罗卜藏鲁雷格隆（lobdzang lurub gelung）、罗卜藏拜尔济格隆（lobdzang bailji gelung）、索那木林亲格隆（sonom rincin gelung）3 人。各项工作共 105 人。这些人是从事核查、校勘、对读、总校阅和把御制序文及《大藏经》目录翻译成藏、蒙古、满、汉四种文体等案头工作，尚不包括从事写版、雕版、裁纸、刷印、装潢、彩绘各项大量具体工作的人员。对看喇嘛（总校阅）为驻京八大胡图克图之首的章嘉胡图克图，依其活动时间推断，应为二世章嘉 · 阿旺罗桑却丹（lCang skya ngag dbang blo bzang chos ldan，1642—1714）。

从藏文题记的角度看，钢和泰男爵曾引用一种北京版《甘珠尔》中的一段题记讨论了北京版《甘珠尔》的刻印人员和时间，并认为康熙三十一年（1692）北京版《甘珠尔》即已刊行于世。[①] 巴多和张智瑜也引用其所见美国哈佛大学燕京图书馆藏第 48 函《第三般若经》同文题记认同这种说法。[②] 此藏文题记汉译如下：

① *On a Peking Edition of the Tibetan Kanjur Which Seems to be Unknown in the West*, pp. 216-217.

② 巴多、张智瑜：《清代官版藏文〈大藏经〉之刊刻考》，《西南民族大学学报（人文社会科学版）》2022 年第 2 期，第 32—33 页。

唵！愿得吉祥！

宿有福泽所生大海中，稀有大悲加持如波涛，祈愿永恒无尽徙多河，浊世众生福泽降殊胜，是时贤劫金色禾穗果，如此妙成经藏之佛语，吉祥殊胜佛宫崇国寺，格隆金巴嘉措等众师，以清净增上意乐之力，令天命金胎康熙宝座，安稳坚固犹如须弥山，以此善我与其他檀越，男男女女之六道众生，去恶趣之束缚得解脱，令速转生于如来净土，佛法总义和文殊怙主，宗喀巴之政教令自在，寿命与权势得愿广大，愿吉祥如意福德圆满！

大清康熙三十一年（1892）阳水猴年宿月①阳水狗胜日肇始，至危宿月②阳土虎喜乐日圆满完成！③

藏文题记下还有一行汉文题记：

大清康熙叁拾壹年仲夏朔日京都崇国寺格龙印吧监佐发心印造。

从此藏、汉跋文可知，崇国寺（vkhrungs kau si），也就是著名的北京藏传佛教寺院大隆善护国寺的一位比丘（dge slong）金巴嘉措（sByin pa rgya mtsho，即汉文之“印吧监佐”）为首的僧团为了祈愿康熙皇帝基业稳固、福寿绵长，施造了这部“经部之甘珠尔”（mdo sdevi bkav vgyur）。

首先要说明的是，西方学者如金 · 史密斯（Gene Smith）、本杰明 · 詹

---

① 此处似为原文笔误，原文作 snrul，当为 snron，即藏历四月十六日至五月十五日，望在心宿。

② 此处似为原文笔误，原文为 mon gru，当为 smin drug，即藏历九月十六日至十月十五日，望在昴宿。

③ 藏文原文：Oṃ swa sti pra dza bhyiḥ/sngon spyad bsod nams las vkhrungs chu gter las // rmad byung thugs rjevi brlabs vphreng cher g.yos te //nam yang zad med smon lam si tāvi klung //snyigs dus skye vgrovi bsod nams zhing mchog tu // babs pavi bskal bzang gser gyi snye mavi vbras // legs par smin pavi mdo sdevi bka vgyur vdi //dpaldan vphags pavi lha khang vkhrungs kau sivi//dge slong sbyin pa rgya mtsho gtso mdzad bavi//dpon slob tshogs kyi lhag bsam dag pavi mthus //gnas bskos gser mngal khang hi gser gyi khrir// ri rab lhun povi lta bu brtan gyur cig [/]/dge vdis bdag sogs rgyu sbyor sbyin bdag dang // pha ma gtso byas vgro drug sems can rnams //gnas ngan len gyi vching ba las grol te //sangs rgyas zhing du myur du skye bar shog / thub bstan spyi dang vjam mgon tsong kha pavi // chos srid zung la dbang bsgyur mes po yi //sku tshe mngav thang srid mthar rgyas pa dang //bkra shis bde legs dpal la spyod par shog /dza yantu / tavi ching khar hi lo sum cu so gcig chu pho sprel lo snrul gyi zla bavi chu pho khyi rgyal gyi nyi ma la dbu gtsugs nas mon gru zla bavi sa pho stag dgav ba nyi mavi bar du legs par bsgrubs pavo /。这也与此版第 48 函《第三般若经》后的藏文和蒙古文跋文内容一致。参见巴多、张智瑜：《清代官版藏文〈大藏经〉之刊刻考》，《西南民族大学学报（人文社会科学版）》，2022 年第 2 期（总第 43 期），第 32 页。

姆斯·诺斯（Benjamin James Nourse）等认定这位金巴嘉措就是曾任第四十六任甘丹赤巴的甘珠尔巴金巴嘉措（bKav vgyur ba sByin pa rgya mtsho，1629—1695）。[①] 这显然与史实不符，因为查甘珠尔巴金巴嘉措之生平，其从未来过北京，也没有更多从事政治事务的历史记载。事实上在文献史料中，清代初期活跃于北京、深入参与沟通清廷与西藏地方政治事务且名金巴嘉措者为藏文材料中记载的巴州活佛色钦曲杰金巴嘉措，然他和蒙古文材料中的席勒图库稜班第大诺们汗乃至伊拉古克三胡图克图等人的史料相互混淆，莫衷一是。[②] 他们活跃的年代都集中在17世纪中期，不大可能晚至17世纪的最后十年。而在康熙朝中期（17世纪末）有一位驻京的次等大喇嘛（可能是副达喇嘛）名"晋巴扎木素"（sbyin pa rgya mtsho）者则最有可能是崇国寺的这位施造者。他和另一位驻京喇嘛乌思尼哈毕咱雅塔（usniq-a bizay-a-yin suburγ-a）之德木齐索诺木臧布曾亲见五世达赖喇嘛，故此在康熙三十五年（1696）被康熙皇帝选中在理藩院主事保住的率领下前往西藏认看五世达赖喇嘛是否仍然在世。[③]

另外，钢和泰男爵等人将这一汉藏文题记理解为崇国寺的金巴嘉措领衔负责刊刻康熙北京版，并在康熙三十一年（1692）完工付梓。《甘珠尔》中大量存在的修版和增加的文本似乎可以理所当然地都被理解为康熙三十九年（1700）基于1692年版的修补版。基于此，钢和泰男爵也注意到了康熙三十九年的汉蒙文题跋中负责刊刻的僧人领衔者中不见金巴加措的名字，他解释这是因为金巴加措的工作并不被宫廷所认可，否则福全不可能忽视他的编辑工作。[④]

这里金巴嘉措领衔的工作从四、五月开始（snrul zla ba[*snron gyi zla ba]）到九、十月（mon gru zla ba[*smin drug zla ba]）结束，这么短的时间大

---

① Benjamin James Nourse, *Canons in Context: A History of the Tibetan Buddhist Canon in the Eighteenth Century*, M.A., University of Virginia, 2009, pp.92-94.

② 陈小强：《金巴嘉措喇嘛事迹考》，《民族史研究》，1999年，第347—359页；若松宽：《〈锡勒图库伦喇嘛传汇典〉初探》，《蒙古学信息》1999年第4期，第18—24页。

③《朔漠方略》卷二十八，第二十四至二十五页载"晋巴扎木素、德木齐索诺木两喇嘛但为彼识达赖喇嘛之面而差之耳。非为行事也。保住联简用尔，此行事关重大。"转引自宝音特古斯：《十八世纪初期卫拉特、西藏、清朝关系研究——以"六世达赖喇嘛事件"为中心》，内蒙古大学博士学位论文，2009年，第16页。司空竺通过检索 Zahiruddin Ahmad 的专著也提到了此人，但仍然着重转引了著名学者金·史密斯（Gene Smith）的观点。

④ *On a Peking Edition of the Tibetan Kanjur Which Seems to be Unknown in the West*, p.220-221, note 1.

概只能是印造，而不可能是雕版，从其下方的汉文题跋也有所体现。而且藏文题记明确说所造之经典系“经部之甘珠尔”，并非包含密续在内的全帙《甘珠尔》，且事实上并非如司空竺（Jonathan A. Silk）在补注中所说的那样，似乎在《甘珠尔》的每一函末尾皆有此题记。[①] 事实上目前所见只出现在般若经部分的末尾（第三甘珠尔经后）。这说明，钢和泰男爵所谓1692年版的《甘珠尔》原本就是不存在的一个概念，当时康熙北京版工程大概只是完成了部分显教经典的刊刻，金巴嘉措并未参与此项工程。他只是作为一个施印者基于某种原因（如为康熙皇帝祈福）未等全藏刊刻、校订完毕，就率先印出一部。因此，他的名字自然也不可能出现在1700年全藏完成后的职官名录中。

二、版本源流

康熙北京版刊刻地为番经厂，后改建为章嘉活佛在京驻锡寺庙嵩祝寺，[②] 因此又被称为嵩祝寺版《甘珠尔》。经版据说保存在北海的大西天大圆镜智宝殿，惜光绪二十六年（1900）八国联军荼毒北京时连同殿宇一并毁损，至民国二十六年（1937）又遭火焚，故只残存少量经版仍藏故宫博物院。[③]

值得特别注意的是，康熙北京版的存世版本并不单一。因为北京版先后在康熙五十六年（1717）、康熙五十九年（1720）、乾隆二年（1737）前后三次进行过厘定，修订了上千处讹误，因而产生了众多的递修本。民族宫所藏的这套康熙北京版从版本上看，与其他版本最大的不同之处在于其每函上夹经板线刻尊像均覆刻自永乐版《甘珠尔》，这是康熙北京版初印本最明显的版本特征。

① *On a Peking Edition of the Tibetan Kanjur Which Seems to be Unknown in the West*, p.216，司空竺注C.

② 嵩祝寺，位于北京地安门内三眼井胡同东门，今已不存。该寺建于康熙五十一年（1712），为清廷赐予章嘉活佛在京的驻锡寺庙。

③ 翁连溪：《清内府刻书研究》，紫禁城出版社，2013年，第133—134页。乾隆三十四年（1769），乾隆皇帝曾下旨典查北京各处所藏书版情形，其中查得嵩祝寺和护国寺仅有藏文和四样字版3111块，内缺119块，而在大西天收贮番藏经版共280083块，作为番经厂的嵩祝寺仅有如此少量的经版实在令人费解，合理的解释是番经厂改为章嘉的座寺后，番经厂的功能也被取代，经厂库藏经版都转至北海保存。见中国第一历史档案馆藏奏销档胶片93，转引自翁连溪：《清代内府刻书图录》，北京出版社，2004年，附录第20页。

康熙北京版是在清宫第一次开雕大藏经，因此主要是在前人的基础上开展工作。当时可资利用的最好印本当即永乐版《甘珠尔》(抑或是永乐版的覆刻本万历版，存疑)。故此，康熙北京版在文字和图像上都与永乐版存在密切关系，显然是顺理成章的事情。至康熙五十六年，清廷开始雕造蒙古文《甘珠尔》，继而在康熙六十年(1721)续雕藏文《丹珠尔》，前者是史无前例的工作，而后者则几乎无从承续前人成果，因为所谓的北京万历版《丹珠尔》极为罕见。可以说，这两次刻印经典的活动是清代宫廷作坊之原创，在装帧上自然开始完全反映作为刊刻施主的清代统治者，以及作为主要施印者的蒙古贵族的审美倾向，故两部经典的扉页绘画完全是纯然清代佛教艺术的风格。康熙北京版《甘珠尔》亦恰好在此时进行了修订改版工作，故此将永乐版样式的版画全部撤去，换成了与这两部藏经完全一致风格的线刻版画，亦在情理之中。

民族文化宫图书馆收藏的这部《甘珠尔》系由故宫博物院调拨，目前故宫还保存有一套完整的北京版《甘珠尔》，然非初印本。据说中国国家图书馆和雍和宫依旧保存有1700年刷印的北京版全帙，然是否确为初印本则未可知。日本大谷大学收藏有1717年至1720年刷印的北京版《甘珠尔》，其影印本于1955—1958年在日本出版，是目前学术界流通最广、最为常用的一套北京版《甘珠尔》。蒙古乌兰巴托国家图书馆亦藏同一时代印制的版本，已经以光碟的形式行布于世。[①] 法国国立图书馆则藏有乾隆二年(1736)刷印的版本。此外，据说北京版《甘珠尔》还有1763年或1765年重印的版本，但具体情况不明。其余所见，皆是卷帙阙损本甚至零本，散存于各大图书馆和民间。由此可见，作为目前仅见的北京版初印本全藏，民族文化宫图书馆所藏版本的价值尤为珍贵。

清代康熙北京版是对明初永乐版《甘珠尔》的覆刻，因此内容编排几乎完全一致。在永乐版《甘珠尔》刊印之前，西藏共编订过三个版本的《甘珠尔》，分别为最早的那塘手写本，由13世纪末[元皇庆二年(1313)，一说1315年，至延祐七年(1320)]那塘寺堪布迥丹日白热

① *The Tempangma Manuscript of the Kangyur, The Peking Edition of the Kangyur, held at the National Library of Mongolia*, Digitally published and distributed by Digital Preservation Society(DPS), Tokyo 2010. 参看 http://www.tibet-dps.org/ 经叶尺寸为 71.7cm×21.2cm。

赤（bCom ldan rig pavi ral gri，1227—1305）及其弟子琛·绛白央（mChims vJam dpal dbyangs，？—1267）、卫巴洛赛（dBus pa blo gsal）的主持下，抄写各地经、律、密咒，收集整理编订，称“那塘古版”《甘珠尔》，现已失传；14世纪前期，夏鲁寺布顿·仁钦珠（Bu ston Rin chen grub，1290—1364）在那塘《甘珠尔》基础上编定夏鲁版《甘珠尔》；在拉萨蔡贡塘寺（Tshal gung thang），万户长门朗多吉（sMan lam rdo rje）于1310—1328年下令编纂《甘珠尔》，后在1347—1351年由蔡巴·贡噶多吉（Tshal pa Kun dgav rdo rje，1309—1364）等编纂，写造了一部完整的《甘珠尔》，并请布顿·仁钦珠校订，贡噶多吉自己编辑了目录，此版共250函，现亦不传。从这部蔡巴《甘珠尔》派生出如下两个系统：一是从永乐版《甘珠尔》（1410）开始的北京版系统。另外一个是钦瓦达孜（Phying ba stag rtse）《甘珠尔》（疑已佚失）。

13世纪以前，藏文大藏经主要以手抄本的形式流传。到了15世纪，第一部印版《甘珠尔》方才问世。此版刊刻于明永乐八年（1410），永乐皇帝为他刚刚逝去的妃子徐氏追求冥福，派专使入藏，将蔡巴《甘珠尔》手抄本带回南京开雕制版。此前，五世噶玛巴活佛得银协巴（bDe bzhin gshegs pa，1384—1415）赴南京，于灵谷寺建普度大斋，资福太祖高皇帝、孝慈高皇后，永乐皇帝请他担任刊刻《甘珠尔》的总纂。每一函均有明成祖所作的《大明皇帝御制藏经赞》及《御制后序》。[①]现经版已佚，印本传世者不多。永乐帝曾分别于永乐十一年（1413）和十四年（1416）赐给大乘法王贡噶扎西（Kun dgav bkra shis）与大慈法王释迦也失（Śakya ye shes）各一套，现各保存于布达拉宫和色拉寺，前者现存106函，后者现存103函。近年又在拉卜楞寺发现一套永乐版《甘珠尔》，只遗失一函。永乐版《甘珠尔》编撰体例与内容对后世的明代景泰泥金写本《甘珠尔》、万历版印本《甘珠尔》、清代康熙《龙藏经》产生了深远影响。

明景泰年间抄写的泥金写本《甘珠尔》原藏故宫中正殿某处，1923年建福宫大火时仅有少数被救出火场，现存故宫博物院图书馆。其所参照的

① 龙达瑞：《波兰亚盖隆大学藏万历版〈甘珠尔〉》，《西南民族大学学报（人文社会科学版）》2017年第1期，第88—93页。周润年：《藏文〈甘珠尔〉的特色》，第三届两岸西藏学研讨会，2009年6月12日，淡江大学西藏研究中心，2009年，第3—4页。

底本可能即是永乐版《甘珠尔》或者永乐版《甘珠尔》的母本。据说孝庄太皇太后于宫廷库房中看到明景泰年间抄写的泥金写本《甘珠尔》，见其已破损不堪，遂命康熙帝遣人重新缮抄。康熙八年（1669）完成，称《龙藏经》，共 108 函，用泥金写成，现收藏于台北故宫博物院，其书写风格、装帧式样几乎全仿景泰泥金写本。①

万历版《甘珠尔》系明万历三十三（1605）以永乐版《甘珠尔》为底本，进行少量修改，在北京重新刊刻，为第二部印版《甘珠尔》②，共 105 函。翌年刊刻《丹珠尔》中的 42 函。现原版无存，仅存少量印本。最近在波兰的克拉科夫（Cracow）雅盖隆（Jagiellonian）大学图书馆发现了不少万历版残片。③

三、图像体系

康熙北京版《甘珠尔》为藏文长条书样式，每叶纵横 14.2 × 58.2 厘米，梵夹装，每函由经衣、护经板和经页组成，较北京故宫藏本少了上下髹朱漆的外护经板。经衣为黄色方形织物，上下护经板以蓝黄两色纸装裱，内页均中间开“合欢门”，覆锦缎经帘，上护经板内页也即扉页，正中为经文题名，两端饰佛教尊像，共计 210 尊。由于为明初永乐版《甘珠尔》的覆刻版本，因此康熙北京版在版本特征上与永乐版《甘珠尔》如出一辙，尤其在藏文字体样式与上夹经板线刻佛像风格上，两者几乎达到了无法分辨的地步，惟妙惟肖地反映出明代初年汉藏佛教艺术风格的典型风貌。进一步细致比对后，会发现两者也存在细微差异，即康熙北京版在每页内文外围增加了边框，并且下护经板增刻财续天母、偌玛堤天母、六臂怙主、黄财神等纯然清代汉藏风格的尊像。

① 李若愚：《火场遗珠——故宫博物院藏景泰七年〈甘珠尔〉经考述》，《故宫博物院院刊》2023 年第 9 期，第 119—127 页。

② 17 世纪前期至 18 世纪前期，产生了多种印版《甘珠尔》，先后有理塘版、卓尼版、北京版、那塘版、德格版等。20 世纪 20 年代又有拉萨版《甘珠尔》出现，是迄今为止最后一部木刻版《甘珠尔》。嘉措、平措、噶玛、丹达、建瓴、丹扎：《拉萨现藏的两部永乐版〈甘珠尔〉》，《文物》1985 年第 9 期，第 85—88、104 页。

③ Mejor M, Helman-Ważny A, Chashab T K, *A Preliminary Report on the Wanli Kanjur: Kept in the Jagiellonian Library, Kraków*, Research Centre of Buddhist Studies, Faculty of Oriental Studies, University of Warsaw, 2010. 另在柏林国家图书馆（Staatsbibliothek zu Berlin）藏有一套《甘珠尔》为 1680 年刊印，这套《甘珠尔》基于万历版《甘珠尔》。

扉画尊像题材涵盖佛、菩萨、本尊、护法、佛母诸多类别，其中佛尊数量与种类居多，初步辨认出的有十方佛、药师七佛、贤劫千佛、三十五佛、三世佛以及《五千五百佛名神咒除障灭罪经》所出诸佛等等。通过比对尊像与康熙北京版全藏目录也即《善逝宝经广示目录》可知，两者关系密切，这些尊像神系的排布主要是对康熙北京版经文内容的图像化，同时继承了早期藏传佛教尊像题材尤其是佛经插图神系的传统。现即以康熙北京版经文内容分类为框架来梳理和释读扉画尊像排布规律与宗教义理。

（一）金刚果乘续部（秘密部）

按此《甘珠尔》之目录《善逝宝经广示目录》，依经典学说见地不同将经典分为密、显两类，即金刚果乘续部（gsang sngags vbras buvi theg pa rgyud kyi dbye ba）与有相因乘经部（mtshan nyid rgyuvi theg pa mdovi dbye ba）。秘密部也即金刚果乘续部，又分为无上瑜伽本续（rnal vbyor chen po bla na med pavi rgyud）、瑜伽本续（rnal vbyor gyi rgyud）、行续（spyod pavi rgyud）、事续（bya bavi rgyud）、旧译密咒（gsang sngags snga vgyur）、现世备急（gnas skabs su nyer mkhovi dbye ba）六种。[①] 每一种密续再渐次细分。

其中，无上瑜伽本续又再分三类，即方便智慧无二本续（thabs shes gnyis su med povi rgyud）、智慧瑜伽母本续（shes rab rnal vbyor mavi rgyud）与方便瑜伽父本续（thabs rnal vbyor phavi rgyud）。秘密部第一函左右两侧扉画分别为文殊智慧萨埵（梵文：Mañjuśrījñānasattva，藏文：vJam dpal ye shes sems dpav）与时轮金刚（梵文：Śrīkālacakra，藏文：dPal dus kyi vkhor lo）两尊，主要对应方便智慧无二本续经典尊神。文殊智慧萨埵尊像名号出自位列康熙北京版秘密部诸密续之首，被誉为一切密续最殊胜的根本经典《文殊智勇识真实名赞》[②]，即汉译《圣妙吉祥真实名经》(《大正藏》1190)，以阐扬文殊师利菩萨智慧及如何获证智慧菩提为经义主旨。文殊智慧萨埵是这部密续最为重要的主尊，因此其图像被置于开篇。尊像一面四臂，菩

① 胡进杉：《台北故宫所藏〈善逝宝经广示日光目录〉述要》，《法光学坛》，台北：法光杂志社，2003 年，第 7 期，第 47—76 页。

② 北京版 No.2, rgyud, ka, 1b1-15b7 (vol.1, p.117)（梵文：*Mañjuśrījñānasattvasya paramārtha nāma saṁgīti*，藏文：*vJam dpal ye shes sems dpavi don dam pavi mtshan yang dag par brjod pa*）。

萨装，四手分持剑、经书、弓与箭，其图像特征与《成就法鬘》(梵文：Sādhanamālā）中真实名文殊（Nāmasaṁgīti Mañjuśrī）成就法相近似，仅在面数上有所区别，《成就法鬘》所收真实名文殊为三面[①]。【图版 001L】时轮金刚（梵文：Śrīkālacakra，藏文：dPal dus kyi vkhor lo）则为以《本续王吉祥时轮》[②] 为代表的时轮密续经典的重要主尊，为藏传佛教密宗四续中最崇高的无上瑜伽密之无二续本尊，故于此绘其身像。此时轮金刚一面二臂三目，持金刚铃杵交拥佛母，左腿屈，右腿伸，分踏白色大自在天与爱欲母。佛母为诸相佛母，手持钺刀与嘎巴拉碗，以两腿右屈左伸之姿站立。【图版 001R】

接续下来的智慧瑜伽母本续主尊上乐金刚（梵文：Cakrasaṃvara，藏文：bDe mchog）与喜金刚（梵文：Hevajra，藏文：Kyevi rdo rje）及其各自佛母金刚亥母（梵文：Vajravārāhī，藏文：Phag mo）和无我母（梵文：Nairātmyā，藏文：bDag med）则分别对应排在秘密部第二、三函扉画中【图版 002L— 003R】，方便瑜伽父本续主尊秘密集会不动金刚（梵文：Guhyasamāja-Akṣobhyavajra，藏文：gSang vdus mi skyod rdo rje）与秘密集会文殊金刚（梵文：Guhyasamāja-Mañjuvajra，藏文：gSang vdus vjam dpal rdo rje）则出现于秘密部第七函函首左右扉画中。值得指出的是，尊像的排布顺序虽然是按照密续分类排布的，但并非严格对应每一函经典，例如秘密集会金刚所对应的密续经典《佛说一切如来金刚三业最上秘密大教王经》主要是在秘密部的第五函[③]。

从图像上来看，秘密部第十一函的毗卢遮那（梵文：Vairocana，藏文：rNam snang）与金刚萨埵（梵文：Vajrasattva，藏文：rDo rje sems dpav）以及第十三函的毗卢遮那和普觉众明主佛（梵文：Vairocana，藏文：rNam snang）则分别作为瑜伽本续与行续的代表尊神出现。【图版 011L— 011R、

① Benoytosh Bhattacharyya, *Sādhanamālā*, Baroda, Oriental Institute, 1925, pp.159-160, no. 82: āryanāmasaṅgītisādhanaṃ samāptam.

② 北京版 No. 4, rgyud, ka, 23b1-141b8 (vol.1, p.127)（梵文：*Parama-ādibuddhoddhrita-śrī-kālacakra-nāma-tantrarājā*，藏文：*mChog gi dang povi sangs rgyas las phyung ba rgyud kyi rgyal po dpal dus kyi vkhol lo*）。

③ 北京版 No. 81, rgyud, ca, 95b5-167a8 (vol.3, p.174)（梵文：*Sarvatathāgatakāyavākcittarahasyo guhyasamāja-nāma-mahā-kalparāja*，藏文：*De bzhin gshegs pa thams cad kyi sku gsung thugs kyi gsang chen gsang ba vdus pa zhes bya ba brtag pavi rgyal po chen po*）。

图版 013L— 013R】

事续经典在主体上又分为如来部（bde bzhin gshegs pavi rigs）、莲花部（pad mavi rigs）和金刚部（rdo rjevi rigs），而从秘密部第十四至二十四函扉画中所现尊像应属此续尊神【图版 014L— 024L】，如从属于如来部密续的药师佛、文殊菩萨、摩利支天、顶髻尊胜佛母、大白伞盖佛母[①]，从属于莲花部的无量寿佛、白度母、但木度母[②]等。

（二）有相因乘经部

康熙北京版中的般若部、大宝积部、华严部、诸经部主要统摄于有相因乘经部，从教理上有相因乘经部可分为中转无相法轮次第（bkav bar ba mtshan nyid med pavi chos kyi vkhor lo bskor bavi rim pa）、三转决定胜义法轮次第（bkav vkhor lo gsum pa don dam rnam par nges pavi chos kyi vkhor lo bskor bavi rim pa）、初转四谛法轮次第（bkav vkhor lo dang po bden pa bzhivi chos kyi vkhor lo bskor bavi rim pa）三类。《甘珠尔》中的般若部《般若波罗蜜多经》（*Shes rab kyi pa rol du phyin pa*）十万颂、二万五千颂、一万八千颂、一万颂等经典隶属于中转无相法轮次第；华严部《大方广佛华严经》（*Sangs rgyas phal po che zhes bya ba shin tu rgyas pa chen povi mdo*）、宝积部（dkon mchog brtsegs pavi bskor）《圣大宝积法门十万颂》（*vPhags pa dkon mchog brtsegs pa chen povi chos kyi rnam grangs levu stong phrag brgya pa*）以及大

① 出自密续经典《药师琉璃光七佛本愿功德经》（梵文：*ārya-nīlāmbaradharavajrapāṇi-kalpa-nāma-dhāraṇī*，藏文：*vPhags pa lag na rdo rje gos sngon po can gyi cho ga zhes bya bavi gzungs*）、《文殊根本续》（梵文：*ārya-mañjuśrīmūlatantra*，藏文：*vPhags pa vjam dpal gyi rtsa bavi rgyud*）、《摩利支天陀罗尼》（梵文：*ārya-mārīcī-nāma-dhāraṇī*，藏文：*vPhags ma vod zer can zhes bya bavi gzungs*）、《最圣灭除一切恶趣尊胜顶髻陀罗尼》（梵文：*ārya-sarvadurgatipariśodhani-uṣṇīṣavijaya-nāma-dhāraṇī*，藏文：*De bzhin gshegs pa thams cad kyi gtsug tor rnam par rgyal ba zhes bya bavi gzungs rtog pa dang bcas pa*）、《一切如来顶髻中出现白伞盖无敌回遮大明咒佛母陀罗尼》（梵文：*ārya-sarvatathāgatoṣṇīṣasitātapatrā-nāma-aparājitāpratyaṁgiramahāviidyārājñī*，藏文：*vPhags pa de bzhin gshegs pa thams cad kyi gtsug tor nas byung ba gdugs dkar mo can zhes bya ba gzhan gyis mi thub ma phyir zlog pavi rig sngags kyi rgyal mo chen mo*），参看北京版 No. 132, rgyud, da, 161a8-162a8 (vol.6, p.98)、No. 162, rgyud, na, 45b4-299a6 (vol.6, p.168)、No. 182, rgyud, pha, 160a4-161a5 (vol.7, p.140)、No. 197, rgyud, pha, 221b7-226b5 (vol.7, p.164)、No. 202, rgyud, pha, 243a3-251a3 (vol.7, p.173)。

② 出自密续经典《大乘无量寿经》（梵文：*ārya-aparimitāyurjñāna-nāma-mahāyāna-sūtra*，藏文：*vPhags pa tshe dang ye shes dpag tu med pa zhes bya ba theg pa chen povi mdo*）、《一切如来救度佛母种种出现本续》（梵文：*sarvatathāgatamātanitāre viśvakarmabhava-tantra-nāma*，藏文：*De bzhin gshegs pa thams cad kyi yum sgrol ma las sna tshogs vbyung ba zhes bya bavi rgyud*），参看北京版 No. 361, rgyud, ba, 243b6-249a5 (vol.7, p.301)、No. 390, rgyud, tsa, 58a5-74a8 (vol.8, p.149)。

乘诸经部（theg pa chen povi mdo sde sna tshogs kyi bskor）、《贤劫经》（*sKal pa bzang po*）、《广大游戏大乘经》（*rGya cher rol pa*）、《解深密经》（*dGongs pa nges par vgrel ba*）、《入楞伽经》（*Lang kar gshegs pa*）、《妙法莲花经》（*Dam pavi chos padma dkar po*）、《大涅槃经》（*Mya ngan las vdas pa chen movi mdo*）、《一切法自性平等戏论禅定王经》（*Chos thams cad kyi rang bzhin mnyam pa nyid rnam par spros pa ting nge vdzin gyi rgyal po*）等经典从属于三转决定胜义法轮次第；小乘诸经部（theg pa chung nguvi mdo sde sna tshogs kyi bskor）的《大正法念住经》（*Dam pavi chos dran pa nyer bzhag chen po*）、《大幻化网经》（*mDo chen mo sgyu mavi dra ba*）、《大空经》（*mDo chen po stong pa nyid chen po*）等与戒律部（vdul bavi bskor）的《戒律事》（*Lung sde bzhi*）、《律分别》（*Lung rnam vbyed*）、《律杂事》（*Lung phran tshegs*）等经典从属于初转四谛法轮次第。

然而，与秘密部不同的是，般若部、大宝积部、华严部、诸经部四部经典的扉画图像并非按经典内容顺序排列，而是将有相因乘经部作为一个整体，择其重要典籍尊像加以排布。例如，在般若部（共 24 函计 48 幅扉画尊像）中开篇为释迦牟尼佛与观音菩萨【图版 025L— 025R】组合，继承了早期梵文贝叶《般若经》图像传统，其后为药师七佛中的法海胜慧游戏神通佛（梵文：Dharmasāgarāgramativikrīḍitābhijñārāja，藏文：Chos rgya mtsho mchog gi blo rnam par rol pa mngon par mkhyen pa）与法海雷音佛（梵文：Dharmakīrtisāgaraghoṣa，藏文：Chos bsgrags rgya mtsho），《金光明经》中宝髻佛（梵文：Ratnaśikhī，藏文：Rin chen gtsug tor can），弥勒（梵文：Maitreya，藏文：Byams pa mgon po），燃灯佛（梵文：Dīpaṃkara，藏文：Mar me mdzad），无量寿佛（梵文：Amitāyus，藏文：Tshe pag med），不动佛（梵文：Akṣobhya，藏文：Mi bskyod pa），不空成就佛（梵文：Amoghasiddhi，藏文：Don yod grub pa）【图版 026L— 027L、030R、031L— 032R】，以及西藏《般若经》常见的释迦牟尼佛与般若佛母的组合【图版 043L— 043R、047L— 047R】。值得注意的是般若部中有五尊佛尊系出自诸经部《五千四百五十三佛名经》[①]，即雷音妙音王佛（vBrug sgra sgra dbyangs kyi rgyal po）、遍知佛（mngon par mkhyen pa）、义成释迦王佛（Don gyis kun grub shag kyavi rgyal po）、宝王藏佛（Rin chen rgyal bavi mdzod）与妙吉祥佛（vJam pavi dbyangs）五尊【图版 033L— 034R、035R】。在华严部（共 6 函计 12 幅扉画尊像）的十二幅尊像中有九尊为贤劫千佛，则是出自诸经部《贤劫经》【图版 056L— 060L】。而在诸经部尊像排布则较为整体而鲜明，主要为三十五佛、十方佛、药师七佛以及过去七佛等佛尊组合【图版 061L— 103R】。

（三）下夹经板护法尊

另在各经函下夹经板上饰有清代宫廷风格的朱印线刻财续天母、偌玛堤天母、六臂怙主、黄财神等尊像，主要为两类，即六臂大黑天及眷属五尊与金刚大自在天等五尊，其造像风格与清康熙八年写造完成的藏文《龙藏经》中第二函与第七函经板彩绘尊像的尊格和绘制风格基本一致。

六臂大黑天及眷属五尊主要包括：六臂大黑天（满文：Itekel mahag'ala，蒙古文：Itegel maqak'ala，藏文：mGon po phyag drug pa）及其眷属欲帝明王（满文：Ragirandza，蒙古文：Raki ranza，藏文：Ta ki rA dza/ vdod pavi rgyal po）、护国护法（满文：Zarabala，蒙古文：Zar-a bala，藏文：KShe Ta pa la）、尊亲护法（满文：Zi namira 蒙古文：Zi namira，藏文：Dzi na mi tra/ Zhing skyong/ rGyal bavi bshes gnyen）和大黑雄威护法（满文：Rakšad g'ala，蒙古文：Raγšad k'ala，藏文：Drag sha nag po）【图版 002b-1—002b-5】。

金刚大自在天等五尊主要有：铜衣天女（满文：Sanggi gusjuma，蒙古文：Sanggi guszum-a，藏文：Zang gi gos gyon ma）、珍宝大自在天（梵文：Maharatnesvara，满文：Maha ratna šowari，蒙古文：Ma ha radna šünri，藏文：Rin chen dbang chen）、金刚大自在天（梵文：Mahavajresvara，满文：Maha bazar šowari，蒙古文：Ma ha bazar šünri，藏文：rDo rje dbang chen）、事业大自在天（梵文：Mahakarmesvara，满文：Maha germa šowari，蒙古

① 即《五千五百佛名神呪除障灭罪经》，梵文：*buddhanāmasahasrapañcaśatacaturtripañcadaśa*，藏文：*Sangs rgyas kyi mtshan lnga stong bzhi brgya lnga bcu rtsa gsum pa*，参见北京版 No. 928, mdo sna tshogs, zu, 1b1-100a7 (vol.36, p.269)。

文：Ma ha k’arm-a šünri，藏文：Phrin las dbang chen）、玉衣天女（满文：Gioi gusjuma，蒙古文：Gioi guszum-a，藏文：g.Yuvi gos gyon ma）等五尊【图版 007b-1—007b-5】。

四、风格来源

《甘珠尔》扉画中，除第二十三函释迦牟尼佛与观音菩萨及其胁侍图像为康熙时期新造外，其余均为永乐版的覆刻图像，因此其扉画图像风格主体为明代永乐时期的藏传佛教造像风格。覆刻本也即翻刻本，是照所依底本原样翻雕，康熙北京版在保持永乐版《甘珠尔》藏文字体与版式样式的基础上，在每页内文外围增加了边框。

康熙北京版扉画尊像主体突出，下承单层或双层覆莲莲台，莲瓣为五瓣或七瓣不等，背后承托圆拱形背光或立柱承托的三联拱形背龛。进一步比对之后会发现，这些覆刻图像在风格样貌上还存在细微差别，主要体现在寂静相与忿怒相的图像中。以佛、菩萨为主体的寂静相尊像，画面多以宝瓶莲花立柱承托的三联拱门为背龛，其后装饰满密的放射形背光、云纹、植物和山石纹样，尊像衣饰上尤其乐于强调衣褶堆叠帛带飘逸的质感，体现出鲜明的汉地艺术风格【图版 001L】；而以本尊护法为主体的忿怒相尊像，背景画面一般简素，仅饰一圈圆拱形背光，尊像四肢粗壮、面容饱满、装饰细密精道，保留了浓郁的尼泊尔造像艺术风格【图版 002L】。

对于前一种样式，海瑟·噶尔美最先将其与创作于 1427 年的江孜白居寺壁画建立联系，指出永乐版《甘珠尔》插图中的三联拱形背龛和两侧由宝瓶柱基承托、顶饰莲花柱头的立柱等元素均可以在白居寺壁画与雕塑中找到相似的例证，这些元素最早在 10 世纪尼泊尔手抄本插图中即有出现。对于永乐版《甘珠尔》插图中尊像背光两侧珠宝嵌饰的三角形焰肩，海瑟也指出是白居寺壁画中的常见元素，并可以追溯至波罗时代的佛教造像。海瑟认为永乐版《甘珠尔》插图融合了汉地艺术特征，反映了同时期西藏中部的造像艺术特征。①

① ［法］海瑟·噶尔美著，熊文彬译：《早期汉藏艺术》，北京：中国藏学出版社，1994 年，第 112—114 页。

插图二　夏鲁寺三门殿西壁
杰尊喜饶迥乃壁画背龛柱式
13 世纪末 14 世纪初

插图三　舞立姿象鼻天
15 世纪中叶
布本设色
西藏中部
68×59 厘米
私人收藏

本文也是在此研究基础上，进一步对其图像元素与风格来源进行探讨。如上所述，从构图风格来讲，康熙北京版《甘珠尔》插图可以分为繁复满密与简素两种风格，在数量上以前者为主体，二百余幅插图中仅有 14 幅为简素的构图风格。而从背龛和背光样式上来看，则主要分为三种，即立柱承托的三联拱形背龛、马蹄形背光以及拱券形背光。

1. 样式 I：立柱承托的三联拱形背龛

这种样式是康熙北京版《甘珠尔》插图构图背景的主体，210 幅插图中，计有 149 幅为这一样式【图版 001L— 001R、004L— 005R、008L— 008R、011L— 014L、015L— 017R、020L— 020R、023L— 024R、043L— 046R、048L— 105R】。背龛主要由两侧立柱与三联拱形龛楣组成，立柱以宝瓶柱

插图四　白居寺祖拉康一层金刚殿壁画（1418—1425）

基，宝瓶中生出的莲茎为柱身，莲茎上再分支出莲花与莲叶，上部以圆形花冠为柱头，顶为托木形制的花台，用以承托上部的三联拱形龛楣；限于画面空间，两侧立柱均表现的是纵立面上的一半。这种龛柱样式是尼泊尔绘画中的重要元素，至少在 14 世纪初夏鲁寺壁画中即已出现【插图二】，但其上多承以装饰华丽的摩羯鱼卷草的拱形龛楣。到了 15 世纪，这一元素在藏传佛教艺术图像中更为流行，也更趋装饰性【插图三】，其上承托的龛楣样式也更为多样，依龛中尊像尊格高低，或繁或简，其中简洁的联拱形龛楣十分习见【插图四】。然而在形制上康熙北京版《甘珠尔》插图中的三联拱形龛楣略有不同，龛楣两端多向内卷曲，有的也向外卷曲【图版 066R、089L】，有的还在尾部装饰以如意云头【图版 070L】，这一形制更接近于白居寺祖拉康道果殿上师塑像中汉式座椅上端的三联拱形搭脑与吉祥多门塔五层四无量宫殿门楣形制【插图五、六】。

这一样式的插画构图虽满密，但通过佛龛与中央主尊背光之间的遮挡关系，增强了画面的层次感与空间感。一般寂静尊的主尊头光与身光内部光素无饰，身光两侧饰三角形焰肩，或为珠宝组成，或内饰刻划纹。海瑟

插图五　白居寺祖拉康二层道果殿祖师塑像（1425—1436）

插图六　白居寺吉祥多门塔五层南无量宫三联拱形门楣

插图七　南宋刻本《佛说寿生经》

插图八　尼泊尔《般若八千颂》经板彩画（10—11 世纪）

插图九　夏鲁寺般若佛母殿壁画（1027）

指出是白居寺壁画中常见元素，并可以追溯至波罗时代的佛教造像。而忿怒尊护法与本尊背光则多满密卷草。龛楣左右上方或饰牡丹、莲花等花叶，或密布葵花花瓣形状的花叶，龛内主尊头身光外布波浪形射线。这一元素应是对宋元时期内地佛经版画的直接传承【插图七】，在 15 世纪的白居寺壁画中亦有相似的表现。

2. 样式 II：马蹄形背光

这一样式主要由主尊背后的头光、身光与马蹄形制的背光组成，这也是元明时期藏传佛教图像中习见的背光样式。集中于般若部 24 函中的前 18 函和第 23 函佛尊与菩萨的扉画中，共计 38 幅【图版 025L—042R、047L— 047R】，除却最后两幅外，其他同样为构图繁复满密的风格，缠枝莲纹、如意云纹、壬字云纹波、波浪形射线以及连环纹等纹样密布于尊像的头光、身光与背光内外。头光与身光外沿饰一圈块状纹饰，应是对明代西藏、尼泊尔艺术中宝石镶嵌装饰的模仿；大背光外沿饰一圈似火焰纹的短小曲线，早至10—11世纪尼泊尔《般若经》经板彩画和11世纪夏鲁寺般若佛母殿壁画中即有出现【插图八、九】。此外，在主尊身光两侧同样饰三角形焰肩，其纹饰还出现了汉地传统的连钱纹。

3. 样式III：拱券形背光

火焰纹边饰的拱券形背光是元明时期藏传佛教图像中忿怒相本尊和护法尊像常见的背光样式。在康熙北京版《甘珠尔》插画中，也同样用作上乐、喜金刚、密集金刚、空行母、怖畏金刚、马哈葛辣以及金刚手等重要本尊和护法的背光样式【图版002L— 003R、005L— 007R、009L— 010R、018L— 018R、021L— 021R】，计有18幅。但不同的是这些插画构图风格以简素为主，背光内外均无纹饰，仅以短小曲线表示背光外沿的火焰纹。这样更加凸显尊像身着骨饰璎珞纹饰的细密与华丽。

值得一提的是，康熙北京版《甘珠尔》所覆刻的底本永乐版《甘珠尔》，虽是第一部刻版藏文《甘珠尔》，但并非最早的刻版藏文佛经。最早的藏文刻版佛经出现于元代宫廷，永乐版《甘珠尔》也是在元版藏文佛经的基础上演变而来，尤其是其对称构图的佛像插图和无边框的经文版式明显受到了元版木刻藏文佛经的影响。[①] 从现存北京雍和宫的《阿毗达磨集论》（1299）[②] 与《中观论根本颂之诠释显句论》（1311—1320）[③] 以及《时轮摄略经》（1293）【插图十、十一】等几部元版藏文佛经，可以看出元明时期藏文宫廷木刻本的渊源与传统承袭关系。元版大多由皇家资助雕造，尺寸及版式基本与永乐版《甘珠尔》相仿佛，《阿毗达磨集论》由卜鲁罕皇后资助在大都刊刻，纵横12×66厘米，首页有两尊佛像，中间有5行藏文，没有外框连接；《中观论根本颂之诠释显句论》由卜鲁罕皇后资助在大都刊刻，纵横12×68厘米，首页有两尊佛像，中间有7行藏文，亦没有外框连接；《时轮摄略经》由邬坚巴大师在大都刊印，纵横11×64厘米，版框60×7.5厘米，正文6行，首页为朱印，有两尊佛像。造像风格上，永乐版《甘珠尔》与元版插画构图基本相仿，元版插画中尊像的尼泊尔造像特征以及背景中满密的装饰风

① 乌日切夫、苏米亚：《元刊藏文文献佛像插图研究》，《美术研究》2021年第1期，第52—58页。
② 雍和宫目录编号：000579，乌日切夫、苏米亚：《元刊藏文文献佛像插图研究》，第52—58页。
③ 雍和宫目录编号：000901，乌日切夫、苏米亚：《元刊藏文文献佛像插图研究》，第52—58页。

插图十　雍和宫藏元刊藏文《阿毗达磨集论》及其弥勒菩萨与无著上师经版画

插图十一　雍和宫藏元刊藏文《中观论根本颂之诠释显句论》及其龙树菩萨与月称上师经版画

格基本被永乐版《甘珠尔》扉画承袭下来，并被进一步强调。相较而言，永乐版《甘珠尔》与康熙北京版《甘珠尔》扉画尊像风格较于元版木刻藏文佛经插画更为繁复，元素更加多样，刻画也更加细腻。①

五、结语

作为历史上第一部印版藏文大藏经《甘珠尔》——永乐版《甘珠尔》的完整覆刻本，清康熙北京版藏文《甘珠尔》具有等量的版本价值。在经典与插画尊像的排布上，整部《甘珠尔》是以蔡巴·贡噶多吉所编定的《善逝宝经广示目录》（1323—1348）为总领，经典依金刚果乘续部与有相因乘经部细分的6部，即秘密部、般若部、大宝积部、华严部、诸经部、戒律部进行划分；而图像主要依金刚果乘续部与有相因乘经部两大类区分排布，也即在秘密部中，图像主要依布顿·仁钦珠四续（无上瑜珈续、瑜伽续、行续、事续）的密续构思加以分类和排布，而在般若部、大宝积部、华严部、诸经部、戒律部5部中，图像则并非依照各部经典区分，而是冠以大乘佛教礼拜仪式中常见诸佛，如十方佛、三十五礼忏佛、药师七佛等。这使得整部《甘珠尔》不仅具有诵读功用，同时更强调其作为《大藏经》的供奉与礼拜功用。

民族文化宫图书馆所藏的康熙北京版是目前所知仅见的这一版本的初印本全藏，与永乐版《甘珠尔》十分接近。其具有多元风貌的木刻插画继承了元代宫廷作坊西天梵相样式，同时也反映了15世纪初明代宫廷与西藏本土汉藏佛教艺术的时代风貌。在清代康熙北京版覆刻之后，明代宫廷造像风格不再流行于清廷，而是迅速改换全新的、清代风格的经版，这应是受到蒙古审美趣味的影响，从一个侧面也反映了汉藏蒙满多元族群互动的脉络和其中的身份作用。

① 乌日切夫在《雍和宫藏元刊两部藏文文献概述》一文中指出，以《阿毗达磨集论》和《时轮摄略经》为代表的元大都早期刊印藏文文献插图造像应是直接参照了藏文泥金写本或普通写本的佛像插图。乌日切夫、田萧雯：《雍和宫藏元刊两部藏文文献概述》，《世界宗教研究》2020年第6期，第185—192页。

【 INTRODUCTION 】

Collection of the Sacred Images: The First Print of the Kangxi Peking Edition of *Kanjur* in the Qing Dynasty and its Illustrations

by YANG Hongjiao and WEI Wen
Translated by HUANG Bo

The Library of Ethnic Cultural Palace (also the Ethnic Library of China) now has a complete collection of the Tibetan *Kangyur* in red print from the Kangxi era of the Qing Dynasty (hereinafter referred to as "Kangxi Peking edition"). This was originally the old collection from the Imperial Storehouse of the Qing Palace, and after liberation, it was transferred from the Palace Museum to the Library of Ethnic Cultural Palace. The Kangxi Peking edition was engraved in the 23rd year of the Kangxi period (1684) by Emperor Kangxi in order to pray for longevity of his grandmother, Grand Empress Dowager Xiaozhuangwen and legal mother, Empress Dowager Xiaohuizhang. In the 31st year of the Kangxi period (1692), part of the Mahayāna sūtras were printed, and completed until the 39th year of the Kangxi period (1700). It was printed in 106 volumes, and since the pages of *Ral pa gyen brdzes kyi rgyud* translated by Bu ston Rin chen grub amount to the number of about one volume, one more volume (Za) was added. The total number of Kangxi Peking edition reached to 107 volumes, and two new texts were added to the Mahāratnakūṭa section (dKon brtsegs). At the same time, more than a thousand corrections were made by means of mending the wood blocks for printing.① According to figures, there are totally 33206 pieces of the pear wood blocks for printing (size 63×19cm). It is said that the Kangxi Peking edition has copied the ancient Tibetan manuscripts collected in Zhwa lu Monastery, which should be Yongle Peking edition of *Kanjur*, that is, originating from the so-called eastern system *Kanjur* of Tshal pa ancient

① Bruce C. Hall, *A Descriptive List of the Tibetan (Tib) Collection in the Rare Books Room of the Harvard-Yenching Library*, (Cambridge, MA: 1980), [3].There is a total of 106 volumes surving in the Kangxi Peking edition of *Kangyur* in the Library of Ethnic Cultural Palace.

manuscripts mentioned by Seishi Karashima.①

There are 107 volumes in the entire collection, and a total of 1055 texts. Among them, the first is the Kangxi Emperor's "Preface to the Imperially Sanctioned Tibetan Buddhist Canon" written in four scripts on the 22nd day of the 8th month of the 23rd year of the Kangxi period, the "Petition for a Preface" submitted by Fuquan, the Prince of Heshuoyu, on the 16th day of the 8th month of the 22nd year of the Kangxi Period (1683), the "Another Petition" from Minister of Rites Jieshan and others on the first day of the ninth month of the 22nd year of the Kangxi period, and the list of 105 officials who participated in the compilation after the publication of the complete collection of the Buddhist Canon on the fourth month of the 39th year of the Kangxi period. Next, there are the main texts of the Buddhist Canon, with 25 volumes of the "esoteric section", 24 volumes of the "Prajñāpāramitā section", 6 volumes of the "Mahāratnakūṭa section", 6 volumes of the "Avataṃsaka section," 32 volumes of "section of various sutras," and 13 volumes of the "Vinaya section," as well as one volume of the catalog *The Precious Scriptures of the Sugata*, *Rays of the Sun Illuminating Widely* (*bDe bar gshegs pavi gsung rab rin po chevi dkar chag bstan pa rgyas pavi nyi vod*) in four scripts of Chinese, Tibetan, Mongolian, and Manchu in the fourth month of the 39th year of the Kangxi period, written by Tshal pa Kun dgav rdo rje (1309-1364), and completed between 1323-1348. Each volume is composed of the sutra cover, the protection plate and the sutra leaf. The sutra protection plate is divided into two pieces, 72 cm in length, 22 cm in width and 2.1 cm in thickness, framed with blue paper. The center of the inner side of the sutra protection plate is hollow, in the first page of the scriptures of each volume, there were vermilion line engraved images on the two ends, which is covered with yellow ground dark flowers and Ruyi cloud pattern brocade, with purple-red silk linen on the inside,② and the lower sutra protection plate is printed with four protector deities. The sutra page has red prints on both sides, surrounded by double columns, with Chinese sutra names and page number on the left side of the column frame, and Tibetan sutra names and page numbers on the right. Through the wall painted four corners of the waist column, on all sides to form the "gate of the open light," the open light of Tibetan Buddhism and other themes are painted in the light, the two sides of the wall are painted with eight auspicious patterns surrounded by lotus, and the two ends are painted with three jewels and arch shaped niche, and the name of each sutra is written in the center of the niche.

The Peking edition of the *Kangyur* in the collection of the Library of Ethnic Cultural

---

① Seishi Karashima, "On the System of Kanjur and Its Importance to the Study of Tibetan Translated Buddhist Sutras", *Chinese Tibetology*, No.3, 2014, p.33. Weng Lianxi, *A Record of Engraving Books in the Inner Palace of the Qing Dynasty*, Beijing Publishing House, 2004, p.23.

② The upper and lower outer sutra protection plates are made of fir wood, with gold and red lacquer, 73.7 cm in length, 23.3 cm in width and 2.5 cm in thickness.

Palace is the only known first printed copy of the said edition of *Kangyur* in its entirety. It is of high value for the purpose of studying different editions, especially the Buddhist images engraved on the front page of each volume in red ink, completely re-carving the divine images engraved on the Yongle *Kangyur*, with a total of more than 200 images. The content and style of these images are no different from the Yongle *Kangyur*, inheriting the style of the Yuan Dynasty court workshop for Indian Buddhist images, and providing us with comprehensive and representative pictorial materials for further research on the Sino-Tibetan Buddhist art of the court in the early 15th century and its influence on posterity. Below, we will sort out and introduce the reasons for the publication, the origins of the different versions, the contents of the images, the styles and their values.

1. Reasons for the Publication

According to the "Imperial Sanctioned Preface" at the beginning, the publication of the Peking edition of *Kangyur* was personally issued by the Kangxi Emperor, and presided over by Fuquan, the Prince Yu of the First Rank. Initially, Fuquan petitioned for the preface on the 16th day of the 8th month of the 22nd year of the Kangxi period, and on the same day, he presented it for imperial review.

The main purpose of this supplication is to elucidate the significance of the emperor himself writing a preface for the Buddhist canon. On the one hand, in ancient China, whenever there was a prosperous era with a wise ruler, especially at the beginning of a dynasty or when the nation's fortunes were on the rise, the emperor would promote and honor Buddhism in order to benefit and humanize all living beings. On the other hand, at the time when the Dowager Empress Xiaozhuangwen and Empress Xiaohuizhang were still alive, publishing Buddhist canon to pray for them a long life was a good opportunity to demonstrate the Confucian political concept of governing the country through filial piety. Thus, it can be seen that Fuquan was expressing the hope that the emperor's own preface would proclaim the continuation of the traditional practices of Chinese emperors in governing the country, and would also demonstrate the legitimacy of the Qing Dynasty and Emperor Kangxi as the inheritors of China's traditional legitimacy. At the same time, he also implied the Qing Dynasty as a "glorious dynasty" and Emperor Kangxi as a "wise and virtuous ruler".

On 18th day of the 8th month of the same year, the Emperor directed the Ministry of Rites to examine the precedent and then make a clear reply. Subsequently, on the 1st day of the ninth month, Minister Jie Shan submitted a written response to Fuquan's supplication, which fully affirmed the great significance of that the emperor wrote the perface for the Buddhist canon as proposed by Fuquan. Hence, Emperor agreed to do it on the 4th day of the 9th month.

In the following year, that is, on the 13th day of the 8th month of the 23rd year of the Kangxi period, the "Preface to the Imperially Sanctioned Tibetan Buddhist Canon" was bestowed and a statement was made. When explaining the origin and cost of the publication of the Buddhist Canon, "the old Tibetan texts has been engraved," refers to going to Tibet to receive Tibetan scriptures and engraving; "the great and high Buddhist Canon, praising the great blessings of the two palaces," refers to engraving the Tibetan Buddhist Canon to pray for fortune and eliminate disaster for the Empress Dowager and the Grand Empress Dowager; "it did not involve the people's money, and the expenses were all out of the imperial harem, not from the Treasury," means that all the expenses used in the publication of the Buddhist Canon are not from private donations and Treasury appropriations, but from the imperial harem.

This preface, with its rhythmical prose and gorgeous rhetoric, should be created by the imperial minister. It is worth noting that although the preface was written for the Tibetan Buddhist Canon, Buddhism was not as the main theme of it, and there was no expression of praise and admiration for Buddhism. On the contrary, the whole article stand on the standpoint of Confucianism, beginning with the high praise to "*Zhouyi*" as the "source of classics", and was quite positive about the theory of *Yin* and *Yang*, and then further introduced the historical narration of Buddhism since the Han Dynasty, which obviously regards Buddhism as one kind of *Yin* and *Yang* techniques. It is said that the promotion of Buddhism is nothing but praying for longevity and blessing. This article argue that, from the national point of view, the Kangxi Emperor was so powerful that he did not need Buddhism to consolidate his rule, and was dismissive of Buddhism to a certain degree. The article further describes the Emperor Kangxi had been tirelessly exploring the ways of governing the country in Confucianism. He did not pay much attention to Buddhism, and it was nothing but to pray for the Grand Empress Dowager and the Empress Dowager's long and blessing life by printing Tibetan Buddhist canon. In fact, this is still a manifestation of Confucian filial piety. The above narration is directly related to Confucian officials advocating Neo-Confucianism in the early Qing Dynasty who stood for the trend of anti-Buddhism. Performing filial piety and emphasizing Buddhist history in Han Chinese narration were aimed to create an imperial image in Chinese tradition for Kangxi Emperor under the Confucian concept. In addition, the narration was totally in the context of Han Chinese Buddhism, without anything related to Tibetan Buddhism, which to some extent also reflected a negative attitude of Confucian scholars towards Tibetan Buddhism.

Fuquan, Prince Yu of the First Rank, was mainly responsible for leading the supervision of the publication of the Buddhist Canon, and the supervising officials were headed by Šulu, a Reader of the Grand Secretariat, with a total of 30 people; among the lamas who examined the texts of the Buddhist Canon, the Lama of the Capital, the Jasak da lama mergen corji was the head, and the chief teacher of Tibetan, Sonom corji, was the vice head. The Tibetan lamas engaged in specific examining work were all from the Huang Temple, headed by Gendun darji gelung, with a total of 40 people, and the chief examiner was Changkya Khutukhtu, and his subordinates included the abbot Lama Wangšuk jimba gelung, Lobdzang baljor gelung, and four other people. The supervisors were headed by Uladai, a Reader of the Grand Secretariat, with a total of 13 people. The officers who proofread the preface and catalog were Dandai, Bairi, and Unggin. The translators of the Tibetan preface and catalog were Usibu and Dengdei. The translators of the Mongolian preface and catalog were Lamjang and Hegeo. The officials scribed the Manchu preface and catalog were Ibari, Dzangšeo, and Cambu. The officials scribed the Chinese preface and catalog were Tsoo jan gi and Wang ki o. The officials scribed the Tibetan preface and catalog were the lama Lobdzang lurub gelung, Lobdzang bailji gelung and Sonom rincin gelung. A total of 105 people worked in various fields. These people were engaged in the work of verifying, proofreading, cross checking, examining, and translating the imperial preface and the catalog of the Buddhist Canon into the four languages of Tibetan, Mongolian, Manchu, and Chinese, not including those engaged in a large number of arduous and specific tasks such as writing, engraving, papercutting, printing, decoration, and painting. The chief examiner was the head of the eight Khutukhtus of Beijing, the Changkya Khutukhtu, and based on the time of his activity, it should be the Second lCang skya Ngag dbang blo bzang chos ldan (1642-1714).

From the perspective of Tibetan inscriptions, Baron Alexander von Staël-Holstein once quoted an inscription in the Peking edition of *Kangyur* to discuss the engraving personnel and time of the Peking edition of *Kangyur*, and believed that it had been published in the 31st year of the Kangxi period. Ba duo and Zhang Zhiyu also cited the same inscription recorded in *Aṣṭasāhasrikāprajñāpāramitā* of the 48th volume collected in the Yenching Library of Harvard University in the United States to agree with this statement.① The Tibetan inscription is as follows:

> Oṃ swa sti pra dza bhyiḥ/sngon spyad bsod nams las vkhrungs chu gter las // rmad byung thugs rjevi brlabs vphreng cher g.yos te //nam yang zad med smon lam si tāvi klung //snyigs dus skye vgrovi bsod nams zhing mchog tu // babs pavi bskal bzang gser gyi snye mavi vbras // legs par smin pavi mdo sdevi bka vgyur vdi //dpaldan vphags pavi lha khang vkhrungs kau sivi//dge

① Ba Duo and Zhang Zhiyu, "Research on the Engraving of the Offcial Tibetan Version of 'The Great Tripitaka' in the Qing Dynasty", *Journal of Southwest Minzu University* (*Humanities and Social Sciences Edition*), No.2, 2022, pp.32-33.

> slong sbyin pa rgya mtsho gtso mdzad bavi//dpon slob tshogs kyi lhag bsam dag pavi mthus //gnas bskos gser mngal khang hi gser gyi khrir// ri rab lhun povi lta bu brtan gyur cig [/]/dge vdis bdag sogs rgyu sbyor sbyin bdag dang // pha ma gtso byas vgro drug sems can rnams //gnas ngan len gyi vching ba las grol te //sangs rgyas zhing du myur du skye bar shog /thub bstan spyi dang vjam mgon tsong kha pavi // chos srid zung la dbang bsgyur mes po yi //sku tshe mngav thang srid mthar rgyas pa dang //bkra shis bde legs dpal la spyod par shog /dza yantu / tavi ching khar hi lo sum cu so gcig chu pho sprel lo snrul gyi zla bavi chu pho khyi rgyal gyi nyi ma la dbu gtsugs nas mon gru zla bavi sa pho stag dgav ba nyi mavi bar du legs par bsgrubs pavo /

Under the Tibetan inscription there is also a Chinese inscription:

> "In in the middle of summer of the 31st year of the Kangxi period, Bhiksu sByin pa rgya mtsho of vKhrungs kau Temple in the Capital Beijing, printed it with the heart."

From this Tibetan and Chinese postscript, it is known that the Sangha community headed by sByin pa rgya mtsho, a bhikku (dge slong) of vKhrungs kau Temple, the famous Tibetan Buddhist monastery Da long shan hu guo Temple in Beijing, printed the Peking edition of *Kangyur* (mdo sdevi bka vgyur), in order to pray for Emperor Kangxi's stable inheritance and long life.

First of all, it should be noted that the western scholars such as Gene Smith and Benjamin James Nourse, etc., have identifed this sByin pa rgya mtsho is just the one, named bKav vgyur ba sByin pa rgya mtsho, who served as the 46th Ganden Tripa (1629-1695).① This is obviously inconsistent with historical facts, because bKav vgyur ba sByin pa rgya mtsho has never come to Beijing according to his biography, and there are no more historical records of being engaged in political affairs. In fact, also according to historical documents, the person named sByin pa rgya mtsho, who was active in Beijing in the early Qing Dynasty and deeply involved in establishing communication between the Qing court and Tibetan region about the political affairs, was the living Buddha of Ba jo Se chen chos rje sByin pa rgya mtsho recorded in Tibetan literature. However, he is confused with the historical documents of Širegetü küreiyen bandida nomon han and

① Benjamin James Nourse, *Canons in Context: A History of the Tibetan Buddhist Canon in the Eighteenth Century*, M.A., University of Virginia, 2009, pp.92-94.

even Ilaγuγsan qutuγtu, etc. in Mongolian materials, and there is no consensus.① The time they were active was concentrated in the mid-17th century and unlikely as late as the last decade of the 17th century. In the middle of the Kangxi period (the end of the 17th century), there was a minor lama stationed in Beijing (probably the Deputy Da Lama) named "sByin pa rgya mtsho", who was most likely to be the printer of vKhrungs kau Temple. He and another lama in Beijing, Usniq-a bizay-a-yin suburγ-a Dem chi bsod nams bzang po had personally met the 5th Dalai Lama, so in the 35th year of the Kangxi period (1696), he was selected by Emperor Kangxi to go to Tibet to see if the Dalai Lama was still alive, headed by the leader of the Court of Colonial Affairs, Bao zhu.②

In addition, Alexander von Staël-Holstein etc., interpret this Chinese and Tibetan inscription as sByin pa rgya mtsho of vKhrungs kau Temple was in charge of engraving the Kangxi Peking edition, and completed it in the 31st year of the Kangxi period. The large amount of revised and additional texts in the *Kanjur* seem to be understood, of course, as revised version of the 39th Year of the Kangxi period based on the version of the 35th year of the Kangxi period. On this basis, Alexander von Staël-Holstein also noted that sByin pa rgya mtsho's name was not included in the list of monk in charge of engraving recorded in the Chinese and Mongolian inscriptions of the 39th year of the Kangxi period. he explained it was because work was not recognized by the court, otherwise Fuquan could not have ignored his editing work.③

Here, the work headed by sByin pa rgya mtsho started in April and May (snrul zla ba[*snron gyi zla ba]) and ended in September and October (mon gru zla ba[*smin drug zla ba]), so it can only be printed in such a short time, and not engraved. This could also be reflected in the Chinese inscriptions below it. Moreover, the Tibetan inscription clearly states that the Canon engraved was "the sutra of the *Kanjur*", not the whole *Kanjur* including the tantra, and in fact, it does not seem to have this inscription at the end of every volume of the *Kanjur*, as Jonathan A. Silk stated in his supplementary note.④ In fact, it only appears at the end of the Prajñāpāramitā section (after the 3rd volume), as what we have seen so far. This shows that the so-called edition of the year 1692 *Kanjur* mentioned by Alexander von Staël-Holstein was originally a concept that did not exist,

① Chen Xiaoqiang, "A Survey on the Deeds of sByin pa rgya mtsho", *Ethnic History Studies*, 1999, pp.347-359. Hiroshi Wakamatsu, "Preliminary Exploration on *The Collection of Šiaregetü küreiyen Lama's Biography*", Mongolian Studies Information, No. 4, 1999, pp.18-24.

② Shuo Mo Fang Lue, vol. 28, pp. 24-25, in Bao yin te gu si, *Research on Relationship between Oirad, Tibet and Qing Court in Early 18th Century, Focused on "the 6th Dalai Lama Event"*, Doctoral Dissertation of Inner Mongolia University, 2009, p. 16. Jonathan A.Silk also mentions this person by searching Zahiruddin Ahmad's monograph, but still highlights the views of the famous scholar Gene Smith.

③ *On a Peking Edition of the Tibetan Kanjur Which Seems to be Unknown in the West*, p.220-221, note 1.

④ *On a Peking Edition of the Tibetan Kanjur Which Seems to be Unknown in the West*, p.216, Jonathan A. Silk's annotation C.

and at that time, of the Kangxi Peking edition project, there was probably only the engraving work of a part of sutra section completed, and also sByin pa rgya mtsho did not participate in the project. He just as a sponsor printed one volume first before the whole canon was engraved and revised for some reason (of blessing the Kangxi emperor?). Therefore, it is not possible for his name to appear in the official list after the completion of the canon in 1700.

2. Origins of Different Editions

The Kangxi Peking edition of *Kangyur* originally stored in the Songzhu Monastery, which was the residence monastery of the Changkya Khutukhtu in Beijing. Later it was transferred to the Beihai Daxitian Dayuanzhijing Treasure Hall. In the 26th year of the Guangxu period (1900), the Buddhist Canon plates were looted, and it further suffered burning in the 26th year of the Republic of China (1937). Most of them no longer exist, and there are still a very small number of these plates collected in the Palace Museum.①

It is worth noting that the surviving editions of the Beijing version are not identical. Since it is said that the Beijing version was finalized three times in the 56th year of the Kangxi period (1717), the 59th year of the Kangxi period (1720), and the second year of the Qianlong period (1737) respectively, they resulted in different editions from the initially printed version. This is especially true in the 56th year of the Kangxi period when the Qing court began to engrave the Mongolian *Kangyur*, and then continued to engrave the Tibetan *Tengyur* in the 60th year of the Kangxi period (1721). The former is an unprecedented work, while the latter seemingly could not continue the achievements of predecessors. The so-called Peking Wanli edition of *Tengyur* was extremely rare, so these two activities of engraving the Buddhist Canon were the original undertakings of the Qing Dynasty court workshop. These activities reflect the aesthetic tendencies of the Qing Dynasty rulers and Mongolian nobles in the book design. Therefore, we can see that the title page portraits of these two Buddhist Canons are completely in the style of Qing Dynasty Buddhist art, and the book design style of the Tibetan *Kangyur* engraved in the 39th year of the Kangxi period is consistent with the style of these two Tibetan Buddhist Canons of the same period, completely replacing the line engraving of the upper sutra holding plate of the early Ming Dynasty and the line engraving of the lower sutra holding plate of the Kangxi period, and replacing them with the same style of colored image from the Tibetan *Tengyur* and the Mongolian *Kangyur*. We can thus call this version the

① Songzhu Temple, located at the east gate of Sanyanjing Hutong in Beijing's Di'anmen, no longer exists. The temple was built in the 51st year of the Kangxi period (1712) as a resident temple in Beijing bestowed by the Qing court to the Changkya Khutukhtu.

revised version for now.

The *Kangyur* in the collection of the Library of Ethnic Cultural Palace was allocated from the Palace Museum, and the Palace Museum still preserves a complete set of the Peking edition of *Kangyur*, but it is not the initial print. It is said that the National Library of China and the Yonghegong Temple hold printed edition of the Peking edition of *Kangyur* engraved in 1700. The Otani University in Japan collectes a printed edition of the Peking edition *Kangyur* engraved from 1717 to 1720. This version was published in Japan in 1955-1958 and now is the most widely circulated and commonly used in academia. In addition, the National Library of Ulaanbaatar, Mongolia, has a complete set of the revised edition, which has been distributed on CD-ROM.① The National Library of France has a print edition of the Peking edition of *Kangyur* of the 2nd year of the Qianlong period (1736). It is said that the Peking edition of *Kangyur* has a reprinted edition in 1763 or 1765, but the specifics are unclear.

The rest that we see are either incomplete copies or even fragments, scattered in major libraries and among private individuals. It can be seen that as the only complete collection of the first printed edition of the Peking *Kangyur*, the version collected in the Library of Ethnic Cultural Palace is particularly valuable.

The Peking edition of *Kangyur* of the Kangxi period of the Qing Dynasty is a re-engraving of the Yongle *Kangyur* in the early Ming Dynasty, so their layouts of the content are completely identical. Before the publication of the Yongle *Kangyur*, there were three editions of the *Kangyur* compiled in Tibet. The earliest manuscript of Tibetan Buddhist Canon was created in the end of the 13th century [the 2nd year of Huangqing during the Yuan (1313), an alternative date is the year 1315, to the 7th year of Yanyou (1320)], and the sutras, vinayas, tantric mantras of different regions were collected, sorted out and compiled under the direction of the abbot of Narthang Monastery, bCom ldan rig pavi ral gri (1227-1305) and his disciples mChims vJam dpal dbyangs (? -1267) and dBus pa blo gsal. It is called the "ancient Narthang edition" of the *Kangyur*, which has not been passed down, and there is also the *Tengyur*, equivalent to the shastras and vinayas in the Chinese Buddhist Canon. In the early 14th century, Bu ston Rin chen grub (1290-1364) of the Zhwa lu Monastery compiled the Zhwa lu *Kangyur* based on the Narthang *Kangyur*. In Lhasa's Tshal gung thang Monastery, sMan lam rdo rje ordered the compilation of the *Kangyur* in 1310-1328, and a complete set of *Kangyur* was then compiled from 1347 to 1351 by Tshal pa Kun dgav rdo rje (1309-1364) and others. Bu ston Rin chen grub was

① *The Tempangma Manuscript of the Kangyur, The Peking Edition of the Kangyur, held at the National Library of Mongolia*, Digitally published and distributed by Digital Preservation Society (DPS), Tokyo 2010. See http://www.tibet-dps.org/ leaf size is 71.7 cm. × 21.2 cm, it is said that the Songzhu Temple also preserved this first engraved print.

then asked to examine it, and Kun dgav rdo rje compiled the catalog himself. There are a total of 250 volumes, and this edition was lost. From this Tshal pa version of the *Kangyur* derives the following two systems: one is the Beijing system starting from the Yongle *Kangyur* (1410), and the other is the Phying ba stag rtse *Kangyur* (now lost).

Before the 13th century, the Tibetan Buddhist Canon mainly circulated in the form of manuscripts. In the 15th century, the first printed edition of the *Kangyur*, the Yongle *Kangyur*, came out, and the Yongle version of the Tibetan Buddhist Canon was also the earliest extant printed copy in Tibetan on copper plate. It was inscribed in the 8th year of the Yongle period of the Ming Dynasty (1410), when the Yongle Emperor sought merits for his recently deceased concubine Xu. He specifically sent an envoy to Tibet to bring the manuscript of the Tibetan Buddhist Canon back to Nanjing, and ordered the *Kangyur* to be made into a copper horizontal plate that can be folded and printed in red ink. Previously, the fifth Karmapa De bzhin gshegs pa (1384-1415) went to Nanjing to establish a great feast for mass liberation at Linggu Temple, to generate merit for the Emperor Taizu and Empress Xiaocigao, and the Yongle Emperor asked him to serve as the chief compiler of the *Kangyur*, each of which included the "Praise of the Buddhist Canon by the Ming Emperor" and the "Epilogue by the Emperor" made by Ming Chengzu.① The plates of this version have been lost, and not many printed copies have survived. In the 11th (1413) and 14th (1416) years of the Yongle period, the Yongle Emperor gave Kun dgav bkra shis and Śhakya ye shes each a set, which are now preserved in the Potala Palace and Sera Monastery respectively, the former with 106 volumes and the later with 103 volumes. It is said that another set of Yongle *Kangyur* has been found in Labrang Monastery in Gansu. The style and content of the Yongle *Kangyur* have a profound impact on the later Jingtai illuminated manuscript *Kangyur*, the Wanli *Kangyur* of the Ming Dynasty, and the Tibetan Dragon Canon (*Longzangjing*) of Kangxi period of the Qing Dynasty.

The illuminated manuscript *Kangyur* copied during the Jingtai period of the Ming Dynasty was originally stored somewhere in the main hall of the Forbidden City. Only a few volumes were rescued from the fire in the Jianfu Palace in 1923, and it is now collected in the library of the Palace Museum.The edition consulted when copying the *Kangyur* manuscript written in gold in the Ming Jingtai period is probably either the Yongle *Kangyur* or the blueprint of the Yongle *Kangyur* (copied from Tibet). It also influenced the compilation of the Kangxi *Longzangjing* in the Qing Dynasty. It is said

① Long Dari: "Wanli Edition kangyur of the Jagiellonian University in Poland", *Journal of Southwest University for Nationalities* (Humanities and Social Sciences Edition), No. 1, 2017, pp. 88-93.] Zhou Runian: "The Characteristics of the Tibetan Language Canon", *The Third Cross-Strait Symposium on Tibetology*, June 12, 2009, Center for Tibet, Tamkang University, 2009, pp.3-4.

that Empress Dowager Xiaozhuang saw the golden Kangyur manuscripts copied during the Ming Jingtai period collected in the palace treasury were damaged, so she asked Emperor Kangxi to send someone to recopy it. That was completed in the 8th year of the Kangxi period (1669), commonly known as the *Longzangjing*, with a total of 108 volumes, written in gold, now in the Palace Museum of Taipei.[①] Its writing style and binding style are almost all imitations of Jingtai *Kangyur*'s illuminated manuscripts.

The Wanli *Kangyur* using the Yongle *Kangyur* as the blueprint, with few modifications, was re-printed in Beijing in the 33rd year of the Ming Wanli period (1605). It is the second printed *Kangyur*, and has a total of 105 volumes.[②] In the following year, 42 volumes from the *Tengyur* were engraved. The original version no longer exists and only a few copies survived. A large number of fragments of the Wanli Buddhist Canon have recently been found in the Jagiellonian University Library in Cracow, Poland.[③]

3. The System of Deities in the Images

The Kangxi Peking edition of *Kangyur* is in the Tibetan traditional looseleaf longbook style, each leaf is 14.2 × 58.2 cm in pothi binding. Each volume is composed of the sutra cover, protection plates and pages. Compared with the collection in the Palace Museum, the outer sutra protection plate with its upper and lower part in vermilion lacquer is absent. The sutra cover is a rectangular shaped yellow fabric. The upper and lower sutra protection plates are covered with blue and yellow papers respectively. The central surface of the inner pages are sunken down, covered in brocade. The inner page of the upper sutra protection plate is also the title page, on which the title of the sutra is inscribed in the center, and the two ends are decorated with images of Buddhist deities, with a total of 210. The inner page of the lower sutra protection plate has images of the six-armed Mahākāla and the his four attendants and the five images of the Mahavajresvara and other Buddhist protectors. Since it is a re-engraved edition of the Tibetan woodcut version of the *Kangyur* in the early Ming Dynasty, it is virtually identical in characteristic to the Yongle *Kangyur*, especially in the style of its Tibetan

① Li Ruoyu,"A Brilliant Pearl Survival from the Fire: the Buddhist Classical Kangyur of Jingtai 7th Year Edition of the Palace Museum", Palace Museum Journal, No. 9, 2023, pp.119-127.

② From the early 17th century to the early 18th century, a variety of printed editions of the *Kangyur* were produced, successively including the Litang edition, the Jone edition, the Beijing edition, the Narthang edition, the Derge edition, and so on. In the twenties of the 20th century, another Lhasa edition of the *Kangyur* appeared, which is the last woodcut version of the *Kangyur* so far. Jiacuo, Pingcuo, Gama, Danda, Jianling, Danzha, "Two Existing Yongle Kanjurs in Lhasa", *Wenwu*, No. 9, 1985, pp.85-88, 104.

③ Mejor M, Helman-Ważny A, Chashab T K, A Preliminary Report on the Wanli Kanjur: Kept in the Jagiellonian Library, Kraków, Research Centre of Buddhist Studies, Faculty of Oriental Studies, University of Warsaw, 2010. There is also a set of *Kangyur* printed in 1680 in the Staatsbibliothek zu Berlin, which is based on the Wanli edition of the *Kangyur*.

writing and the style of the Buddha images carved on the upper sutra plate. The two are almost indistinguishable, vividly reflecting the typical style of Sino-Tibetan Buddhist art in the early Ming period. After further detailed comparisons, one will find that there are still slight differences between the two, in that the Peking edition of *Kangyur* has added a border frame around the interior text of each page, and the lower sutra protection plate has added the carvings of tutelary deities like the Vasudhārā (Lha mo nor rgyun), Lha mo re ma ti, Six-armed Mahākāla (mGon po phyag drug), and the Yellow Jambhala in the Sino-Tibetan style of the Qing Dynasty.

The images on the title page include many categories such as Buddhas, Bodhisattvas, yidams, Buddhist protectors, and Buddha mothers, among which the number and types of Buddhas are mostly identified. They can be preliminarily identified as the Buddhas of the ten directions, the seven medicine Buddhas, the thousand Buddhas of the present kalpa, the thirty-five Buddhas, the Buddhas of the three times, and Buddhas from the *Buddhanāmasahasrapañcaśatacaturtripañcadaśa*. By comparing the images with the Kangxi Peking edition of *Kangyur* catalog, that is, the *bDe bar gshegs pavi gsung rab rin po chevi dkar chag bstan pa rgyas pavi nyi vod*, we can see that the two are closely related, and the arrangement of these images is mainly a visualization of the content of the Peking edition of *Kangyur*, while inheriting the tradition of early Tibetan Buddhist images, especially the image system of the deities in the Buddhist Canon. Now, we use the classification of the texts in the Kangxi Peking edition of *Kangyur* as a framework to sort out and interpret the rules of arrangement of the images on the title page and their religious connotations.

(1) Tantra Section of the Fruit Vehicle (Esoteric Section)

According to the catalog *bDe bar gshegs pavi gsung rab rin po chevi dkar chag bstan pa rgyas pavi nyi vod* written by Tshal pa Kun dgav rdo rje in this *Kangyur*, it is divided into two categories, namely the Tantra section of the Fruit Vehicle (gsang sngags vbras buvi theg pa rgyud kyi dbye ba) and the Sutra section of the Cause Vehicle (mtshan nyid rgyuvi theg pa mdovi dbye ba). The esoteric section, also known as the Tantra section of the Fruit Vehicle, is further divided into Anuttarayoga Tantra (rnal vbyor chen po bla na med pavi rgyud), Yoga Tantra (rnal vbyor gyi rgyud), Carya Tantra (spyod pavi rgyud), Kriya Tantra (bya bavi rgyud), formerly translated esoteric mantras (gsang sngags snga vgyur), and temporarily important section (gnas skabs su nyer mkhovi dbye ba).[1] Each

① Hu Jinshan, "General Remarks on *The Precious Scriptures of the Sugata, Rays of the Sun Illuminating Widely* Catalogue Kept at the Palace Museum in Taipei", *Dharma Light Lyceum*, Fa-kuang Institute of Buddhist Studies, 2003, Vol.7, pp.47-76.

kind of those tantras is then further detailly divided into categories.

Among them, the Anuttarayoga Tantra is also divided into three categories, namely, the non-dual tantra of method and wisdom (thobs shes gnyis su med povi rgyud), the mother tantra of wisdom (shes rab rnal vbyor mavi rgyud), and the father tantra of method (thabs rnal vbyor phavi rgyud). The portraits on the left and right sides of the first volume of the first page of the esoteric section are Mañjuśrījñānasattva (vJam dpal ye shes sems dpav) and Śrīkālacakra (dPal dus kyi vkhor lo), which mainly correspond to the deities of the non-dual tantra of method and wisdom. The name of Mañjuśrījñānasattva comes from the first of the tantras in the esoteric section of the Kangxi Peking edition of *Kangyur*, which is reputed to be the most remarkable text of the tantras, the *Mañjuśrījñānasattvasya-paramārtha-nāma-saṃgīti* (*vJam dpal ye shes sems dpavi don dam pavi mtshan yang dag par brjod pa*), translated as *Shen miao jixiang zhenshi mingjing* (圣妙吉祥真实名经) in Chinese (Taisho No. 1190), which contains the doctrine of expounding the wisdom of Bodhisattva Mañjuśrī and how to attain enlightenment.① Mañjuśrījñānasattva is the most important yidam of this tantra, so its image is placed at the beginning of the esoteric section. The image has one face and four arms, wearing bodhisattva clothing. The four hands hold a sword, a sutra on a lotus, a bow, and an arrow. Its pictorial features are similar to the images of Nāmasaṃgīti Mañjuśrī in the *Sādhanamālā*, differing only in the number of faces. The Nāmasaṃgīti Mañjuśrī image collected in the *Sādhanamālā* has three faces.② [Plate 001L] The Śrīkālacakra (dPal dus kyi vkhor lo) is an important yidam of *Parama-ādibuddhoddhrita-śrī-kālacakra-nāma-tantrarājā*, which is representative of the Kālacakra tantric literature. To the right side of the title page of the first volume in the esoteric section is an image with one face, two arms, three eyes, and two bodies.③ The Kālacakravajra holds his vajra and bell and embraces the Buddha mother, with the left leg bent and the right leg extended, stepping on Maheśvara and Kamakhya separately. The Buddha Mother is the sNa tshogs yum, holding the Karttṛkā and Kapāla, standing with her legs bent on the right and extended on the left. [Plate 001R]

The main deities for the mother tantra of wisdom, the Cakrasaṃvara (bDe mchog) and the Hevajra (Kyevi rdo rje), as well as their respective Buddha mothers Vajravārāhī (Phag mo) and Nairātmyā (bDag med), are separately placed in the title pages' pictures of the second and third volumes of the esoteric section [Plates 002L to 003R]. The main deities for the father tantra of method, the Guhyasamāja-Akṣobhyavajra (gSang vdus mi skyod rdo rje) and the Guhyasamāja-Mañjuvajra (gSang vdus vjam dpal rdo rje) appear in the

① Peking Edition No.2, rgyud, ka, 1b1-15b7 (vol.1, p.117).

② Benoytosh Bhattacharyya, *Sādhanamālā*, Baroda, Oriental Institute, 1925, pp. 159-160, no. 82: āryanāmasaṅgītisādhanaṃ samāptam.

③ Peking Edition No. 4, rgyud, ka, 23b1-141b8 (vol.1, p.127).

pictures on the left and right sides of the title page of the seventh volume of the esoteric section. It is worth pointing out that although the images are arranged according to the tantric classification, it does not strictly correspond to each volume. For example, the tantric text corresponding to the Guhyasamāja, the *Sarvatathāgatakāyavākcittarahasyo guhyasamāja-nāma-mahā-kalparāja* (*De bzhin gshegs pa thams cad kyi sku gsung thugs kyi gsang ba vdus pa zhes bya ba brtag pavi rgyal po chen po*) is listed in the fifth volume of the esoteric section.①

In terms of the images, the Vairocana (rNam snang) and Vajrasattva (rDo rje sems dpav) in the 11th volume of the esoteric section, and the Vairocana (rNam snang) in the 13th volume appear as representative deities of the Yoga Tantra and the Carya Tantra respectively. [Plates 011L to 011R, 013L to 013R]

The main body of the Kriya Tantra is divided into the Tathāgata section (bde bzhin gshegs pavi rigs), the lotus section (pad mavi rigs and rdo rjevi rigs), and the Vajra section (rdo rjevi rigs) and the deity images that appear in the pictures of the 14th to 24th volumes of the esoteric section should belong to this type of tantra [Plates 014L to 024L]. Examples include the medicine Buddha, Bodhisattva Mañjuśrī, Marīcī, Uṣṇiṣavijaya, and Uṣṇīṣasitātapatrā who belong to the Tathāgata section, and Amitābha, the White Tara, and Khadiravani②, who belong to the lotus section.③

(2) Sutra Section of the Cause Vehicle

The Prajñā section, the Mahāratnakūṭa section, the Avataṃsaka section and the section of various sutras fall under the sutra section of the Cause Vehicle in the Peking edition of *Kangyur*. From its doctrine, it can be divided into three categories; the second turning of the wheel on no self-nature (bkav bar ba mtshan nyid med pavi chos kyi vkhor clo bskor bavi rim pa), the third turning of the wheel on the definitive truth (bkav vkhor lo gsum pa don dam rnam par nges pavi chos kyi vkhor lo bskor bavi rim pa), and the first turning of the wheel on the four noble truth (bkav vkhor lo dang po bden pa bzhivi chos kyi vkhor clo bskor bavi rim pa). The Ten Thousand Verses, Twenty-five Thousand Verses, Eighteen Thousand Verses, and Ten Thousand Verses of the *Shes rab kyi pa rol du phyin pa* of the Prajñā section in the *Kangyur* belong to the second turning of the wheel on no self-

① Peking Edition No. 81, rgyud, ca, 95b5-167a8 (vol.3, p.174).

② From *Ārya-aparimitāyurjñāna-nāma-mahāyāna-sūtra*, *Sarvatathāgatamātanitāre viśvakarmabhava-tantra-nāma*, Peking Edition on No. 361, rgyud, ba, 243b6-249a5 (vol.7, p.301); No. 390, rgyud, tsa, 58a5-74a8 (vol.8, p.149).

③ From *Ārya-nīlāmbaradharavajrapāṇi-kalpa-nāma-dhāraṇī*, *Ārya-mañjuśrīmūlatantra*, *Ārya-mārīcī-nāma-dhāraṇī*, *Ārya-sarvadurgatipariśodhani-uṣṇiṣavijaya-nāma-dhāraṇī*, *Ārya-sarvatathāgatoṣṇīṣasitātapatrā-nāma-aparājitāpratyaṁgiramahāviidyārājñī*, Peking Edition No. 132, rgyud, da, 161a8-162a8 (vol.6, p.98); No. 162, rgyud, na, 45b4-299a6 (vol.6, p.168); No. 182, rgyud, pha, 160a4-161a5 (vol.7, p.140); No. 197, rgyud, pha, 221b7-226b5 (vol.7, p.164); No. 202, rgyud, pha, 243a3-251a3 (vol.7, p.173).

nature. Texts like the *Sangs rgyas phal po che zhes bya ba shin tu rgyas pa chen povi mdo* of the Avataṃsaka section, *vPhags pa dkon mchog brtsegs pa chen povi chos kyi rnam grangs levu stong phrag brgya pa* of the Mahāratnakūṭa section (dkon mchog brtsegs pavi bskor), and the *sKal pa bzang po, rGya cher rol pa, dGongs pa nges par vgrel ba, Lang kar gshegs pa, Dam pavi chos pad ma dkar po, Mya ngan las vdas pa chen movi mdo, Chos thams cad kyi rang bzhin mnyam pa nyid rnam par spros pa ting nge vdzin gyi rgyal po* of the various Mahayana sutras section (theg pa chen povi mdo sde sna tshogs kyi bskor) belong to the third turning of the wheel on the definitive truth. Texts like the *Dam pavi chos dran pa nyer bzhag chen po, mDo chen mo sgyu mavi dra ba, mDo chen po stong pa nyid chen po* of the various Hinayana sutras section (theg pa chung nguvi mdo sde sna tshogs kyi bskor) and texts from the Vinaya section (vdul bavi bskor) like the *Lung sde bzhi, Lung rnam vbyed, Lung phran tshegs* belong to the first turning of the wheel on the four noble truth.

However, unlike the esoteric section, the images of the four sections of Prajñā, Mahāratnakūṭa, Avataṃsaka and various sutras are not arranged in order of the content of the texts. Instead, the Cause Vehicle of the Sutras was treated as a whole, and the deity images selected from important texts, mainly images of Buddhas were arranged. For example, in the Prajñā section (a total of 48 images in the title pages in 24 volumes), the opening is a combination of the images of Śākyamuni and Avalokiteśvara [Plates 025L to 025R], which has inherited the tradition of the images of the early Sanskrit palm-leaf *Prajñāpāramitāsūtra*. This is followed by two of the seven Medicine Buddhas, Dharma sāgarāgramativikrīḍitābhijñārāja (Chos rgya mtsho mchog gi blo rnam par rol pa mngon par mkhyen pa) and Dharmakīrtisāgaraghoṣa (Chos bsgrags rgya mtsho); Ratnaśikhī (Rin chen gtsug tor can), Maitreya (Byams pa mgon po), Dīpaṃkara (Mar me mdzad), Amitābha (Tshe pag med), Akṣobhya (Mi bskyod pa), and Amoghasiddhi (Don yod grub pa) from the *Suvarṇaprabhāsottamasūtrendrarājaḥ* [Plates 026L to 027L, 030R, 031L to 032R]; and the combination of Śākyamuni and Prajñāpāramitā (Sher phyin ma) commonly seen in the Tibetan *Prajñāpāramitāsūtra* [Plates 043L to 043R, 047L to 047R]. It is worth noting that there are five Buddhas in the Prajñā section from the *Buddhanāmasahasrapañcaśatacaturtripañcadaśa*, namely the five images of vBrug sgra dbyangs kyi rgyal po, mNgon par mkhyen pa, Don gyis kun grub shag kyavi rgyal po, Rin chen rgyal bavi mdzod and vJam pavi dbyangs [Plates 033L to 034R, 035R].[①] Among the twelve images of the Avataṃsaka section (a total of 12 images in the title pages in 6 volumes), the main figures are nine Buddhas from the *Bhadrakalpika-sūtra* in the various sutras section [Plates 056L to 060L]. The arrangement of images in the

① *Buddhanāmasahasrapañcaśatacaturtripañcadaśa*, Peking Edition No. 928, mdo sna tshogs, zu, 1b1-100a7 (vol.36, p.269)

various sutras section is more complete and distinct, mainly including the thirty-five Buddhas, the Buddhas of the ten directions, the seven medicine Buddhas and the seven Buddhas of the past [Plates 061L to 103R].

(3) Buddhist Protective Deities on the Lower Sutra Protection Plate

In addition, the Qing Dynasty court-style red print lines engraved the images of deities like the Vasudhārā (Lha mo nor rgyun), the Lha mo re ma ti, the Six-armed Mahākāla (mGon po phyag drug), and the Yellow Jambhala. These fall into mainly two categories, i.e., the five images of the Six-armed Mahākāla and his attendants and the five images of the Mahavajresvara and other Buddhist protectors. Their drawing style is largely the same as those found in the second and the seventh volumes of the *Longzangjing* completed in the 8th year of the Kangxi period of the Qing Dynasty.

The five images of the Six-armed Mahākāla and his attendants include: the Six-armed Mahākāla (Manchu: Itekel mahag'ala, Mongolian: Itegel maqak'ala, Tibetan: mGon po phyag drug pa) and his attendants Kāmarāja (Manchu: Ragirandza, Mongolian: Raki ranza, Tibetan: Ta ki rA dza/ vDod pavi rgyal po), Kṣetrapāla (Manchu: Zarabala, Mongolian: Zar-a bala, Tibetan: KShe Ta pa la), Jinamitra (Manchu: Zi namiraC, Mongolian: Zi namira, Tibetan: Dzi na mi tra/ Zhing skyong/ rGyal bavi bshes gnyen), and Mahākāla-Raudrantaka (Manchu: Rakšad g'ala, Mongolian: Raγšad k'ala, Tibetan: Drag sha nag po) [Plates 002b-1 to 002b-5].

The five images of the Mahavajreśvara and other tutelary deities include: Goddness in Bronze Clothes (Manchu: Sanggi gusjuma, Mongolian: Sanggi guszum-a, Tibetan: Zang gi gos gyon ma), Mahāratneśvara (Manchu: Maha ratna šowari, Mongolian: Ma ha radna šünri, Tibetan: Rin chen dbang chen), Mahākarmeśvara (Manchu: Maha germa šowari, Mongolian: Ma ha k'arm-a šünri, Tibetan: Phrin las dbang chen), and Goddness in Turquoise Clothes (Manch: Gioi gusjuma, Mongolian: Gioi guszum-a, Tibetan: g.Yuvi gos gyon ma) [Plates 007b-1 to 007b-5].

4. Origin of the Style

In the images of the title pages of the Kangxi Peking edition of *Kangyur*, except for the images of Śākyamuni, Bodhisattva Avalokiteśvara and their assistants, which were newly created in the Kangxi period, the rest were re-engraved images of the Yongle edition. Therefore, the image style of the title pages is mainly the Tibetan Buddhist art style of the Yongle period of the Ming Dynasty. On the basis of maintaining the writing style of the Tibetan text and layout style of the Yongle *Kangyur*, the Kangxi Peking edition of *Kangyur* has added a border frame around the inner text of each page.

The title page's image of the Kangxi Peking edition of *Kangyur* features a prominent main body of the deity, held by a single or double-layered lotus throne with five or seven petals, and backed by a round arched backlight or a triple arched niche by supported by a column. Further comparison shows that there are still slight differences in the style of these re-engraved images, mainly reflected in the images of the silent and wrathful figures. In the silent images primarily featuring Buddhas and Bodhisattvas, the picture is mostly backed by a triple arch supported by a column decorated in the style of vase lotus, and the back is decorated with dense rays of light, cloud patterns, plants and mountain stone patterns, and the costumes of the deity images tend to put emphasis on the natural texture of the stacked silk band of the clothes, reflecting distinctive Chinese art style [Plate 001L]. In regard to the image of the wrathful deities primarily featuring the Yidams and tutelary deities, the background picture is generally simple. It is only decorated with a circle of arched halo. The deity has thick limbs and a plump face, with detailed decoration, retaining a strong Nepalese art style [Plate 002L].

For the former style, Heather Karmay first linked it to the Gyantse Pelkor Chode Monastery mural painting created in 1427, pointing out that elements such as the triptych arched niches in the illustrations of the Yongle *Kangyur* and the columns on both sides supported by a vase base and crowned with a lotus capital can be found in the murals and sculptures of the Pelkor Chode Monastery. These elements first appeared in the illustrations of 10th-century Nepalese manuscripts. In regard to the illustrations found in the Yongle *Kangyur* that depicted triangular shaped flaming shoulders with jewelry inlays on both sides of the deity's backlight, Heather also pointed out that this is a commonly seen element in the murals of the Pelkor Chode Monastery and can be traced to the Buddhist images of the Pala period. Heather thinks that the illustrations of the Yongle *Kangyur* also incorporated Sino art style, reflecting the characteristic of the art style of the central Tibet of the same time.[①]

Based on this research, this paper further discusses the origin of image elements and styles. As mentioned above, in terms of composition style, the illustrations of the Yongle *Kangyur* can be divided into two styles: complex and simple, the former makes up the main body in terms of quantity, and only fourteen of the more than 200 illustrations falls under simple compositional styles. From the perspective of the body halo and head halo, they are mainly divided into three types, namely triple arch niches supported by standing columns, horseshoe shaped back halo and arch coupon backlights.

Style I: Niche with a Triple Arch Supported by Columns

This style basically makes up the main body of the background scenery of the

① Heather Karmy, *Early Sino-Tibetan Art*, Aris and Phillips Ltd. Warminster, 1975, pp.55-61.

illustration composition of the Yongle *Kangyur*, and 149 of the 210 drawings are in this style. The back is mainly composed of two sides of the column and a triple arched niche [Plates 001L to 001R, 004L to 005R, 008L to 008R, 011L to 014L, 015L to 017R, 020L to 020R. 023L to 024R, 043L to 046R, 048L to 105R]. The column has a treasure vase at the bottom serving as support. The lotus stem spawning from the vase is the column body. The lotus stem then branches off into lotus flowers and lotus leaves. The upper portion has a round corolla as the capital of the pillar, and the top is a *tuomu*-shaped flower platform to support the niche with a triple arch; due to the limits of space in the picture, the columns on both sides represent the upper half of the vertical surface. This style of niches is an important element in Nepalese painting, appearing at least in the murals of the Zhwa lu Monastery in the early 14th century, but it is often supported by arched niches decorated with ornate Capricorn of rolled tail. By the 15th century, this element became more popular and decorative in Tibetan Buddhist art images, and the niche styles on it were more diverse, depending on the height of the statue in the niche, their complexity, among which the simple joint arched niche was very common. However, in terms of shape, the triple arched niche in the illustration of the Yongle *Kangyur* is slightly different, the two ends of the niche are curled inward, while some are also curled outward [Plates 066R, 089L], and some are also decorated with a *Ruyi* cloud [Plate 070L] at the end. This style is closer to the triple arch at the upper end of the Sino style seat in the statue of the Lama of the Lam ’bras Lhakang in the Pelkor Chode Monastery and the shape of the lintel of the auspicious multi-gate pagoda and five-story of four-immeasurable palace.

Although the illustrations and composition of this style is packed, the relationship between the Buddha shrine and the halos of the main deity at the center enhances the layering and spatial sense of the picture. Generally, the head halo and the inside of the body halo of the Silent Deity are not ornamented, and the two sides of the body halo are decorated with triangular flame shoulders, composed of jewelry, or the engraved with patterns at the interior. Heather points out that it is a common element in the murals of Pelkor Chode Monastery and can be traced back to Buddhist statues dating back to the Pala period. The wrathful deities and the halos of Buddha figures are full of dense curly grass. Above the left and right sides of the niche, it is decorated with peonies, lotuses and other flower leaves, or densely covered with sunflower petal-shaped leaves, and exterior of the halos of the head and body of the main deity in the niche is covered with wave shaped rays. This element is probably directly inherited the Buddhist scripture engravings in China during the Song and Yuan dynasties, and is similarly expressed in the 15th-century Pelkor Chode Monastery murals.

Style II: Horseshoe Shaped Back Halo

This style is mainly composed of the head halo, body halo, and the horseshoe shaped back halo behind the main deity. This is also the back halo style practiced in Tibetan Buddhist images during the Yuan and Ming periods. Concentrated in the Buddha and Bodhisattva images of the first 18 volumes and volume 23 of the 24 volumes of the Prajñaparamita section [Plates 025L to 042R, 047L to 047R]. With the exception of the last two pictures, the other are also complex and densely packed, with entwined lotus patterns, ruyi cloud patterns, cloud patterns like the character *ren* (壬), wavy rays and chain patterns, which densely covers the inside and outside the head halo, the body halo and back halo of the deities. The head halo and body halo are decorated with a circle of block ornaments on the outside of the circle, which should be an imitation of the inlaid gem decoration in Tibetan Nepalese art in the Ming period; The outer edge of the large back halo is decorated with a small short curve resembling a flame pattern, which appeared in the sutra plates of the Prajñāpāramitā Sutras of Nepal as early as the 10th and 11th centuries and in the murals of the Hall of Prajñāpāramitā in the Zhwa lu Monastery. Furthermore, triangular flame shoulders are also decorated on both sides of the main deity's body, and the traditional Sino style of overlapping coins also appeared among the decorations.

Style III: Arch Shaped Halo

The arched shaped halo with a flame patterned border is a common halo style for statues of the wrathful yidams and protector deities of the Dharma in Tibetan Buddhist images during the Yuan and Ming dynasties. In the illustrations of the Yongle *Kangyur*, it is also used as the halo style of important Buddha-figures and protectors such as Cakrasaṃvara, Hevajra, Guhyasamāja, Ḍākinī, Yamāntaka, Mahākāla, and Vajrapāṇi [Plates 002L to 003R, 005L to 007 R, 009L to 010 R, 018L to 018 R, 021 L to 021R]. However, the difference is that the composition style of these illustrations is mostly simple, and there are no decorations inside and outside the halo, and only short curves represent the flame pattern on the outer edge of the halo. This further highlights the delicate and elegant decoration of the statue with bone ornaments.

It is worth mentioning that as the first engraved Tibetan *Kangyur*, the Yongle *Kangyur* is not the earliest engraved Tibetan Buddhist scriptures. The earliest Tibetan engraved Buddhist scriptures appeared in the court of the Yuan Dynasty, and the Yongle *Kangyur* also evolved on the basis of the Yuan edition of Tibetan Buddhist scriptures. The former's symmetrical composition of Buddha image illustrations and texts without border frame obviously have been influenced by the Yuan woodcut edition of the Tibetan Buddhist canons.① Several Yuan Tibetan Buddhist scriptures such as the *Abhidharmasamuccaya* (1299),② *Prasannapadā* (1311-1320),③ and *Kalachara Tantra* (1293) now collected in the Yonghegong Temple in Beijing, show the origin and the lineage of Tibetan woodcuts in the Yuan and Ming courts. Most of the Yuan versions were carved with imperial funding, and the size and layout were largely similar to the Yongle *Kangyur*, and the *Abhidharmasamuccaya* was funded by Empress Bulugan and engraved in Dadu, 12 × 66 cm in size, with two Buddha images on the title page, five lines in Tibetan in the middle, and without a border frame. The *Prasannapadā* was funded by Empress Buluhan and engraved in Dadu, 12 × 68 cm in size, with two Buddha images on the title page, seven lines of Tibetan in the middle, with no border frame. The *Kalacakra Tantra* was printed by U rgyan pa in Dadu, 11 × 64 cm in size, with a frame of 60 × 7.5 cm. It has 6 lines of main text. The first page is printed in red, and there are two Buddha images. In terms of image style, the composition of the Yongle *Kangyur* is largely similar to that of the images of the Yuan version. The Nepalese characteristics of the images in the Yuan version and the dense decorative style in the background are largely inherited by the title-page images of the Yongle *Kangyur* and further emphasized. In comparison, the Yongle *Kangyur* title-page image style is more complex than the illustration of the woodcut Tibetan Buddhist scriptures in the Yuan version, with more diverse elements and more delicate carvings.④

5. Conclusion

As the complete re-engraved edition of the Yongle *Kangyur*, which is the first printed version of the Tibetan *Kangyur* in history, the Kangxi Peking edition of *Kangyur* in the Qing Dynasty also has the same value. In the arrangement of texts and illustrated images, the entire *Kangyur* is based on the *bDe bar gshegs pavi gsung rab rin po chevi dkar chag bstan pa rgyas pavi nyi vod* (1323-1348) compiled by Tshal pa Kun dgav rdo rje. The texts are classified into six sections based on the tantra section of Fruit Vehicle and the sutra section of the Cause Vehicle, namely the esoteric, the Prajñāpāramitā, the Mahāratnakūṭa, the Avataṃsaka, the various sutras, and the Vinaya. The images are

① Uzhichev and Sumya, "A Study on the Illustration of Buddha Statues in Tibetan Literature in the Yuan Dynasty", *Fine Arts Research*, 2021, No. 1, pp.52-58.

② Item number: 000579.

③ Item number: 000901.

④ Uzhichev and Tian Xiaowen, "Overview of Two Tibetan Texts Printed during Yuan Dynasty in Yonghegong Temple", *Studies in World Religions*, 2020, No.6, pp.185-192. In this paper, Uzhichev pointed out that the illustrations of Tibetan literature in the early period of Yuan Dynasty, represented by *Abhidharmasamuccaya and Prasannapadā*, should directly refer to the illustrations of Buddhist statues in Tibetan gold manuscripts or ordinary manuscripts.

mainly classified and arranged according to the tantra section of the Fruit Vehicle and the sutra section of the Cause Vehicle. In the esoteric section, the images are mostly based on the four tantras structure of Bu ston Rin chen grub (Anuttarayoga Tantra, Yoga tantra, Carya tantra, and Kriya Tantra), while in the five sections of Prajñāpāramitā, the Mahāratnakūṭa, the Avataṃsaka, the various sutras, and the Vinaya, the images are not classified according to the texts under each section, but on the Buddhas commonly found in Mahayana Buddhist rituals, such as the Buddhas of the Ten Directions, the Thirty-Five Confessional Buddhas, and the Seven Medicine Buddhas. This gave the entire *Kangyur* not only a recitation function, but even more emphasized its function for offering and paying homage as the Buddhist canon.

The Kangxi Peking edition of *Kangyur* collected in the Library of Ethnic Cultural Palace is the only known complete first print of this version and is very close to the Yongle *Kangyur*. Its diverse woodcut illustrations have inherited the style of the Indian Buddhist images from the Yuan Dynasty court workshop, and also reflected the Sino-Tibetan Buddhist art style of the Ming court and Tibet in the early 15th century. After the re-engraving of the Kangxi Peking edition of *Kangyur* in the Qing Dynasty, the style of Ming court images was no longer popular in the Qing court, but quickly changed to a new style of the Qing Dynasty. This was probably influenced by Mongolian aesthetic taste, and also indirectly reflected the respective identities and functions of the Sino, Tibetan, Mongolian, and Manchu ethnic groups in the context of their interaction.

།།འཇམ་དཔལ་ཡེ་ཤེས་སེམས་དཔའ་ལ་ན་མོ།།

001L
S: Mañjuśrījñānasattva
T: vJam dpal ye shes sems dpav
C: 文殊智慧薩埵

།།དཔལ་དུས་ཀྱི་འཁོར་ལོ་ལ་ན་མོ།།

真實名經第一

001R

S: Śrīkālacakra

T: dPal dus kyi vkhor lo

C: 吉祥时轮

བདེ་མཆོག་ལ་ནམོ།།

002L
S: Saṃvara
T: bDe mchog
C: 上乐

祕密經第二卷 上一

ཕག་མོ་ལ་ན་མོ།།

002R
S: Vārāhī
T: Phag mo
C: 亥母

||ཀྱེའི་རྡོ་རྗེ་ལ་ན་མོ||

003L
S: Hevajra
T: Kyevi rdo rje
C: 喜乐金刚

秘密經第三卷 上一

||བདགམེདམཡནམོ||

003R

S: Nairātmyā

T: bDag med ma

C: 无我母

004L
S: Vajradhara
T: rDo rje vchang
C: 金刚持

004R
S: Vajrasattva
T: rDo rje sems dpav
C: 金刚萨埵

ན་རོ་མཁའ་སྤྱོད་ལ་ན་མོ།

005L
S: Nārodākinī
T: Na ro mkhav spyod
C: 捺啰空行［母］

祕密經第五卷 上一

མེ་ཏི་མཁའ་སྤྱོད་ལ་ན་མོ།

005R

S: Maitridākinī

T: Me Ti mkhav spyod

C: 弥底空行 [母]

||ཕག་མོ་ཞལ་གཉིས་མ་ལ་ན་མོ||

006L

S: Dvimukha-vārāhī

T: Phag mo zhal gnyis ma

C: 二面亥母

祕密經第六卷上一

||ཀུ་རུ་ཀུ་ལེ་ལ་ན་མོ||

006R

S: Kurukullā

T: Ku ru ku le

C: 智行佛母

007L
S: Guhyasamāja-Akṣobhyavajra
T: gSang vdus mi skyod rdo rje
C: 秘密集会不动金刚

祕密經第七卷上一

|| གསང་འདུས་འཇམ་དཔལ་རྡོ་རྗེ་ལ་ན་མོ ||

007R

S: Guhyasamāja-Mañjuvajra

T: gSang vdus vjam dpal rdo rje

C: 秘密集会文殊金刚

॥མི་གཡོ་བ་བླ་མེད་ལ་ནོ॥

008L
S: Acala
T: Mi g.yo ba bla med
C: 无上不动忿怒

祕密経苐八卷上一

||རྣམ་འཇོམས་ལ་ན་མོ||

008R

S: Vajravidāraṇa

T: rNam vjoms

C: 摧碎忿怒

འཇིགས་བྱེད་དཔའ་བོ།

009L
S: Bhairava
T: vJigs byed
C: 怖畏忿怒

祕密經第九卷 上二

ག ཤེདདམརཡནུམོ།།

009R
S: Rakta-Yamāri
T: gShed (gShen) dmar
C: 红色怖畏

༄ཕྱག་བཞི་པ་ལ་ན་མོ།

010L
S: Caturbhuja-Mahākāla
T: Phyag bzhi pa
C: 四臂马哈葛辣

010R

S: Vajrapāṇi

T: Phyag na rdo rje

C: 金刚手

||རྣམ་སྣང་ལ་ན་མོ།

011L
S: Vairocana
T: rNam snang
C: 毗卢遮那

秘密經第十一卷 上一

རྡོ་རྗེ་སེམས་དཔའ་ལ་ན་མོ།

011R
S: Vajrasattva
T: rDo rje sems dpav
C: 金刚萨埵

||ཁམས་གསུམ་རྣམ་རྒྱལ་ལ་ན་མོ||

012L
S: Trailokyavijaya
T: Khams gsum rnam rgyal
C: 降三世

秘密経第十二卷　上一

རྡོ་རྗེ་རིན་ཆེན་ལ་ན་མོ།

012R
S: Vajraratna
T: rDo rje rin chen
C: 金刚宝

རྣམ་སྣང་ལ་ན་མོ།།

013L
S: Vairocana
T: rNam snang
C: 毗卢遮那

祕密經第十三卷　上二

རྣམ་སྣང་ལ་ན་མོ།།

013R
S: Vairocana
T: rNam snang
C: 普觉众明主佛

ༀ། འཇམ་དཀར་ལ་ན་མོ།

014L
S: Sita-Mañjughoṣa
T: vJam dkar
C: 白色文殊菩萨

祕密經第十四卷上一

༄། འཇམ་དཔལ་སྨྲ་སེང་གེ།

014R

S: Vādisiṁha-Mañjughoṣa

T: vJam dpal smra seng

C: 妙吉祥语狮子

015L
S: Vajravidāraṇa
T: rNam vjoms
C: 摧碎忿怒
题记被掩，应为摧碎金刚

015R
S: Vajradharma
T: rDo rje chos
C: 金刚法
题记被掩，应为金刚法

||རྣམ་པར་སྣང་མཛད་ལ་ན་མོ||

016L
S: Vairocana
T: rNam par snang mdzad
C: 毗卢遮那

016R
S: Mañjughoṣa
T: vJam dbyangs
C: 文殊菩萨

||ཚེ་དཔག་མེད་ལ་ན་མོ||

017L
S: Amitāyus
T: Tshe dpag med
C: 无量寿佛

祕密經第十七卷 上一

||སྨན་ལྷ་ལ་ན་མོ||

017R
S: Bhaiṣajyaguru
T: sMan lha
C: 药师佛

018L
S: Jñānanātha
T: Ye shes mgon po
C: 智慧怙主

柲密經第十八卷上一

||རི་མ་ཏི་ལ་ན་མོ||

018R
S: Remati
T: Ri ma ti
C: 日麻替

||ཐུགས་རྗེ་ཆེན་པོ་ལ་ན་མོ||

019L
S: Mahākaruṇā-Avalokiteśvara
T: Thugs rje chen po
C: 大悲观世音菩萨

祕密經第十九卷上二

||དོནཞགསལ་ན་མོ||

019R
S: Amoghapāśa
T: Don yod zhags pa
C: 不空羂索

020L
S: Hayagrīva
T: rTa mgrin
C: 马项忿怒

秘密經第二十卷上二

||རལ་ཅིག་མ་ལ་ན་མོ།||

020R
S: Ekajaṭī
T: Ral cig ma
C: 独髻母

།།ཁྲོ་གཉེར་ཅན་ལ་ན་མོ།།

021L
S: Bhṛkuṭī
T: Khro gnyer can
C: 颦眉母

021R
S: Mārīcī
T: Vod zer can
C: 摩利支天

022L
S: Maitreya
S: Śākyamuni
S: Mañjuśrī
T: rJe btsun byams pa
T: Shā kya thub pa
T: vPhags pa vjam dpal
C: 弥勒尊者
C: 释迦牟尼佛
C: 圣者妙吉祥

022R
S: Tārā
S: Avalokiteśvara
S: Tārā-vikrānta Krodharāja
T: vPhags ma sgrol ma
T: Byang chub sems dpav sbyan ras gzigs
T: Khro bovi rgyal po sgrol ma sa non pa
C: 圣度母
C: 观世音菩萨
C: 忿怒王主地度母

023L

S: Sita-Tārā

T: sGrol ma dkar mo

C: 白度母

023R
S: Khadiravaṇī-Tārā
T: Sod (seng) lded (ldeng) nags sgrol
C: 佀木度母

||གཙུག་ཏོར་རྣམ་རྒྱལ་ལ་ན་མོ||

024L
S: Uṣṇīṣavijayā
T: gTsug tor rnam rgyal
C: 顶髻尊胜母

祕密經第二十四卷上一

།།གདུགས་དཀར་ཅན་ལ་ན་མོ།

024R
S: Sitātapatrā
T: gDugs dkar can
C: 白伞盖母

025L
S: Śākyamuni
T: Shag kya thub pa
C: 释迦牟尼佛

025R
S: Avalokiteśvara
T: sPyan ras gzigs
C: 观世音菩萨

026L

S: Dharmasāgarāgramativikrīḍitābhijñārāja

T: Chos rgya mtsho mchog gi blo rnam par rol pa mngon par mkhyen pa

C: 法海胜慧游戏神通佛

大般若經第二卷　上第一

ཆོས་བསྒྲགས་རྒྱ་མཚོ་ལ་ན་མོ༎

026R

S: Dharmakīrtisāgaraghoṣa

T: Chos bsgrags rgya mtsho

C: 法海雷音佛

རིན་ཆེན་གཙུག་ཏོར་ཅན་ལ་ན་མོ།

027L
S: Ratnaśikhī
T: Rin chen gtsug tor can
C: 宝髻佛

大般若経第三巻 上第一

||·འོད་དཔག་མེད་ལ་ན་མོ་||

027R
S: Amitaprabha
T: Vod dpag med
C: 无量光佛

འོད་ཞི་འོད་སྣང་དཔལ་ལ་ན་མོ།།

028L
S:
T: Vod zhi vod snang dpal
C: 光熄光耀吉祥佛

大般若經第四卷上一

||ཐུགས་ཟླ་བའི་དཀྱིལ་འཁོར་ན་མོ||

028R
S:
T: Thugs zla bavi dkyil vkhor
C: 心月中围佛

ཆོས་ཀྱི་འོད་ཟེར་པང་མོས་རབ་བརྒྱན་ལ་ན་མོ།

029L
S:
T: Chos kyi vod zer pang (pad) mos rab brgyan
C: 法光莲花庄严佛

大般若經第五卷　上一

།ཤཱཀྱ་ཐུབ་པ་ལ་ན་མོ།

029R
S: Śākyamuni
T: Shag kya thub pa
C: 释迦牟尼佛

འོད་དཔག་མེད་ལ་ན་མོ།

030L
S: Amitaprabha
T: Vod dpag med
C: 无量光佛

大般若經第六卷 上一

བྱམས་པ་མགོན་པོ་ལ་ནྨོ།

030R
S: Maitreyanātha
T: Byams pa mgon po
C: 弥勒怙主佛

།མི་བསྐྱོད་པ་ལ་ནམོ།།

031L
S: Akṣobhya
T: Mi bskyod pa
C: 不动佛

大般若經七卷　上一

||དོན་ཡོད་གྲུབ་པ་ལ་ན་མོ||

031R

S: Amoghasiddhi

T: Don yod grub pa

C: 不空成就佛

ཚེ་དཔག་མེད་ལ་ན་མོ།།

032L
S: Amitāyus
T: Tshe pag med
C: 无量寿佛

大般若經第八卷 上一

༄།མར་མེ་མཛད་ལ་ན་མོ།།

032R
S: Dīpaṃkara
T: Mar me mdzad
C: 燃灯佛

འབྲུག་སྒྲ་སྒྲ་དབྱངས་ཀྱི་རྒྱལ་པོ་ལ་ན་མོ།

033L
S: *Nirghoṣrāja
T: vBrug sgra sgra dbyangs kyi rgyal po
C: 雷音妙音王佛

大般若經第九卷 上一

མངོན་པར་མཁྱེན་པ་ལ་ན་མོ། །

033R
S: *Ābhijñā[rāja]
T: mngon par mkhyen pa
C: 法海胜慧游戏神通佛

དོན་གྱིས་ཀུན་གྲུབ་ཤག་ཀྱའི་རྒྱལ་པོ་ལ་ན་མོ།།

034L
S: *Sarvārthasiddhi-śakya-rāja
T: Don gyis kun grub shag kyavi rgyal po
C: 义成释迦王佛

大般若經第十卷 上

རིན་ཆེན་རྒྱལ་བའི་མཛོད་ལ་ན་མོ།།

034R

S:

T: Rin chen rgyal bavi mdzod

C: 宝王库佛

༄།།རིན་ཆེན་ཡོན་ཏན་སྣ་ཚོགས་ལ་ན་མོ།།

035L
S: *Ratnaviśvaguṇa
T: Rin chen yon tan sna tshogs
C: 诸功德宝佛

大般若經第十卷 上一

།འཇམ་པའི་དབྱངས་ལ་ན་མོ། །

035R
S: Mañjughoṣa
T: vJam pavi dbyangs
C: 妙音佛

སྣང་བ་མཐའ་ཡས་ལ་ན་མོ།།

036L
S: Amitābha
T: sNang pa mthav yas
C: 无量光佛

036R
S: Śākyamuni
T: Shag kya thub pa
C: 释迦牟尼佛

037L
S: Akṣobhya
T: Mi bskyod pa
C: 不动佛

大般若經第十三卷 上二

རིན་ཆེན་འབྱུང་ལྡན་ལ་ན་མོ།།

037R

S: Ratnasaṃbhava

T: Rin chen vbyung ldan

C: 宝生佛

མ་ར་མེ་མཛད་ལ་ན་མོ།།

038L
S: Dīpaṃkaraḥ
T: Mar me mdzad
C: 燃灯佛

大般若経第十四卷 上一

འོད་དཔག་མེད་ལ་ན་མོ།།

038R
S: Amitābha
T: Vod dpag med
C: 无量光佛

མངན་དང་མུན་པ་རབ་ཏུ་སེལ་བ་ལ་ན་མོ།།

039L
S:
T: mNgan dang mun pa rab tu sel ba
C: 除舛暗佛

039R
S:
T: Sems can thams cad kyi mthong mngon par dgav ba
C: 令一切有情见即欢喜佛

སྒྲིབ་པ་རྣམ་པར་སེལ་བ་ལ་ན་མོ

040L
S: Sarvanīvaraṇaviṣkambhī
T: sGrib pa rnam par sel ba
C: 除盖障佛

第二般若經第二卷 上一

འཁོར་བ་འཇིག་ལ་ན་མོ

040R
S: Krakucchanda
T: vKhor ba vjig
C: 拘留孙佛

སེང་གེ་ལ་ན་མོ།

041L
S: Siṃha
T: Seng ge
C: 师子佛

第二般若經第三卷　上二

།སེང་གེའི་ང་རོ་ལ་ན་མོ༔

041R
S: Simhanāda
T: Seng gevi da (nga) ngo (ro)
C: 师子吼佛

ནམ་མཁའ་ལ་ན་མོ།

042L
S: Gagana
T: Nam mkhav
C: 虚空佛

第二般若经第四卷 上一

ནམ་མཁའ་མཛོད་ལ་ནམོ།

042R
S: Gaganagañja
T: Nam mkhav mdzod
C: 虚空库佛

སངས་རྒྱས་ཤཱཀྱ་ཐུབ་པ་མཐོང་བ་དོན་ལྡན་ལ་ན་མོ།།

043L
S: Śākyamuni
T: Sangs rgyas shākya thub pa mthong ba don ldan
C: 见即获益佛释迦牟尼佛

第二大般若經第一卷 上六

ཡུམ་ཆེན་མོ་ཤེས་རབ་ཀྱི་ཕ་རོལ་དུ་ཕྱིན་པ་ལ་ན་མོ།།

043R
S: Prajñāpāramitā
T: Yum chen mo shes rab kyi pha rol du phyin pa
C: 般若佛母

|| སངས་རྒྱས་རྡོ་རྗེས་རྣམ་པར་གནོན་པ་ལ་ན་མོ ||

044L
S: *Vajra-vikaṭa
T: Sangs rgyas rdo rjes rnam par gnon pa
C: 金刚猛利佛

第一大般若經第二卷 上一

།།སངས་རྒྱས་ལོག་པར་དད་སེལ་ལ་ན་མོ།།

044R

S: Krakucchanda

T: Sangs rgyas log par dad sel

C: 除邪信佛（拘留孙佛别名）

045L
S: Amitābha
T: Vod dpag med
C: 无量光佛

第二大般若經第三卷上一

||མཐོང་བ་དོན་ལྡན་ལ་ན་མོ།|

045R

S: Amoghadarśin

T: mThong ba don ldan

C: 见即获益佛

||རིན་ཆེན་འབྱུང་ལྡན་ལ་ན་མོ||

046L
S: Ratnasaṃbhava
T: Rin chen vbyung ldan
C: 宝生佛

第二大般若經第四卷上一

རྣམ་པར་སྣང་མཛད་ལ་ན་མོ

046R
S: Vairocana
T: rNam par snang mdzad
C: 毗卢遮那

ཤཱཀྱ་ཐུབ་པ་ལ་ན་མོཾ།།

047L
S: Śākyamuni
T: Shākya thub pa
C: 释迦牟尼佛

第三般若經一卷 上一

ཡུམ་ཆེན་མོ་ལ་ན་མོ།།

047R

S: Prajñāpāramitā

T: Yum chen mo

C: 大佛母（般若佛母）

||སངས་རྒྱས་ཤཱཀྱ་ཐུབ་པ་ལ་ན་མོ||

048L

S: Śākyamuni

T: Sangs rgyas shākya thub pa

C: 释迦牟尼佛

諸般般若經第一卷上一

||བྱང་ཆུབ་སེམས་དཔའ་རྡོ་རྗེ་རྒྱལ་མཚན་ལ་ན་མོ།||

048R
S: Bodhisattva Vajraketu
T: Byang chub sems dpav rdo rje rgyal mtshan
C: 金刚幢菩萨

049L
S: Śākyamuni
T: Sangs rgyas shākya thub pa
C: 释迦牟尼佛

049R
S: Ākāśagarbha
T: Byang chub sems dpav nam mkhavi snying po
C: 虛空藏菩薩

སངས་རྒྱས་མི་འཁྲུགས་པ་ལ་ན་མོ། །

050L
S: Akṣobhya
T: Sangs rgyas mi vkhrugs pa
C: 不动佛

050R
S: Avalokiteśvara
T: Byang chub sems dpav spyan ras gzigs
C: 观世音菩萨

051L
S: Buddha Lokeśvara
T: Sangs rgyas vjig rten dbang po
C: 世间自在佛

大寶積經第三卷 上一

||བྱང་ཆུབ་སེམས་དཔའ་སྒྲིབ་པ་རྣམ་པར་སེལ་བ་ལ་ན་མོ།||

051R
S: Sarvanīvaraṇaviṣkambhī
T: Byang chub sems dpav sgrib pa rnam par sel ba
C: 除盖障菩萨

||སངས་རྒྱས་ཀུན་གཟིགས་པ་ལ་ན་མོ།||

052L
S: Samantadarśin
T: Sangs rgyas kun gzigs
C: 普照佛

大寶積經第四卷 上一

།།བྱང་ཆུབ་སེམས་དཔའ་བྱམས་པ་ལ་ན་མོ།།

052R
S: Maitreya
T: Byang chub sems dpav byams pa
C: 弥勒菩萨

053L
S: *Buddha Vikasitanetra
T: Sangs rgyas spyan rgyas pa
C: 广目佛

大寶積經第五卷上一

༄། བྱང་ཆུབ་སེམས་དཔའ་འཇམ་དབྱངས་ལ་ན་མོ། །།

053R
S: Mañjughoṣa
T: Byang chub sems dpav vjam dbyangs
C: 文殊菩萨

སངས་རྒྱས་སྤོས་དང་མེ་ཏོག་ལ་དབང་བ་ལ་ན་མོ། ||

054L
S: *Gandhapuṣpeśvara
T: Sangs rgyas spos dang me tog la dbang ba
C: 主香花佛

054R
S: Samantabhadra
T: Byang chub sems dpav kun tu bzang
C: 普贤菩萨

སངས་རྒྱས་རྡོ་རྗེས་རྣམ་པར་རྣོན་པ་ལ་ན་མོ

055L

S: *Vajra-vikaṭa

T: Sangs rgyas rdo rjes rnam par rnon pa

C: 金刚猛利佛

華嚴經第一卷 上

སངས་རྒྱས་སྤྱན་ལིགས་ལ་ནམོ།།

055R
S: Buddha Sulocana
T: Sangs rgyas spyan ligs (legs)
C: 妙明佛

སངས་རྒྱས་ས་ལའི་དབང་པོ་ལ་ན་མོ།

056L
S: Sālendra[rāja]
T: Sangs rgyas sa lavi dbang po
C: 娑罗主佛

華嚴經第二卷 上一

སངས་རྒྱས་སྟོབས་ཆེན་ལ་ནམོ

056R
S: Mahābala
T: Sangs rgyas stobs chen
C: 大力佛

057L
S: Siṃha
T: Sangs rgyas seng ge
C: 师子佛

華嚴經第三卷上一

||སངས་རྒྱས་རྒྱུ་སྐར་རྒྱལ་པོ་ལ་ན་མོ||

057R
S: Nakṣatrarāja
T: Sangs rgyas rgyu skar rgyal po
C: 宿王佛

སངས་རྒྱས་རབ་བསྟན་ལ་ནམོ།

058L

S: Supratiṣṭhita

T: Sangs rgyas rab bstan (brtan)

C: 坚固佛

華嚴經第四卷上二

སངས་རྒྱས་རྩི་སྨན་ལ་ན་མོ།།

058R
S: Oṣadhī
T: Sangs rgyas rtsi sman
C: 脩药佛

སངས་རྒྱས་མེ་ཏོག་གཉིས་ལ་ན་མོཿ

059L
S:
T: Sangs rgyas me tog gnyis pa
C: 华氏佛

華嚴經第五卷上一

སངས་རྒྱས་སྙན་པའི་རྟོག་ལ་ནམོ།

059R
S:
T: Sangs rgyas snyan pavi rtog
C: 名相佛

‖ སངས་རྒྱས་མེ་ཏོག་ཙན་ལ་ནམོ ‖

060L
S:
T: Sangs rgyas me tog rtsan (can?)
C: 持花佛

華嚴經第六卷 上一

|| བྱང་ཆུབ་སེམས་དཔའ་སའི་སྙིང་པོ་ལ་ན་མོ ||

060R
S: Kṣitigarbha
T: Byang chub sems dpav savi snying po
C: 地藏菩萨

སངས་རྒྱས་ཤཱཀྱ་ཐུབ་པ་ལ་ན་མོ།

061L
S: Śākyamuni
T: Sangs rgyas shākya thub pa
C: 释迦牟尼佛

賢劫千佛名經一卷上一

སངས་རྒྱས་རྡོ་རྗེ་སྙིང་པོ་ལ་ན་མོ།

061R
S: Vajragarbha
T: Sangs rgyas rdo rje snying po
C: 金刚藏佛

།རིན་ཆེན་འོད་འཕྲོས་ན་མོ།།

062L
S: Ratnārcis
T: Rin chen vod vphros
C: 宝焰佛

大遊戲經一卷 上一

།དཔལ་དགྱེས་པ་ལ་ན་མོ༎

062R
S: Vīranandin
T: dPal dgyes
C: 吉祥喜乐佛

ཀླུ་དབང་གི་རྒྱལ་པོ་ལ་ན་མོ།

063L
S: Nāgeśvararāja
T: Klu dbang gi rgyal po
C: 龙自在王佛

聖婆伽梵廣智經一卷上

||དཔའ་བོའི་སྡེ་ལ་ན་མོ་||

063R
S: Vīrasena
T: dPav bovi sde
C: 勇猛军佛

|| རིན་ཆེན་མེ་ལ་ན་མོ ||

064L
S: Ratnāgni
T: Rin chen me
C: 宝火佛

聖思善大聖經　上一

||རིན་ཆེན་ཟླ་འོད་ལ་ན་མོ།||

064R

S: Ratnacandraprabha

T: Rin chen zla vod

C: 宝月光佛

||མཐོང་བ་དོན་ཡོད་ལ་ན་མོ||

065L
S: Amoghadarśī
T: mThong ba don yod
C: 现无愚佛

||རིནཆེནཟླབལནམོ||

大聖廣開真義經一卷上 六

065R
S: Ratnacandra
T: Rin chen zla ba
C: 宝月佛

066L
S: Vimalā
T: Dri med ba
C: 无垢佛

066R
S: Vigatamala
T: Dri mad dbal ba (Dri ma dang bral ba)
C: 离垢佛

||དཔལ་སྦྱིན་ལ་ན་མོ||

067L
S: Śūradatta
T: dPal (dPav) sbyin
C: 勇施佛

妙法蓮華經一卷 上一

ཚངས་པ་ལ་ན་མོ།།

067R
S: Brahma
T: Tshangs pa
C: 净行佛

ཚངས་པས་བྱིན་ལ་ན་མོ།

068L
S: Brahmadatta
T: Tshang pas byin
C: 梵施佛

大般涅槃経第一卷 上

།ཆུ་ལྷ་ལ་ན་མོ།།

068R
S: Varuṇa
T: Chu lha
C: 水王佛

ཆུ་ལྷ་ལ་ན་མོཾ། །

069L

S: Varuṇadeva

T: Chu lha (Chu lhavi lha)

C: 水天佛

大般涅槃經第二卷 上二

དཔལ་བཟང་ལ་ན་མོ། །

069R
S: Bhadraśrī
T: dPal bzang
C: 贤吉祥佛

ཙན་དན་དཔལ་ལ་ན་མོ།།

070L
S: Candanaśrī
T: Tsan dan dpal
C: 旃檀吉祥佛

大般涅槃經第三卷上一

གཟི་བརྗིད་མཐའ་ཡས་ལ་ན་མོ།།

070R
S: Anantaujas
T: gZi brjid mthav yas
C: 无边威德佛

།།འོད་དཔལ་ལ་ན་མོ།།

071L
S: Prabhāsaśrī
T: Vod dpal
C: 光吉祥佛

聖禪定王經一卷 上一

|| མྱ་ངན་མེད་པའི་དཔལ་ལ་ན་མོ ||

071R
S: Aśokaśrī
T: Mya ngan med pavi dpal
C: 无忧吉祥佛

||སྲེད་མེད་ཀྱི་བུ་ལ་ན་མོ||

072L
S: Nārāyaṇa
T: Sred med kyi bu
C: 那罗延佛

見在諸佛禪定經一卷 上一

||མེ་ཏོག་དཔལ་ལ་ན་མོ||

072R

S: Kusumaśrī

T: Me tog dpal

C: 华吉祥

073L

S: Brahmajyotivikrīḍitābhijña

T: Tshangs pavi vod zer rnam par rol pas mngon par mkhyen pa

C: 净照明游戏神通佛

聖入不思議咒一卷上一

||པད་མའི་འོད་ཟེར་རྣམ་པར་རོལ་པས་མངོན་པར་མཁྱེན་པ་ལ་ན་མོ||

073R

S: Padmajyotirvikrīḍitābhijña

T: Pad mavi vod zer rnam par rol pas mngon par mkhyen pa

C: 莲华光游戏神通佛

||ནོར་དཔལ་ལ་ན་མོ||

074L
S: Dhanaśrī
T: Nor dpal
C: 财吉祥佛

義海菩薩請問經一卷 上

||དྲན་པའི་དཔལ་ལ་ན་མོ||

074R

S: Smṛtiśrī

T: Dran pavi dpal

C: 念吉祥佛

||ཚངས་པ་ཤིན་ཏུ་ཡོད་གྲགས་ལ་ནམོ||

075L
S: Suparikīrtitanāmagheyaśrī
T: Tshangs pa shing tu yod grags
C: 梵德称佛

大梵天王請問經一卷上一

།།དབང་པོ་ཏོག་གི་རྒྱལ་མཚན་གྱི་རྒྱལ་པོ་ལ་ན་མོ།།

075R

S: Indraketudhvajarāja

T: dBang po tog gi rgyal mtshan gyi rgyal po

C: 因陀罗顶幢王佛

|| ཤིན་ཏུ་རྣམ་པར་གནོན་པ་ལ་ན་མོ ||

076L

S: Suvikrāntaśrī

T: Shin tu rnam par gnon pa

C: 善游步功德佛

文殊菩薩問佛經一卷 二

།།གཡུལ་ལས་ཤིན་ཏུ་རྣམ་པར་རྒྱལ་བ་ལ་ན་མོ།།

076R
S: Yuddhajaya
T: gY.ul las shing tu rnam par rgyal ba
C: 斗战胜佛

།།ཀུན་ནས་སྣང་བ་བཀོད་པའི་དཔལ་ལ་ན་མོ།།

077L
S: Samantāvabhāsavyūhaśrī
T: Kun nas snang ba bkod pavi dpal
C: 周匝庄严功德佛

聖明五般若大聖經一卷上

||རིན་ཆེན་པད་མོ་རྣམ་པར་གནོན་པ་ལ་ན་མོ||

077R
S: Ratnapadmavikramī
T: Rin chen pad mo rnam par gnon pa
C: 宝莲华胜游步佛

||རྣམ་པར་གནོན་པ་གཤེགས་པ་ལ་ན་མོ||

078L
S: Vikrāntagāmī
T: rNam par gnon pa gshegs pa
C: 善游步佛

大聖信力增入印經一卷上一

།།སངས་རྒྱས་འཕགས་པ་རི་དབང་གི་རྒྱལ་པོ་ལ་ན་མོ།།

078R
S: Śailendrarāja
T: Sangs rgyas vphags pa ri dbang gi rgyal po
C: 妙住山王佛

||རྗེས་སུ་སྤྱོད་པ་ལ་ན་མོ||

079L
S: Anucārin
T: rJes su spyod pa
C: 随应佛

明

滿最器戒破說罪業大聖經卷上一

||མངོན་པར་འཕགས་པའི་རྒྱལ་པོ་ལ་ན་མོ།||

079R

S: Abhyudgatarāja

T: mNgon par vphags pavi rgyal po

C: 显圣王佛

།།འཁོན་དང་རྒྱགས་པ་རྣམ་པར་གནོན་པ་ལ་ན་མོ།།

080L

S:

T: vKhon dang rgyags pa rnam par gnon pa

C: 善灭净谶佛

080R

S: Ratnāṅgavyūhadyuti

T: Rin chen gZugs bkod vod snang

C: 宝身光辉佛

།བདུད་དང་ཡིད་གཉིས་ཀུན་འཇོམས་ལ་ན་མོ། །

081L

S:

T: bDud dang yid gnyis kun vjoms

C: 坏魔慢独步佛

||ཕྱིར་མི་ལྡོག་པའི་འཁོར་ལོའི་དཔལ་ལ་ན་མོ||

大聖收正法經一卷 上二

081R

S: *Avaivartikacakrasambhavaśrī?

T: Phyir mi ldog pavi vkhor lovi dpal

C: 初发心不退转轮成首佛

||རིན་ཆེན་གདུགས་འཕགས་སྣང་ལ་ན་མོ||

082L
S: Ratnacchattrodgata
T: Rin chen gdugs vphags snang
C: 宝盖照空佛

大聖法王經 卷上 一

||བྱང་ཆུབ་སེམས་དཔའ་འདུལ་ལ་ན་མོ||

082R

S:

T: Byang chub sems dpav vdul

C: 开化菩萨佛

||ཏིང་ངེ་འཛིན་མངོན་འཕགས་རྒྱལ་པོ་ལ་ན་མོ།|

083L
S: *Samādhi-ārya-rāja
T: Ting nge vdzin mngon vphags rgyal po
C: 无畏灭冥佛

三千四百五十三箇佛名經一卷三

||ཐེ་ཚོམ་སྤྱོད་མཛད་ལ་ན་མོ།||

083R
S: *Prathamacittotpādasaṃśayacchedika?
T: The tshom spyod mdzad
C: 初慈决疑佛

༄༅། །རྣམ་པར་གཟིགས་ལ་ན་མོ། །

084L
S: Vipaśyin
T: rNam par gzigs
C: 毗婆尸佛

百拜懺悔經卷上 一

084R
S: Śikhin
T: gTsug gtor can
C: 尸弃佛

ཐམསཅདསྐྱོབལནམོ།།

085L
S: Viśvabhū
T: Thams cad skyob
C: 毗舍浮佛

聖勝法念住經第一卷 上二

འཁོར་བ འཇིག་ལ་ན་མོ།།

085R
S: Krakucchanda
T: vKhor ba vjig
C: 拘留孙佛

།།གསར་ཐུབ་ལ་ན་མོ།།

086L
S: Kanakamuni
T: gSar (gSer) thub
C: 拘那含牟尼佛

聖勝法念住經第二卷 上

།།འོད་སྲུངས་ལ་ན་མོ།།

086R

S: Kāśyapa

T: Vod srungs

C: 迦叶佛

087L
S: Śākyamuni
T: Shākya thub pa
C: 释迦牟尼佛

聖勝法念住經第三卷上一

།།བྱམས་པ་ལ་ན་མོ།།

087R

S: Maitreya

T: Byams pa

C: 弥勒佛

088L
S: Śikhin
T: Rin chen gtsug tor
C: 尸弃佛

佛出現經一卷上一

།། རིན་ཆེན་རྒྱལ་བའི་མཛོད་ལ་ནམོ།།

088R
S: *Ratnajinagañja
T: Rin chen rgyal bavi mdzod
C: 宝王库佛

||རིན་ཆེན་ཟླ་བ་ལ་ན་མོ||

089L

S: Ratnacandrapadmapratimaṇḍitapaṇḍita?tejaḥsvaraghoṣarāja

T: Rin chen zla ba

C: 宝月智严光音自在王佛

།། མཚན་ལེགས་ལ་ན་མོ།།

因果經第一卷 上

089R

S: Suparikīrtitanāmaśrīrāja

T: mTshan legs

C: 善名称吉祥王佛

གསེར་བཟང་དྲི་མེད་ལ་ན་མོ།

090L
S: Suvarṇabhadravimalaratnaprabhāsavrata
T: gSer bzangs dri med
C: 金色宝光妙行成就佛

因果經第二卷　上二

090R
S: Aśokottamaśrī
T: Mya ngan med mchog dpal
C: 无忧胜吉祥佛

||ཆོས་གྲགས་རྒྱ་མཚོ་ལ་ན་མོ||

091L
S: Dharmakīrtisāgaraghoṣa
T: Chos grags rgya mtsho
C: 法海雷音佛

説綱波等百悟經一卷上一

||མངོན་མཁྱེན་རྒྱལ་པོ་ལ་ན་མོ||

091R

S: Dharmasāgarāgramativikrīḍitābhijñārāja

T: mNgon mkhyen rgyal po

C: 法海胜慧游戏神通佛

།།སངས་རྒྱས་ཤཱཀྱ་ཐུབ་པ་ལ་ན་མོ།།

092L
S: Śākyamuni
T: Sangs rgyas shākya thub ba
C: 释迦牟尼佛

律師戒行經第一卷上一

།སངས་རྒྱས་རྣམ་པར་གཟིགས་ལ་ན་མོ།།

092R
S: Vipaśyin
T: Sangs rgyas rnam par gzigs
C: 毗婆尸佛

॥ཤཱཀྱ་ཐུབ་པ་ལ་ན་མོ།॥

093L
S: Śākyamuni
T: Shākya thub pa
C: 释迦牟尼佛

佛説稱悟福力經一卷上一

།།སྨན་པའི་རྒྱལ་པོ་ལ་ན་མོ།།

093R

S: Bhaiṣajyaguru-Vaiḍūryaprabhārāja

T: sMan pavi rgyal po

C: 药王佛

༄། །ཤར་ཕྱོགས་ཀྱི་སངས་རྒྱས་རིན་ཆེན་འབྱུང་གནས་ལ་ན་མོ། །

094L
S: Ratnasaṃbhava
T: Shar phyogs kyi sangs rgyas rin chen vbyung gnas
C: 东方宝生佛

094R
S: Śikhin
T: Sangs rgyas gtsug tor can
C: 尸弃佛

ལྷོ་ཕྱོགས་ཀྱི་སངས་རྒྱས་མྱ་ངན་མེད་པའི་དཔལ་ལ་ན་མོ།

095L
S: Aśokaśrī
T: Lho phyogs kyi sangs rgyas mya ngan med pavi dpal
C: 南方无忧吉祥佛

律師戒行經第三卷上一

སངས་རྒྱས་ཐམས་ཅད་སྐྱོབ་ལ་ན་མོ།།

095R
S: Viśvabhū
T: Sangs rgyas thams cad skyob
C: 毗舍浮佛

ནུབ་ཕྱོགས་ཀྱི་སངས་རྒྱས་རིན་ཆེན་འོད་འཕྲོ་ལ་ན་མོ།།

096L

S: Ratnārcis

T: Nub phyogs kyi sangs rgyas rin chen vod vphros

C: 西方宝焰佛

096R
S: Krakucchanda
T: vKhor ba vjig
C: 拘留孙佛

བྱང་ཕྱོགས་ཀྱི་དས་རྒྱས་རྒྱལ་བའི་དབང་པོ་ལ་ནམོ།།

097L

S: Jinendra

T: Byang phyogs kyi das (sangs) rgyas rgyal bavi dbang po

C: 北方胜者自在佛

律師戒行經第五卷上一

སངས་རྒྱས་གསེར་ཐུབ་ལ་ན་མོ།།

097R

S: Kanakamuni

T: Sangs rgyas gser thub

C: 拘那含牟尼佛

098L
S: Samādhihastyuttaraśrī
T: (Shar) Byang phyogs kyi sangs rgyas ting nge vdzin gyi glang po dam pavi dpal
C:（东）北方禅定净象吉祥佛

律師戒行經第六卷上

༄ན་མོ་སངས་རྒྱས་འོད་སྲུངས་ལ་ན་མོ།

098R

S: Kāśyapa

T: Sangs rgyas vod vsrungs

C: 迦叶佛

099L
S: Padmottaraśrī
T: Shar lho mtshams kyi sangs rgyas pad mo dam pavi dpal
C: 东南隅净莲吉祥佛

律師戒行經第七卷上一

|| སངས་རྒྱས་མར་མེ་མཛད་ལ་ན་མོ། ||

099R
S: Dīpaṃkara
T: Sangs rgyas mar me mdzad
C: 燃灯佛

ལྷོ་ནུབ་ཀྱི་སངས་རྒྱས་ཉི་མའི་དཀྱིལ་འཁོར་སྣང་བ་དམ་པའི་དཔལ་ལ་ན་མོ༎

100L

S: Sūryamaṇḍalapratibhāsottamaśrī

T: Lho nub kyi sangs rgyas nyi mavi dkyil vkhor snang ba dam pavi dpal

C: 西南日轮净耀吉祥佛

||སངས་རྒྱས་བྱས་ས་བམ་སད་བོ་ལ་ན་མོ་||

100R

S: Maitreya (?)

T: Sangs rgyas byas sa bam sad bo (byams pa mgon po?)

C: 弥勒佛（？）

ནུབ་བྱང་གི་སངས་རྒྱས་གདུགས་དམ་པའི་དཔལ་ལ་ན་མོ༎

101L
S: Chattrottamaśrī
T: Nub byang gi sangs rgyas gdugs dam pavi dpal
C: 西北净伞吉祥佛

律師戒行經第九卷上一

སངས་རྒྱས་སྨན་གྱི་བླ་བཻ་ཌཱུ་རྱའི་འོད་ཀྱི་རྒྱལ་པོ་ལ་ན་མོ།།

101R
S: Bhaiṣajyaguru-Vaiḍūryaprabhārāja
T: Sangs rgyas sman gyi bla bai du ryavi vod kyi rgyal po
C: 药师琉璃光佛

102L
S: Padmaśrī
T: Vog phyogs kyi sangs rgyas bang mo (pad mo) dam bavi dpal
C: 下方净藏吉祥佛

律師戒行經第十卷上一

སངས་རྒྱས་ཀུན་ཏུ་བཟང་པོ་ལ་ན་མོ།

102R
S: Samantabhadra
T: Sangs rgyas kun du bzang po
C: 普贤佛

སྟེང་ཕྱོགས་ཀྱི་སངས་རྒྱས་དགའ་བའི་དཔལ་ལ་ན་མོ།།

103L
S: Ānandaśrī
T: sTeng phyogs kyi sangs rgyas dgav bavi dpal
C: 上方乐吉祥佛

律師戒行經第十一卷上一

སངས་རྒྱས་ཀུན་ཏུ་གཟིགས་ལ་ནམོ།།

103R
S:
T: Sangs rgyas kun tu gzigs
C: 遍照佛

104L
S: Akṣobhya
T: Sangs rgya (s) mi vkhrugs pa
C: 不动佛

律師戒行經第十二卷上一

འཕགས་པ་འོད་བསྲུངས་ལ་ན་མོ།།

104R

S: Kāśyapa

T: vPhags pa vod bsrungs

C: 圣者迦叶

105L
S: Amitābha
T: Sangs rgyas vod dpag med
C: 无量光佛

律師戒行經第十三卷上一

105R
S:
T: vPhags pa nye ba vkhor
C: 圣者优波离

002b-1
S: Ṭakkirāja
T: Ta ki rA dza/ vdod pavi rgyal po
Mg: Raki ranza
Mn: Ragirandza
C: 欲帝明王

002b-2
S: Kṣetrapāla
T: Kshe Ta pa la
Mg: Zar-a bala
Mn: Dzarabala
C: 护国护法

002b-3
S: Ṣaḍbhuja-Mahākāla
T: mGon po phyag drug pa
Mg: Itegel maqak'ala
Mn: Itegel mahag'ala
C: 六臂大黑天

002b-4
S: Jinamitra
T: Dzi na mi tra/ Zhing skyong/ rGyal bavi bshes gnyen
Mg: Zi namira
Mn: dzy namira
C: 尊亲护法

002b-5
S: Rakṣakāla
T: Drag sha nag po
Mg: Raγšad k'ala
Mn: Rakšat g'ala
C: 大黑雄威护法

007b-1
S:
T: Zang gi gos gyon ma
Mg: Sanggi guszum-a
Mn: Sanggi gusjuma
C: 铜衣天女

007b-2
S: Mahāratneśvara
T: Rin chen dbang chen
Mg: Ma ha radna šori
Mn: Maha ratna šowari
C: 珍宝大自在天

007b-3
S: Mahāvajreśvara
T: rDo rje dbang chen
Mg: Ma ha bazar šori
Mn: Maha badzar šowari
C: 金刚大自在天

007b-4
S: Mahākarmeśvara
T: Phrin las dbang chen
Mg: Ma ha k'arm-a šori
Mn: Maha germa šowari
C: 事业大自在天

007b-5

S:

T: g.Yuvi gos gyon ma

Mg: gyui guszum-a

Mn: Gioi gusjuma

C: 玉衣天女

附　录

北京康熙版《甘珠尔》序疏与职官名录录文（四体对照）

一、汉文录文

御制番藏經序

朕聞。羲爻既衍。遠開經籍之源。禹範旋披。弘啟文章之籥。溯淳風於太古。恢景運於中天。大義微言。較日星而並燦。靈篇寶籙。偕嶽瀆以爭奇。既至祐國庇民。有祝史受釐之冊。和風甘雨。有陰陽占候之家。總皆以崇有為歸。遂各著闡幽之論。若夫十方四諦之門。三明六通之業。夢金人於漢帝。白馬馱來。序聖教於唐宗。青蓮湧出。琅函東度。登黃珉碧玉之壇。金疊南翻。建獅子龍王之會。竺蘭授記。宗風振四十二章。元奘載歸。勝果揚六百餘部。用度閻浮之域。長留震旦之區。原其流衍弘綱意在挽回末俗。依然忠孝言言祛妄存眞。亦曰仁慈念念勝殘去殺心。燈夜炳則照徹昏衢。意蘂晨飄則凉生火宅。雖殊途而一致實。異派而同原。兼以諷誦仙輪。仰祝靈長之祚。敷宣教鐸。俯垂濟渡之航。固所瞻依。寧無裨補。是知乾綱在握。無俟藉響於法螺。而當泰宇方隆。並可徵休

頁一

於香象矣。朕探索古今。研窮謨典。皇風帝緒之策。時掣牙籤。名山秘笈之藏。更披玉軸。雞籌報曉。資啟沃於經帷。鳳炬分宵。備詢謀於冊府。憲章所係。討蒐文獻之遺。儒術攸崇。紹明理性之學。際茲車書一統。庶幾軌物咸遵。至於意樹心蓮。未展貝多之葉。鶴林鹿苑。偶臨般若之臺。究玉鏡之圓光。覽金繩之妙諦。伏惟　太皇太后。遐齡永錫。齊心舍衛之城。皇太后。純嘏殷流。報禮祇洹之役。曩者林衡授矩。無非桂棟梅梁。于焉竹素成編。盡是彫談奧辯。供億靡勞於蔀屋。不涉民財。經營悉出於芝宮。非關內帑。念眞乘之慧業宜宣。而梵唄之潮音未廣。乃稽歷古傳燈之録。更輯千山印鉢之篇。番藏舊文爰加鐫刻。錄縹裝就。八解高超。黃錦開時。七花遠邁。誠以導蠙暉於紫幄。分璇彩於黃圖。助啟芳詮。廣崇大藏。

頌兩宮之景福。延萬姓之鴻庥。式弁簡端。用資褒讚云爾。

頁二

康熙二十三年八月二十二日

頁三

請序疏

和碩裕親王臣 福全等謹 題。為釋藏名經奉 命鐫梓。恭請 御製序文。宣示永久事。竊惟。迦維誕瑞。象法王肇開八正五乘。毗邪摩詰授受遠矣。自漢帝夢感金仙。遣使天竺。釋典諸書之流傳於中土者。幾二千年。其間雖歷唐宋隆盛之朝亦多闡明褒讚。非徒廣揚佛教。正欲藉以慈育萬有也。恭遇我 皇上聰明睿知。秉自性生。峻德神功侔於覆載。治化翔洽威烈弘敷。日月照臨之頁下。罔不沾濡 渥澤。奉朔貢琛。而 聖度淵沖。日加兢業。宵衣旰食。勤政愛民。複以 萬幾餘閒。研精六經。綜覽群史。闢圖疇未發之淵微。鑑治運相循之理數。以至星官地志諸子百家稗乘緯書仙經貝葉。莫不丙夜詳探究其旨奧。故能學洞陰陽。博極古今。時而 宸襟游豫 睿藻琳琅。落筆千言。炳彪雲漢。所謂道備典謨。義兼風雅。煌煌乎統千聖而集成。苞三才而建極已。乃若 寶墨瑤箋。龍翔鳳翥。運羲畫之奇。陋漢章之體。又餘事也。邇者 特沛洪慈。重刊番藏名經。用廣利益。蓋以上凝 太皇太后 皇太后萬壽無疆之禎。下錫四海臣民億萬載之祉。但四流六度妙理難詮。非得天語發揮。下土塵迷何由共開覺路。昔

頁一

唐太宗敕名僧。翻譯經文六百餘部。特製序文。明太祖親撰佛母像讚。永樂中校刻大藏眞經。皆當開國盛時。表章梵典。況我 皇上仁敬孝慈。迥非唐明三君所能比擬萬一。 宸翰所頒。便可燭照諸天。康濟率土。伏祈 皇上俯念佛果 特賜御製經序文。弁諸經首。開示顓蒙。昭垂萬禩。庶慧日賴 奎章而並煥。慈雲同 聖澤以長流矣。為此具本謹題請 旨。

和 碩 裕 親 王臣 福 全

內閣侍讀學士食二品俸加四級臣 烏喇代

宗人府右司掌印理事官加一級臣 覺羅舜拜

工科掌印給事中加二級臣 雅齊納

監察御史加二級臣 伊拉哈

監察御史加三級臣 耿 額

兵 部 郎 中臣 圖那什希

康熙二十二年八月十六日具

題本月十八日奉　旨禮部詳察典例確議具奏

頁二

覆請序疏

禮部尚書臣介山等謹　題。為釋藏名經奉　命鐫梓。恭請　御製經序文。宣示永久事。禮科抄出和碩裕親王福全等題。前事內開。竊惟迦維誕瑞。象法王肇開八正五乘。毗邪摩詰授受遠矣。自漢帝夢感金仙。遣使天竺。釋典諸書之流傳於中土者。幾二千年。其間雖歷唐宋隆盛之朝亦多闡明褒讚。非徒廣揚佛教。正欲藉以慈育萬有也。恭遇我　皇上聰明睿知。秉自性生。峻德神功侔於覆載。治化翔洽威烈弘敷。日月照臨之页下。罔不沾濡　渥澤。奉朔貢琛。而　聖度淵沖。日加兢業。宵衣旰食。勤政愛民。複以　萬幾餘閒。研精六經。綜覽群史。闡圖疇未發之淵微。鑑治運相循之理數。以至星官地志諸子百家稗乘緯書仙經貝葉。莫不丙夜詳探究其旨奧。故能學洞陰陽。博極古今。時而　宸襟游豫　睿藻琳琅。落筆千言。炳彪雲漢。所謂道備典謨。義兼風雅。煌煌乎統千聖而集成。苞三才而建極已。乃若　寶墨瑤箋。龍翔鳳翥。運羲畫之奇。陋漢章之體。又餘事也。邇者　特沛洪慈。重刊番藏名經。用廣利益。蓋以上凝　太皇太后　皇太后萬壽無疆之禎。下錫四海臣民億萬載之祉。但四流六度妙理難詮。

頁一

非得　天語發揮。下土塵迷何由共開覺路。昔唐太宗敕名僧。翻譯經文六百餘部。特製序文。明太祖親撰佛母像讚。永樂中校刻大藏真經。皆當開國盛時。表章梵典。況我　皇上仁敬孝慈。逈非唐明三君所能比擬萬一。宸翰所頒。便可燭照諸天。康濟率土。伏祈　皇上俯念佛果　特賜御製經序文。弁諸經首。開示顓蒙。昭垂萬禩。庶慧日賴　奎章而並煥。慈雲同　聖澤以長流矣。為此具本謹題請　旨。等因康熙二十二年八月十六日題。本月十八日奉　旨。禮部詳察典例確議具奏欽此遵同於本月十九日到部該臣等議。得和碩裕親王福全等疏稱。釋典流傳中土幾二千年。歷唐宋隆盛之朝。闡明褒讚。非徒廣揚佛教。正欲藉以慈育萬有。恭遇　皇上聰明睿知。秉自性生。峻德神功侔於敷載。萬幾餘閒。研精六經。綜覽群史。乃至諸子百家仙經貝葉。莫不丙夜詳探究其旨奧。邇者　特沛洪慈。重刊番藏經名。用廣利益。上凝　太皇太后　皇太后萬壽無疆之禎。下錫四海臣民億萬載之祉。昔唐太宗敕名僧。翻譯經文六百餘部。特製序文。明太祖親撰佛母像讚。永樂中校刻大藏眞經。皆當開國盛時。表章梵典。我　皇上仁敬孝慈。逈非唐明三君所能比

頁二

擬萬一。伏祈　皇上俯念佛果　特賜御製經序文。弁諸經首。開示顓蒙。昭垂萬禩。等因臣等。竊惟釋典諸書。充牣祕藏。雖教有顯密之分。宗有性相之異。要其指歸。在於利濟萬品化導群生。歷代帝王。往往為之流通宣布。或命翻譯。或命鐫梓。其教賴以弗替。至於闡揚道風恢弘勝果。尤在親製文辭冠之。簡冊方足。令神人欽仰遠邇瞻依。考唐太宗貞觀二十二年。沙門元奘等。將梵經六百五十七部譯畢。帝親製三藏聖教序。石刻至今猶存。明太祖御製文集內有佛母讚。又有心經序。及蓮華菩薩藏世界諸讚。明成祖校刻大藏眞經。有藏經讚。及正宗大覺妙經四部經華嚴經眞實名經諸序。弁諸梵冊。俱載藏函。又考唐憲宗。有心地觀經序。宋太宗有御製妙覺集五卷。眞宗有釋典御集一部。並藏諸琳宮。傳示不朽。恭惟。我　皇上。功同覆載。道貫天人。極深研幾理。無隱而不燭。知來藏往籍。無奧而不探。　聖學淵徵　天章鴻麗。誠非前代帝王所能比擬萬一。茲者體天地好生之心。擴聖人止孝之量。上為　兩宮禔福。下為萬姓降祥　特命刊刻釋藏名經。流通海內。顧釋典難諳。梵書乍布。必得　天語褒揚。方可炳著日月允宜俯從。王等所請　御製經序文。冠諸經首。俾瑯函寶笈沾被

頁三

龍光昭示天壤永永無極。誠　昌朝之盛事　聖代之曠典也。臣等未敢擅便謹題請　旨。

禮部尚書臣介山
尚書臣沙澄
左侍郎臣額星格
經筵講官左侍郎兼翰林院學士臣楊正中
右侍郎加二級臣沙海
經筵講官右侍郎兼翰林院學士臣陳廷敬
祠祭清吏司郎中臣何棅
員外郎加二級臣常在
員外郎臣桑格
員外郎加一級臣蔡音達
員外郎臣郭世隆
員外郎臣蕭永藻
主事臣王敬臣
主事加一級臣費暘古
主事臣徐人鳳
康熙二十二年九月初一日具

題本月初四日奉　旨依議

頁四

職名

奉　旨補造大藏經承造

和碩裕親王臣福　全

監脩官員

司　　　　　業臣阿勒卑忒胡

內閣侍讀學士臣舒　輅

禮科掌印給事中臣阿什譚

刑科掌印給事中臣赫　壽

督察院監察御史臣色德里

督　察　御　史臣麻　色

督　察　御　史臣薩音布

刑　部　郎　中臣温　察

工　部　郎　中臣六　相

吏部員外郎臣恩　霱

兵部員外郎臣馬朝賛

廣善庫員外郎臣蘇　泰

員　　外　　郎臣德成格

主　　　　　事臣永　福

主　　　　　事臣佟吉圖

吏部筆帖式臣白保住

禮部筆帖式臣福　祿

兵部筆帖式臣吉爾賽

刑部筆帖式臣爾　格

筆　　帖　　式臣蘇爾度

筆　　帖　　式臣唐　艾

工部筆帖式臣察補護

督察院筆帖式臣能　格

筆　　帖　　式臣瓦爾達

筆　　帖　　式臣劉　住

筆　　帖　　式臣劉　思

筆　　帖　　式臣劉一元

戶科筆帖式臣 興 圖
禮科筆帖式臣 瓦洪泰

頁上一

刑科筆帖式臣 騰 格

對看喇嘛

章 家 胡 圖 圖
住持喇嘛王舒克津巴格隆
住持喇嘛羅卜臧巴爾柱格隆
德睦齊羅卜臧那木渣格隆
敦魯布拉布淡蘭占巴
錯爾秦臧布蘭占霸
旦巴賽爾濟格隆

大清康熙叁拾玖年肆月 吉日刊成

頁下一

校閱經字喇麻

總管京都喇麻班第查薩克大喇麻墨爾根綽爾濟
總管京都喇麻班第查薩克大喇麻番文總教習索諾穆綽爾濟
番文副教習官食四品俸式臣 石 頭

對讀經字喇麻

根敦達爾扎格龍
羅卜藏拜爾濟格龍
索諾穆林親格龍
羅卜藏魯雷格龍
阿瓦僧格格龍
羅卜藏混格格龍
羅卜藏巴爾諸利格龍
寸爾親木藏般格龍
旦木巴喇喜格龍
羅卜藏喜洛格龍
薩木旦林親格龍
金木巴巴爾諸利格龍
羅卜藏崔扎爾格龍

林親索諾木格龍
崔爾奇木巴爾叭利格龍
崔爾奇木雲旦格龍
崔爾奇木喇喜格龍
格勒克林親格龍
喇喜林親格龍
阿王金木巴格龍
旦木巴喇穆旦格龍
阿王金木巴格龍
藏般崔爾奇木格龍
羅木藏作德叭格龍
雲旦林親格龍
盆素林親格龍
羅卜藏丹達利格龍
金木巴索諾木格龍
業喜巴爾諸利格龍
崔木拍爾藏般格龍
喇喜達爾扎格龍

頁上一

索諾木尖山格龍
崔木拍爾藏般格龍
羅卜藏達爾齊格隆
藏般尖山格隆
羅卜藏泥瑪格龍
索諾木尊雷格龍
喇喜藏般格龍
尊雷林親格龍
羅卜藏拍爾雷格龍
番文官學生　多爾濟

頁下一

校閲序目錄官

內閣侍讀學士加三級臣 丹　代
內閣侍讀學士食三品俸加二級臣 拜　禮

內閣侍讀學士食三品俸加六級臣 翁 英

翻譯番文序目錄官

番文副教習官食四品俸臣 石 頭

翻譯漢字目錄官

內閣辦事中書臣 武熙布

內閣辦事中書臣 登 德

翻譯蒙古字序目錄官

內閣辦事中書加二級食六品俸臣 喇睦璋

內閣辦事中書加一級食六品俸臣 黑 鈞

滿文謄錄官

內閣辦事中書加四級食五品俸臣 伊巴禮

內閣辦事中書臣 增 壽

內閣辦事中書臣 禪 布

蒙古文謄錄官

內閣辦事中書臣 韶 構

漢文謄錄官

內閣辦事中書加一級臣 曹貞吉

內閣辦事中書臣 王敁沃

番文謄錄喇麻

羅卜藏魯雷格隆

羅卜藏拜爾濟格龍

索那木林親格隆

頁一

總理監修大藏經

和碩裕親王臣 福 全

監修官

內閣侍讀學士食二品俸加四級臣 烏拉代

宗人府右司掌印理事官加一級臣 覺羅舜拜

理事官加一級臣 覺羅李歷馬

工科掌印給事中加二級臣 雅齊納

都察院監察御史加一級臣 伊拉哈

監察御史加三級臣 耿 額

兵部郎中臣 圖把什希

內閣撰文中書加一級臣 華 色

宗人府六品筆帖式加一級臣 胡溫哲
七品筆帖式加二級臣 常保
都察院七品筆帖式加二級臣 駙密達
筆帖式臣 納彥泰
兵部七品筆帖式加二級臣 吳蘭

二、藏文录文及转写

（一）藏文录文

御制序文

༄༅།།རྒྱལ་པོའི་མཛད་པའི་བོད་ཀྱི་བཀའ་འགྱུར་གྱི་འབྲི་སྦྱངས། ངེད་ཐོས་ན། མང་བཀུར་གྱི། རི་མོའི་རྒྱས་པར་བྱེད་པ་ལ། མདོ་དང་གསུང་རབ་ཀྱི་དབུ་འགྲུང་རིང་ནས་བྱེ་བའོ།། ཡུའི་ཧུང་ཕན་དར་བ་ལ། ཡི་གེའི་དབྱིབས་ཆེན་པོ་བརྩམ་པ་མངོན་པར་བྱེད་པའོ།། སྔོན་གྱི་འཛངས་སྲོལ་ཤིན་ཏུ་རྩད་ཆོད་དེ། འཇིག་རྟེན་བར་པ་ལ་སྣང་སྲིད་བྱེ་བའི་དོན། ལུགས་ཆེན་པོ་གསང་ཆོག། ཉི་མ་སྐར་མ་དང་བཅས་གཤིབ་པར་ལྡན་ཅིག་ཏུ་གསལ། ངོ་མཚར་ཅན་གྱི་ལེའུ་ཡི་གེའི་གཙོ་རི་དང་རྒྱ་མཚོ་ལ་འགྲན་ཟླ་ལྡན་ཅིག་ཡར་འཕགས་སོ།། ཡང་མངའ་ཞབས་བསྒོམས་པ་འབངས་རྣམས་སྐྱབས་པ་ཡིན་ཀྱང་། གསོལ་འདེབས་པའི་གླིན་པོའི་སྨོན་ལམ་འདེབས་པའི་ཡི་གེ་ཡོད། ཆར་ཆུ་ལེགས་པར་མཐུན་པར་བྱས་ནས། གནམ་སའི་བབ་རྣམས་ལྷ་མཁན་ཡང་འདུག། ཇི་ལྟར་ནའང་ཡོད་པ་གཉེར་བའི་དོན་ཐམས་ཅད་གཅིག་ཏུ་བྱ་བའི་ཕྱིར། དེ་རྣམས་སོ་སོའི་གསང་བ་གསལ་བར་བརྗོད་པའི་བྲིས་སོ།། གང་ཞིག་ཕྱོགས་བཅུ། འཕགས་པའི་བདེན་པ་བཞི། སྣང་བ་གསུམ། མངོན་ཤེས་དྲུག་ཡིན་ན། ཧན་དུས་ཀྱི་མིང་ཏེ། གསེར་གྱི་མི་རྨིབ་ལ། རྟ་དཀར་ཐོག་ལ་བཀལ་ཏེ་ཁྱེར་ནས་འོང་།། ཐང་དུས་ཀྱི་ཐའི་ཙུང་འཕགས་པའི་བསླབ་བྱའི་མཛད་སྦྱངས་བྲིས་པ་ཡིས། པདྨ་སྟོན་པོ་རྒྱས་པར་འབྱུང་། གཡང་དྲེའུ་ཡི་པོ་ཏི་ཤར་ཕྱོགས་ལ་སླེབ་ཅིང་། གཡང་དྲེའི་སྟོན་པོའི་གླིབ་མོའི་དཀྱིལ་འཁོར་ལ་གཙོ་བོར་བྱས་སོ།། གསེར་གྱི་གླེགས་བམ་ལྷོ་ཕྱོགས་སུ་བསྒྱུར་ནས། སེང་གེ་དང་འབྲུག་གི་ཚོགས་ཀྱང་བཞེངས་། ཙུ་ལན་གྱི་བསླབ་བྱས་རིམ་པར་བརྒྱུད་དེ། ཐོག་མར་ལེའུ་བཞི་བཅུ་ཞེ་གཉིས་སྐྱངས་སོ།། ཡུན་ཙང་གི་ཁྱེར་འོང་ནས། འཇགས་པར་བཀོད་པའང་པོ་ཏི་དྲུག་བརྒྱ་ལྷག་པར་

页上一

གྱུར་པ་གྲགས་པ། འཇིག་རྟེན་རྣམས་རྟོག་པར། ཤར་ཕྱོགས་ལ་རྟག་ཏུ་བཞུགས་སོ།། དེའི་རིམ་པར་བརྒྱུད་ནས། ཆེ་བར་གྲགས་པའི་མདོར་བསྡུས་པ་ནན་ཏུ་བྱས་ན། བསམ་པ་ནི་སྙིགས་དུས་སྣང་ལྡོག་པ་ཡོད། དེ་ཁའི་དྲང་པོར་སྲི་ཞུ་བྱ་སྟེ། ཚིག་རྣམས་ཕྱིན་ཅི་ལོག་པ་བསལ་ཏེ་བདེན་པ་ལ་འཛོག་གོ། དེ་ཁའི་བྱམས་དང་སྙིང་བརྩེ་ཡོད་པའི་སྟབས། བསམ་རེ་བཞིན་ཏུ་ལོག་ལྟ་ཐམས་ཅད་བཅོམ་པར་གསོད་པ་ཡང་བཞག། སེམས་ཀྱི་མར་མེ་མཚན་མོར་བསལ་ན། ལམ་ནག་པོ་ཐལ་སྟེ་བསལ། སེམས་ཀྱི་རྒྱུ་ནང་བར་བསྐྱེད་ན། མེའི་ར་བ་ནས་བསིལ་བར་གྱུར། ལམ་ཇེ་སྙེད་མི་འདྲ་ནའང་དོན་གཅིག་ཡིན། ངེས་པར་ཡལ་ག་གཞན་ཡིན་ཀྱང་རྩེ་མོ་ནི་གཅིག་ཡིན། ཡང་འཕགས་པའི་ཆོས་ཀྱི་རྣམ་པར་སྨིན་པ་བཤད་དོ།། གོང་མ་རྣམས་ལ་ཡུན་རིང་དུ་འབྱུང་བའི་སྲོལ་ལ་གསོལ་འདེབས་ཤིང་། བསླབ་བྱར་བསྒྲགས། འོག་མ་རྣམས་ལ་ཕན་པར་སྤྲལ་བའི་གྲུབ་ཐོབ་པར་བགྱིད། ངེས་པར་ཕྱོགས་ནས་བརྩོན་པའི་ཕྱིར། ཕན་པ་སྟོན་པ་མེད་པ་ཅི། འདི་ལ་ལྷའི་མདོར་བསྡུས་

བཟུང་སྟེ། ཇི་ཙམ་བཀོད་པ་སངས་རྒྱས་ཀྱི་དུང་གི་སྒྲ་ལས་བཅལ་བའི་སྤྱོད་པ་མེད་ན་ཡང་། ས་གཞི་རྣམས་ཀྱི་ཕྱིར་བདེ་བ་ལ་བརྣ་སྦྱོད་ཀྱི་ཕྱིར། ཡང་ངོ་མཚར་ནི་སྤྱོས་ཀྱི་དད་ལ་ཤེས་ནའང་འགྱུར་རོ།། ངས་སྔོན་དང་ད་ལྟ་རྣམས་བརྗོན་པར་ཕྱུང་སྟེ། མདོ་དང་དཔེ་ནན་ཏན་ཞིབ་ཏུ་བྱས། ཧྲང་གསུམ་དང་། ཧི་ལྡའི་ཡི་གེ་དུས་རྣམས་ལ་དབྱེ་ནས་ལྷས་ཀྱང་། མིང་ཅན་རི་ལ་སྨས་ཏེ་བཞག་པའི་མདོ་ཡང་བློའི་བཤད་མོད། ཛོ་རང་གི་དུས་བཞེངས་སྟ་ཞིང་འཆང་རྗོད་རྗོམ་པའི་གནས་སར་རྒྱས་པར་བྱེད་པའི་དྲན་པ་བཅལ། མཚན་མར་མི་སྨར་ནས་ཡི་གེའི་ཁང་པར་རྒྱུན་དུ་བཅལ་ནས་ཞིབ་པར་ཇོགས། བཙའ་ཁྲིམས་ལུགས་སྲོལ་ལ་འབྲེལ་བ་

页下一

ཡིན་ནའང་། མདོ་དང་ཡི་གེར་རིམ་པར་བརྒྱུད་པ་ནན་ཏུ་བཅལ། ཡི་གེའི་ལུགས་ལ་གཙོ་བོ་ཡིན་ན། རང་བཞིན་གྱི་ལུགས་ཀྱི་བསླབ་བྱ་རིམ་པར་བརྒྱུད་ནས་གསལ་མོད། ད་ལྟ་ཤིང་ཧྲ་དང་ཡི་གེ་གཅིག་ཏུ་བསྡུས་པའི་ཕྱིར། ཇི་ལྟར་ན་དཔེ་དང་དབྱིབས་ལ་ཀུན་ཀྱང་འབྲང་། ཡང་བློ་ཡི་ཤིང་སེམས་ཀྱི་མེ་ཏོག། ཏ་ལའི་ལོ་མའི་ཆོས་ལ་མ་མཐོང་ནའང་། ཁྲུང་ཁྲུང་གི་ཚལ་ཤ་བའི་ར་བ། ཕར་ཕྱིན་གྱི་སྟེགས་བུ་ལ་རེ་ཤིག་འདིག་ཏེ་ལྟོས་པའི་དོན། གཡང་དྲིལ་བསྐོར་མོའི་མེ་ལོང་གི་གཟུགས་མཐོང་ནས། ངོ་མཚར་ཅན་གྱི་གསེར་ཐག་གི་སྤྱོད་པ་ནན་ཏུ་བྱས། ནན་ཏུ་བསམ་ན།། ཐའི་ཧྲང་ཐའི་ཧྲུའི་སྐུ་ཚེ་བསོད་ནམས་ཡུན་རིང་དུ་འཕེལ་ནས། གྲོང་ཁྱེར་མཉམ་ཡོད་དུ་ཐུགས་དགའ་གོ།། ཧྲང་ཐའི་ཧྲུའི་བསོད་ནམས་ཆེན་པོ་ཁྱད་དུ་དར་ནས། རྒྱལ་བུ་རྒྱལ་བྱེད་ཀྱི་ཚལ་དུ་ཚུལ་བཞིན་དུ་དྲིན་བཟབ་པོ།། སྔོན་ལས་བྱེད་ཀྱི་ཁྲིམས་རའི་བློན་པོ་རྣམས་ལུགས་བཞིན་དུ་མཐུན་པར་བྱས་པ་ནི། ཐམས་ཅད་ཀུའི་ཤེས་བྱ་བའི་ཤིང་གི་ཕོག། མེས་ཤེས་བྱ་བའི་ཤིང་གི་གདུང་ཡིན་ཀྱང་། ད་ལྟར་སྒྲུབ་པའི་ཆོས་ལ་ཡོད་པ་ནི། ཀུན་ལ་ཡ་མཚན་གཏམ་པའི་གསང་ཚིག། སྐྱེ་བོ་དམན་པ་རྣམས་སྤྱུག་པར་མ་བྱས་ཏེ། འབངས་རྣམས་ཀྱི་ཧྲས་མ་འགྲུག་བར་ལས་བྱེད་རྣམས་ལ་ནང་གི་མཛོད་ནས་བསྟན་ཅིང་། ཕྱིའི་མཛོད་ནས། འགྲུལ་ཅག་བཏང་བའང་མེད། ཡང་དག་བསླབ་བྱའི་ངོ་མཚར་ཅན་གྱི་སྲོལ་གྲགས་པར་བྱེད་པ་འོས་པ་བསམ་ནས། ཆོས་འདོན་པ་དང་། གཙོ་བོ་སྒྲ་དབྱངས་ཆེ་བར་མ་བྱུང་ནའང་། དེ་རྣམས་སྔོན་ནས་ཚུན་ཆད་བསླབ་བྱ་རིམ་པར་བརྒྱུད་པའི་ཡི་གེ་ནན་ཏུ་བྱས་ནས། ཡང་

页上二

སངས་རྒྱས་སྟོང་རྩ་ཕན་ཚུན་རིམ་པར་བརྒྱུད་པའི་ལེའུ་ལ་བསྡུས་ཤིང་བོད་ཆོས་ཉིད་པའི་བར་བཀོས་སོ།། གོས་ཆེན་སྨུམ་ལྡང་སྒྲིགས་པར་བྱས་ནས། བཀྲ་ཤིས་བརྟག་བརྒྱད་ལྡན་པའི་ཐོན་ཐི་སེར་པོའི་ན་བཟའ་ཕུད་པར་བྱས། མེ་ཏོག་སྣ་བདུན་གྱི་རི་མོ་ཅན་ཁྱད་འཕགས་བྱས་སོ།། ནང་གི་ཕོ་བྲང་ལ་ཡང་དག་ངོ་མཚར་ཅན་གྱི་འོད་ཟེར་ཁྱབ་ཅིང་། ཤིན་ཏུ་མཛེས་བ་ནི། ཀུན་ལ་བསྒྲགས་བར་བྱ་སྟེ། འགྲེལ་པའི་ཚིག་ལ་བསྟན་ནས་རྒྱས་པར་བྱེད་ཅིང་། བཀའ་འགྱུར་དར་བྱེད་པ་གཙོ་བྱས་ནས།། ཐའི་ཧྲང་ཐའི་ཧྲུའི་དང་ཧྲང་ཐའི་ཏུ་གཉིས་ལ་ཡ་མཚན་བཀྲ་ཤིས་གསོལ་འདེབས་པ་རིགས་ཉུས་ཁྲི་ཕྲག་རྣམས་ལ་བསོད་ནམས་ཆེན་པོ་གནས་པར་བགྱིའོ་ཞེས། དེ་རྣམས་ཆོས་ཀྱི་དབྱུར་འབྲི་ཞིང་། བསྟགས་པར་བསྟོད་པ་བསྟན་ཡོད།། བདེ་སྐྱིད་ཀྱི་ལོ་ཉེར་གསུམ། སྟོན་ཟླ་འབྲིང་པོའི་ཉི་ཤུ་གཉིས་ལ།

页下二

請序疏

༄།། མཛད་བྱང་ཞུ་བའི་ཡི་གེ་བཙའ་ཁྲིམས་ཀྱི་བློན་པོ་ཕུ་རྟོན་ཨེལ་གེན་མཁྱེན་དབང་དག་གི་ཞུ་བ་ནི། ལུང་གི་རྗེས་འབྲང་ནས། བཀའ་འགྱུར་ཀྱི་པར་བཞེངས་པའི་དོན། རྒྱལ་པོའི་མཛད་པའི་བྲིས་སྒྲུངས་བཀོད་ནས་ཡུན་རིང་

བརྒྱུད་པར་བྱ་བའི་ཕྱིར་ནན་དུ་ཞུ་བ་ནི། བསྔས་ནས། རྒྱ་གར་ཡུལ་དུ་ལས་ཀྱི་དབང་གི་ངོ་མཚར་སྤྲུལ་པའི་རྣམ་འཕྲུལ་ཐོག་མར་བྱུང་ལ། འཕགས་ལམ་ཡན་ལག་བརྒྱད། ཐེག་པ་རིམ་པ་ལྔ་རྣམས་ཡངས་པ་ཅན་དང་སུ་ཀླའི་ཡུལ་དུ་དབུ་བཙུགས་ནས་གཏད་པ་དང་བླངས་པ་ཤིན་ཏུ། རིང་མོད། རྒྱ་ནག་གི་ཏན་དང་མིང་ཞེས་བྱ་བའི།། རྒྱལ་པོའི་དུས་སུ། འཕགས་པ་གསེར་གྱི་མདོག་ཅན་ཐྲི་བ་ལས། རྒྱ་གར་ཡུལ་ལ་ཕོ་ཉ་མངགས་ནས། བསྟན་པའི་ལུགས་སྲོལ་གྱི་ཡིག་ཆོགས་མང་པོ་དང་ཆོགས་བཅད་རྣམས་རིམ་པར་ཡུལ་དབུས་སུ་བརྒྱུད་ནས། ལོ་ཉི་སྟོང་ཉེ་བ་བྱུང་ཞིང་། འདི་ཡི་འཚམས་སུ་ཐང་དང་སུང་གི་རྒྱལ་སྐབས་གསལ་བར་བསྔགས་པར་བསྟོད་པ་ཇི་ཙམ་མང་ཡང་། སངས་རྒྱས་ཀྱི་བསྟན་པ་དར་ཞིང་རྒྱས་པ་གཅིག་བུའི་དོན་དུ་འང་མིན་ཅིང་།ཆེད་དུ་འདིས་ཀྱང་རྣམ་པ་ཁྲི་ཕྲག་མང་པོ་སྤེལ་བའི་དོན་ཡིན་ལ། གོང་མ་སྐྱེ་ཙམ་ཉིད་ནི་ཐུགས་མཁྱེན་པ་མཁས་པའི་རང་བཞིན་ཡིན་པ་ལ། རྟུལ་ཕོད་ཡོན་ཏན་ངོ་མཚར་ཆེ་བ་ནི། གནམ་ས་དང་འགྲན་ཟླ་བའི། བཅའ་ཁྲིམས། སླབ་སྟོན་ལེགས་པར་འགྱུར་བའི། དཔལ་གྱི་སྙན་གྲགས་ཆེན་པོ་མངོན་པར་མཐོ་བའི། ཉི་ཟླ་ཁྱབ་པའི་ས་སྟེང་དུ་གནང་སྦྱིན་གྱི་ཁྱབ་པར་དང་དུ་བླངས། ལོ་དང་ཟླ་བའི་དུས་ཀྱི་རྗེས་འབྲང་ནས། ཁྲལ་གྱི་རིག་མི་འཛིན་པའང་མེད། འདི་ལྟར་ནའང་། གོང་མའི་ཐུགས་བདག་གིར་མེད་པས། ཉིན་རེ་བཞིན་ཤིན་ཏུ་ཉེན་ནས། གཞེངས་སྤྲ་ཞིང་གསོལ་ཕྱི་བ། གཞུངས་དོན་ཆེད་དུ་གཉེར་ཞིང་འབངས་ལ་བརྩེ་སྐྱོངས་ཆེ། ཡང་ཁྲི་ཕྲག

页上一

མང་པོའི་དོན་དབྱེ་བའི། དལ་སྐབས་སུའང་། འཛིག་རྟེན་བསྟན་ཆོས་དྲུག་དང་བསྟན་ཆོས་མང་པོ་བསྒྱུར་ནས་ནན་ཏུ་གཟིགས་པས། ཡིག་རིས་སུ་མ་ཐོན་པའི་གསང་བ་ཕྲ་མོ་ཡང་ཕྱེ་བ་ཡིན།གཞུང་དང་སྲིད་པ་ཕན་ཚུན་རིམ་པར་བརྒྱུད་པའི་ལུགས་ཀྱི་རྣམ་གྲངས་མ་མཁྱེན་པའང་མེད། ཡང་གནམ་སའི་ལུགས་དང་། རྒྱ་ནག་ཟི་མིང་ཅན་གྱི་ཡི་གེ། ཁྲིམ་བརྒྱའི་ཡི་གེ་ཤེས་རྫོགས་ཤིང་། སྤྱིའི་དོན་རྒྱ་སྐད་ཀྱི་གནས་འཕགས་པའི་ཆོས་ཤིང་ཏ་ལའི་ལོ་མའི་ཡི་གེ་སོགས། སྲོད་དང་ཐོ་རང་དུས་སུ་ནན་ཏན་ཞིབ་ཏུ་བྱས་ནས། སླབ་པའི་ཐབས་ཤེས་རྫོགས་ཤིང་། ཟབ་པའི་མ་ཕྱེ་བའང་མེད། སྟོན་དང་ད་ལྟ་རྣམས་རྫོགས་པར་མཁྱེན། བདག་པོའི་ཐུགས་བརྗོན་པིར་རེག་པ་ཙམ་གྱི་བརྒྱ་ཕྲག་བཅུའི་ཚིགས་སོགས་འབྱུང་བ། གནམ་གྱི་དགུ་ཚིག་བཞིན་དུ་དངས་ཤིང་ལྷ་བའི་ཚིག་མི་ཤེས། ངེས་པར་ཧི་ཡན་ཏུ་ཡི་དཔེ་ཕུང་མི་ཡི་ལུགས་རྫོགས་པར་བྱས་པ་ནི། འཕགས་པ་སྟོང་གཅིག་ཏུ་འདུས་པའི་བདག་ཉིད་ཆེན་པོ་མངོན་སུམ་གསལ་བར་སྒྲུབས་པའང་ཡིན་ཞིང་། ཡོན་ཏན་གསུམ་གཞི་གཅིག་ཏུ་གཞེངས་པས་སོ། དེ་ལྟར་ནའང་། གཡང་དྲིལ་སྨྱུ་གུའི་རིན་ཆེན་ཡི་གེ་འབྲུག་འཕར་ཞིང་། ཀ་ལན་ད་ཀའི་གར་ལྟར། མང་བཀུར་རྒྱལ་པོའི་བཏབ་པའི་ཡ་མཚན་ཞིག། ཏན་གྱི་རྒྱལ་པོས་བརྩམ་ནས་བྲིས་པའི། དཔེ་ཡང་མོག་པོར་མཛད་མོད་དོན་འདི་ཡང་དལ་སྐབས་སུ་བྱས་པ་ཡིན་ལ། ད་ལྟ་ཡང་བརྩེ་བ་ཆེན་པོའི་སྒོ་ནས་ཁྱབ་ཅིང་། ཆེད་དུ་བསམ་ན་བཀའ་འགྱུར་གྱིས་པར་བཀོས་པས་ཕན་ཡོན་ཆེན་པོའི། གོང་མ་ཐའི་ཙུང་ཐའི་ཙུ་ཐའི་ཙུ་རྣམས་ལོ་ཁྲི་ཐུབ་པའི་བཀྲ་ཤིས་དཔག་མེད་ཡུན་རིང་དུ་འབྱུང་བར་གྱུར་ཅིག། ས་སྟེང་གི་བློན་འབངས་འོག་མ་རྣམས་ལ་ཡང་། ལོ་འབུམ་གྱི་བར་དུ་འབྱུང་བའི་བཀྲ་ཤིས་ཐོབ་པར་གྱུར་ཅིག། ཆེད་དུ་འབྲས་གནས

页下一

བཞི། པར་ཕྱིན་དྲུག་གི་ཟབ་དོན་རྟོགས་པར་དཀའ། ལྷའི་ལུང་གིས་གསལ་བར་མ་བསྟན་ན། མ་རིག་པའི་འཁྲུམ་བཞིན་བླུན་པོའི་སྐྱེ་བོ་དམན་པ་རྣམས་རྟོགས་ལམ་ཇི་ལྟར་རྙེད། སྟོན་ཐང་གི་དུས་ཀྱི་ཐའི་ཙུང་གིས་ཧོ་ཤང་མིང་ཅན་ལ་ལུང་ཕབ་སྟེ། གླེགས་བམ་དྲུག་བརྒྱ་ལྷག་པར་བསྒྱུར་ནས། ཁྲིས་སྦྱངས་ཆེད་དུ་བྱས་པ་ཡིན་ལ། མིང་དུས་ཀྱི་ཐའི་ཙུས། འཕགས་མའི་ཐང་ཀ་ལ་བསྟོད་ཚིག་འང་འདུག། ཡུང་ལོའི་དུས་སུ་འདི་ཐམས་ཅད་མངའ་འབངས་རྒྱས་པའི་ཡར་ཆོས་ལ་བཀའ་འགྱུར་ཞུ་དག་བྱས་ནས་པར་དུ་བཀོས། བོད་ཀྱི་ལུགས་སྲོལ་གྱི་བཏགས་མངོན་པར་བྱས་སོ། གོང་མའི་སྲི་ཞུ་བཀུར་སྟི

བྱམས་དང་སྦྱིན་པ་ཐང་དང་མིང་གི་རྒྱལ་པོ་གསུམ་གྱིས་ཆ་ཁྲིས་ཀྱང་། ཆ་གཅིག་འདྲ་བར་ག་ལ་ནུས། གོང་མའི་མཛད་པའི་ཕྲིས་སྦྱངས་གནང་ན་ནམ་མཁའ་ཐམས་ཅད་འོད་ཁྱབ་ཅིང་། ས་གཞི་ཐམས་ཅད་ལ་ཕན་བདེ་འབྱུང་སྲིད། ཞུ་བ་ནི། གོང་མའི་སངས་རྒྱས་ཀྱི་བསྟན་པ་དགོངས་ནས། ཆེད་དུ་རྒྱལ་པོའི་མཛད་པའི་ཕྲིས་སྦྱངས་གནང་ལ་ཆོས་ཀྱི་དབུར་བཞག་ནས། མ་རིག་པའི་ཐུན་པོ་རྣམས་ལ་རྒྱས་པར་བསྟན། ལོ་ཁྲིའི་བར་དུ་རིམ་པར་བརྒྱུད་ན་ཇི་ལྟར་ལགས། འདི་ལྟར་ན་དངས་པའི་ཉི་མས། བདག་པོའི་ཡི་གེ་འབབ་ཞིག་ལ་བརྩོན་པར་བརྩེ་བའི་ཕྲིན་གྱིས། གོང་མའི་སྐུ་བསོད་དང་མཉམ་པོར་ཡུན་རིང་དུ་འབྱུང་སྲིད། འདིའི་དོན་དུ་ཞུ་ཡིག་ཕྲིས་ནས་ནན་ཏན་དུ་ཞུ་བ་ནི། ལུང་གི་ཞུ་བ་ཡིན་ལ། བདེ་སྐྱིད་ཀྱི་ལོ་ཞེར་གཉིས། སྟོན་ཟླ་འབྲིང་པོའི་བཅུ་དྲུག་ཉིན། བཅའ་ཁྲིམས་ཀྱི་བློན་པོ་ཕུ་ཚྭན་ཨེལ་གེན་མཁྱེན་དབང་། ནང་གི་ཁྲིམས་རའི་ཡི་གེའི་བློན་པོ་རིམ་པ་གཉིས་པ་ཡིན་ཞིང་། རིམ་པ་གཉིས་

页上二

པའི་ཐོགས་ཟ་བའི་རིམ་པ་བཞི་བསྣན་པའི་ཞུ་ལ་ཏའི། ཙུང་ཤེན་ཕུ་ཁྲིམས་རའི་གཡས་ཕྱོགས་ཀྱི་ཐེའི་དོན་དཔྱོད་པའི་ཐེལ་འཛིན་གྱི་བློན་པོ་རིམ་པ་གཅིག་བསྣན་པའི་བློན་པོ་ཀྲོ་རོ་ཤོམ་དཔེའི་ལས་བྱེད་ཀྱི་ཁྲིམས་རའི་ཐེལ་འཛིན་སླ་མཁན་བློན་པོ་རིམ་པ་གཉིས་བསྣན་པའི་བློན་པོ་ཡ་ཆི་ན། དཔྱིས་པར་བལྟ་བའི་བློན་པོ་རིམ་པ་གཉིས་བསྣན་པའི་ཨི་ལ་ཏ། དཔྱིས་པར་བལྟ་བའི་བློན་པོ་རིམ་པ་གསུམ་བསྣན་པའི་ཀེང་གེའི། དམག་གི་ཁྲིམས་རའི་དོན་དཔྱོད་པའི་བློན་པོ་ཐུབ་པ་སྐྱབས་དག་གིས་ཞུ་བ། ཞུས་མ་ཐག་པའི་ཟླ་བའི་བཅོ་བརྒྱད་ལ་ལུང་། གཞུང་གི་ཁྲིམས་རར་སྐྱོལ་གསལ་བར་བྱས་ནས་ནན་ཏན་དུ་གྲོས་ཀྱི་ལ་ཞུས་གསུངས་བྱུང་།

页下二

覆请序疏

༄།། མཛད་བྱང་སྐོར་ཞུ་བའི་ཡི་གེ། གཞུང་གི་ཁྲིམས་རའི་བློན་པོའི་གཙོ་བོ།། བློན་པོ་བཅས་སན་དག་གི་ནན་གྱི། ཞུ་བ་ནི། ལུང་གི་རྗེས་འབྲང་ནས་བཀའ་འགྱུར་གྱི་པར་བཞེངས་པའི་དོན།། རྒྱལ་པོའི་མཛད་པའི་འཕྲི་སྦྱངས་ཡུན་རིང་བརྒྱུད་པར་བྱ་བའི་ཕྱིར། ནན་དུ་ཞུ་བ་ནི། གཞུང་གི་ཁྲིམས་རའི་ཁོ་ཡ་མུན་ནས་དཔེ་ཕྲིས་ནས་འབྱུང་། བཅའ་ཁྲིམས་བློན་པོ་ཕུ་ཚྭན་ཨེལ་གེན་མཁྱེན་དབང་དག་གི། དོན་འདིའི་ཕྱིར་དུ་ཞུ་བ་ནི། བལྟས་ན། རྒྱ་གར་ཡུལ་དུ་ལས་ཀྱི་དབང་གི་ངོ་མཚར་སྤྲུལ་པའི་རྣམ་འཕྲུལ་ཐོག་མར་འབྱུང་ལ། འཕགས་པའི་ལམ་ཡན་ལག་བརྒྱད། ཐེག་པ་རིམ་པ་ལྔ་རྣམས་ཡངས་པ་ཅན་དང་མུཧྲའི་ཡུལ་དུ་དབུ་བཙུགས་ནས། གཏད་པ་དང་དུ་བླངས་པ་ཤིན་ཏུ་རིང་སྲིད། རྒྱ་ནག་གི་ཏན་མིང་ཞེས་བྱ་བའི་རྒྱལ་པོའི་དུས་སུ། འཕགས་པ་གསེར་གྱི་མདོག་ཅན་རྗེ་བ་ལས། རྒྱ་གར་ཡུལ་ལ་པོ་ཉ་མངགས་ནས་བསྟན་པའི་ལུགས་སྲོལ་གྱི་ཡིག་ཚོགས་མང་པོ་དང་ཚོགས་བཅད་རྣམས་རིམ་པར་ཡུལ་དབུས་སུ་བརྒྱུད་ནས། ལོ་ཉི་སྟོང་ཉེ་འབྱུང་ཞིང་། འདི་ཡི་མཚམས་སུ་ཐང་དང་སུང་གི་རྒྱལ་སྐབས་གསལ་བར་བསྔགས་པར་བསྟོད་པ་ཇི་ཙམ་མང་ཡང་། སངས་རྒྱས་ཀྱི་བསྟན་པ་དར་ཞིང་རྒྱས་པ་གཅིག་བུའི་དོན་དུ་འང་མིན་ཅིང་། ཆེད་དུ་འདིས་ཀྱང་རྣམ་པ་ཁྲི་ཕྲག་མང་པོའི་དོན་ཡིན་ལ། གོང་མ་སྐྱེ་ཙམ་ཉིད་ནི་ཐུགས་མཁྱེན་པ་མཁས་པའི་རང་བཞིན་ཡིན་པ་ལ། རྟུལ་ཕོད་ཡོན་ཏན་ངོ་མཚར་ཆེ་བ་ནི། གནམ་དང་འགྲན་ཟླ་བའི། བཅའ་ཁྲིམས་སླབ་སྟོན་ལེགས་པར་འཕྱོར་བའི། དཔལ་གྱི་སྣང་གྲགས་ཆེན་པོ་མངོན་པར་མཐོ་བ་ས་སྟེང་དུ་ཁྱབ་པའི་གནང་སྦྱིན་དང་དུ་བླངས། ལོ་དང་ཟླ་བའི་དུས་ཀྱི་རྗེས་འབྲང་ནས། ཁྲལ་གྱི་རིག་མི་འཛིན་པའང་མེད། འདི་

页上一

ལྟར་ནའང་། གོང་མའི་ཐུགས་བདག་གིར་མེད་པས། ཉིན་རེ་བཞིན་ཤིན་ཏུ་ཉེན་ནས། གཞེངས་སྤྲ་ཞིང་གསོལ་ཕྱི་བ། གཞུངས་དོན་ཆེད་དུ་གཉེར་ཞིང་འབངས་ལ་བརྩེ་སྐྱོངས་ཆེ། ཡང་ཁྲི་ཐྲག་མང་པོའི་དོན་དབྱེ་བའི་དལ་སྐབས་སུའང་འཛིག་རྟེན་བསྟན་ཆོས་དྲུག་དང་བསྟན་ཆོས་མང་པོ་བསླབ་ནས་ནན་ཏུ་གཟིགས་པས། ཡིག་རིས་སུ་མཐོན་པའི་གསང་བ་ཐྲ་མོ་ཡང་ཕྱེ་བ་ཡིན་གཞུང་དང་སྲིད་པ་ཕན་ཚུན་རིམ་པར་བརྒྱུད་པའི་ལུགས་ཀྱི་རྣམ་གྲངས་མ་མཁྱེན་པའང་མེད། ཡང་གནས་སའི་ལུགས་དང་རྒྱ་ནག་ཟེ་མིང་ཅན་གྱི་ཡི་གེ། ཁྲིམ་བརྒྱའི་ཡི་གེ་སྤྱིའི་དོན་དང་རྒྱ་སྐད་ཀྱི་གནས། འཕགས་པའི་ཆོས་ཤིང་ཏ་ལའི་ལོ་མའི་ཡི་གེ་སོགས། སྲིད་དང་ཐོ་རང་དུས་སུ་ནན་ཏན་ཞིབ་ཏུ་བྱས་ནས། སླབ་པའི་ཐབས་ཤེས་ཇོགས་ཤིང་། ཟབ་པའི་མ་ཕྱེ་བའང་མེད་པས། སྔོན་དང་ད་ལྟ་རྣམས་ཇོགས་ཤིང་མཁྱེན། རེ་རེའི་སྐབས་སུ། བདག་པོའི་ཐུགས་བརྩམ་བིར་རིག་པ་ཙམ་གྱི་བརྒྱ་ཕྲག་བཅུའི་ཤོག་སོགས་འབྱུང་བ་ནི། གནམ་གྱི་དགུ་ཚིགས་བཞིན་དུ་དངས་ཤིང་བལྟ་བའི་ཚོག་མི་ཤེས། ངེས་པར་ཧི་ཡན་ཐུ་ཡི་དཔེ་ཤུང་མི་ཡི་ལུགས་ཇོགས་པར་བྱས་པ་ནི། འཕགས་པ་སྟོང་གཅིག་ཏུ་འདུས་པའི་བདག་ཉིད་ཆེན་པོ་མངོན་སུམ་གསལ་བར་སྨྲབས་པའང་ཡིན་ཞིང་། ཡོན་ཏན་གསུམ་གཞི་གཅིག་ཏུ་བཞེངས་པས་སོ།། དེ་ལྟར་ནའང་། གཡང་དྲིལ་མྱུ་གུའི་རིན་ཆེན་ཡི་གེ་འབྲུག་འཕར་ཞིང་། ཀ་ལན་ད་ཀའི་གར་ལྟར། མང་བཀུར་རྒྱལ་པོའི་བཏབ་པའི་ཡ་མཚན་ཐིག ཏན་གྱི་རྒྱལ་པོས་བརྩམ་ནས་བྲིས་པའི་དཔེ་ཡང་མོག་པོར་མཇེད་མོད། དོན་འདི་ཡང་དལ་སྐབས་སུ་བྱས་པ་ཡིན་ལ། ད་ལྟ་ཡང་བརྩེ་བ་ཆེན་པོའི་སྒོ་ནས་ཁྱབ་ཅིང་། ཆེད་དུ་བསམ་ན་སྐྱར་བཀའ་འགྱུར་གྱི་པར་བཀོས་

页下一

པས་ཕན་ཡོན་ཆེན་པོ། གོང་མ་ཐའི་ཏྲང་ཐའི་ཙུ་ཏྲང་ཐའི་ཙུ་རྣམས་ལོ་ཁྲི་ཐུབ་པའི་བཀྲ་ཤིས་དཔག་མེད་ཡུན་རིང་དུ་འབྱུང་བར་གྱུར་ཅིག ས་སྐྱོང་གི་བློན་འབངས་འོག་མ་རྣམས་ལ་ཡང་། ལོ་འབྲུམ་གྱི་བར་དུ་འབྱུང་བའི་བཀྲ་ཤིས་ཐོབ་པར་གྱུར་ཅིག ཅེས་སོ། སྤྱིར་འབྲས་གནས་བཞི། ཕར་ཕྱིན་དྲུག་གི་ཟབ་དོན་རྟོག་པར་དཀའ། ལྷའི་ལུང་གི་གསལ་བར་མ་བསྟན་ན། མ་རིག་པའི་འཁྲུམ་བཞིན་བླུན་པོ་སྐྱེ་བོ་དམན་པ་རྣམས་ཇོགས་ལམ་ཇི་ལྟར་རྟེད། སྔོན་ཐང་གི་དུས་སུ་ཐའི་ཙུང་གིས་ཧྭ་ཤང་མིང་ཅན་ལ་ལུང་ཕབ་སྟེ། གླེགས་བམ་དྲུག་བརྒྱ་ལྷག་པར་བསྒྱུར་ནས། འབྲི་སྤྲུངས་ཆེད་དུ་བྱས་པ་ཡིན་ལ། མིང་དུས་ཀྱི་ཐའི་ཙུའི་འཕགས་མའི་ཐང་ཀ་ལ་བསྟོད་ཚིག་བྱས་པའང་འདུག ཡུང་ལོའི་དུས་སུ་བཀའ་འགྱུར་ཆེན་པོ་ཞུ་དག་ཞིབ་པར་བྱས་ནས་བཀོས་པ་འདི་ཐམས་ཅད་མངའ་འབངས་རྒྱས་པའི་ཡར་ཆོས་ལ། བོད་ཀྱི་ལུགས་སྲོལ་གྱི་བརྟགས་མངོན་པར་བྱས་སོ། གོང་མའི་སྲི་ཞུ་བཀུར་སྟི་བྱམས་དང་སྦྱིན་པ་ནི་ཤིན་ཏུ་ཁྱད་པར་འཕགས། ཐང་དང་། མིང་གི་རྒྱལ་པོ་གསུམ་གྱིས། ཆ་ཁྲིས་ཀྱང་ཆ་གཅིག་འདྲ་བར་ག་ལ་ནུས། གོང་མའི་མཛད་པའི་བྲིས་སྤྲུངས་གནང་ན་ནམ་མཁའ་ཐམས་ཅད་འོད་ཁྱབ་ཅིང་། ས་གཞི་ཐམས་ཅད་ལ་ཕན་བདེ་འབྱུང་མོད། ཞུ་བ་ནི། གོང་མའང་སངས་རྒྱས་ཀྱི་བསྟན་པ་དགོངས་ནས། ཆེད་དུ་རྒྱལ་པོའི་མཛད་པའི་བྲིས་སྤྲུངས་གནང་ལ། ཆོས་ཀྱི་དབུར་བཞག་ནས། མ་རིག་པའི་བླུན་པོ་རྣམས་ལ་རྒྱས་པར་བསྟན། ལོ་ཁྲིའི་བར་དུ་རིམ་པར་བརྒྱུད་ན་ཇི་ལྟར་ལགས། འདི་ལྟར་ན་དངས་པའི་ཉི་མས། བདག་པོའི་ཡི་གེ་ལ་འབབ་ཞིག་གསལ་ནས། བརྩེ་བའི་སྤྲིན་གྱིས། གོང་མའི་སྐུ་བསོད་དང་མཉམ་པོར་ཡུན་རིང་དུ་འབྱུང་མོད། འདིའི་

页上二

དོན་དུ་ཞུ་ཡིག་འབྲི་ནས་ནན་ཏན་དུ་ཞུ་བ་ནི། ལུང་ཞུས་ལགས། ཞེས་བདེ་སྐྱིད་ཀྱི་ལོ་ཉེར་གཉིས། སྟོན་ཟླ་འབྲིང་པོའི་བཅུ་དྲུག་ལ་ཞུས་ལགས། ཟླ་བ་འདི་ཁའི་བཅྭ་བརྒྱད་ལ། ལུང་གཞུང་གི་ཁྲིམས་རའི་སྲོལ་གསལ་བར་དབྱེ་ནས་ནན་དུ་གྲོས་བྱས་ནས་ཞུས་ཟེར། འདིས་རྗེས་འབྲང་ནན་གྱིས། ཟླ་བ་འདི་ཁའི་བཅུ་དགུར་གཞུང་གི་ཁྲིམས་ར་ལ་ཕབ་བྱུང་། བློན་པོ་བདག་ཅག་གི་གྲོས་བྱས་པ་ནས། བཅའ་ཁྲིམས་ཀྱི་ཕུ་རྟོན་ཨེལ་གེན་ཆེན་ཕྱང་དག་གི་ཞུ་བའི་ཡི་གེ་ལ། སླབ་བྱ། ཤོ་ལོ་ཀ་ཡུལ་དབུས་སུ་བརྒྱུད་ནས་ལོ་ཉིས་སྟོང་ཉེ་བ་སོང་། ཐང་དང་། སུང་གི་རྒྱལ་སྐབས་གསལ་བར་བརྟགས་པར་བསྟོད་པ་ནི། སངས་རྒྱས་

ཀྱི་བསྟན་པ་དར་ཞིང་རྒྱས་པ་གཅིག་པུའི་དོན་དུའང་མིན། ཆེད་དུ་འདིས་ཀྱང་རྣམ་པ་ཁྲི་ཕྲག་མང་པོ་སྤེལ་བའི་དོན་ཡིན་ལ། གོང་མ་སྐྱེ་ཙམ་ཉིད་ནི་མཁྱེན་པ་མཁས་པའི་རང་བཞིན་ཡིན་པ་ལ། རྟུལ་ཕོད་ཡོན་ཏན་ཆེ་བ་ནི། གནམ་ས་དང་འགྲན་ཟླ་བའི། ཁྲི་ཕྲག་མང་པོའི་དོན་དགེ་བའི་དཔལ་སྐབས་སུའང་འཇིག་རྟེན་བསྟན་ཆོས་དྲུག་དང་བསྟན་ཆོས་མང་པོ་བསྒྱུར་ནས་ནན་དུ་གཟིགས་པས། ཟི་མང་པོའི་ཡི་གེ། ཁྲིམ་བརྒྱའི་ཡི་གེ་འཕགས་པའི་ཆོས། ཤིང་ཏ་ལ་ལོ་མའི་ཡི་གེ་སོགས། སྤྱོད་དང་ཐོ་རང་དུས་སུ་ནན་ཏན་ཞིབ་ཏུ་བྱས་ནས། ཟབ་པའི་བསམ་པ་མ་ཕྱེ་བ་ཅིག་ཡང་མེད། ད་ལྟར། ཆེད་དུ་བརྩེ་བ་ཆེན་པོའི་སྒོ་ནས་ཁྱབ་ཅིང་། བཀའ་འགྱུར་གྱིས་པར་ཡང་སྐར་བཀོས་པའི་ཕན་ཡོན་ཆེན་པོ་ནི། གོང་མ་ཐའི་ཙུང་ཐའི་ཙུ། ཙུང་ཐའི་ཙུའི་ལོ་ཁྲི་ཐུབ་པའི་བཀྲ་ཤིས་དཔག་མེད་ཡུན་རིང་དུ་འབྱུང་བར་གྱུར་ཅིག ས་སྐྱོང་གི་བློན་འབངས་འོག་མ་ལ་ཡང་། ལོ་འབུམ་གྱི་བར་དུ་འབྱུང་བའི་བཀྲ་ཤིས་ཐོབ་པར་གྱུར་ཅིག སྔོན་ཐང་གི་དུས་ཀྱི་ཐའི་ཙུང་གིས། ཏོ་ཤང་མིང་ཅན་

页下二

ལ་བཀའ་ཕབ་སྟེ། གླེགས་བམ་དྲུག་བརྒྱ་ལྷག་བསྒྱུར་ནས། བྲིས་སྦྱངས་ཆེད་དུ་བྱས་པ་ཡིན་ལ། མིང་དུས་ཀྱི་ཐའི་ཙུ། འཕགས་མའི་ཐང་ཀ་ལ་བསྟོད་ཚིག་བྱས་པའང་འདུག། ཡུང་ལོའི་དུས་སུ་བཀའ་འགྱུར་ཆེན་པོ་ཞུ་དག་ཞིབ་པར་བྱས་ནས་བཀོས་པ། འདི་ཐམས་ཅད་མདའ་འབངས་རྒྱས་པའི་ཡར་ཆོས་ལ། བོད་ཀྱི་ལུགས་སྲོལ་གྱི་བརྟགས་མངོན་པར་བྱས་སོ།། གོང་མའི་སྲི་ཞུ་བཀུར་སྟི་བྱམས་དང་སྦྱིན་པ་ནི་ཤིན་ཏུ་ཁྱད་པར་འཕགས། ཐང་དང་མིང་གི་རྒྱལ་པོ་གསུམ་གྱི་ཆ་ཁྲི་ཡང་ཆ་ཅིག་འདྲ་བར་ག་ལ་ནུས། ཞུ་བ་ནི། གོང་མ་སངས་རྒྱས་ཀྱི་བསྟན་པ་དགོངས་ནས། ཆེད་དུ་རྒྱལ་པོའི་མཛད་པའི་བྲིས་སྦྱངས་གནང་ལ་ཆོས་ཀྱི་དབུར་བཞག་ནས། མ་རིག་པའི་བླུན་པོ་རྣམས་ལ་རྒྱས་པར་བསྟན། ལོ་ཁྲིའི་བར་དུ་རིམ་པར་བརྒྱུད་ན་ཇི་ལྟར་ལགས། བདག་ཅག་བློན་པོ་རྣམས་ཀྱིས་བལྟས་ན། ཚིགས་བཅད་དང་སླབ་བྱའི་ཡི་གེ་མང་པོ། བཀའ་འགྱུར་ལ་མ་ཚང་བ་ཅི་ཡང་མེད། སླབ་བྱར། གསལ་བར། གསང་བ། དགེ་བར་བྱ་བའི་སྲོལ་རང་བཞིན་རྣམ་པར་སྤྱོད་པ་ནི་གཞན་ནའང་དེའི་བསམ་པའི་ཚད་ཁྲི་ཕྲག་གི་བྱ་བའི་དོན་དུ་འགྲོ་རྣམས་སྨིན་པར་བྱས་ནས་འཁྲིད་ཡོད། སྐབས་སྐབས་ཀྱི་གོང་མ་རྣམས་ཀྱི་རྒྱུན་དུ་རྒྱས་པར་ཁྱབ་སྟེ། ཁ་ཅིག་གི་ནི་བསྒྱུར་བ་དང་། ཁ་ཅིག་གི་ནི་པར་དུ་བཀོས་ནས་དེ་རྣམས་སླབ་བྱ་རྣམས་ཆད་པ་མེད་པར་བྱས། ཕྱིར་ཡང་སླབ་བྱའི་ལུགས་ལྷག་པར་གྲགས་སྲོལ་རྣམས་དར་བ་ལ། ཐེ་ཚོམ་མེད་པར་རང་གི་མཛད་སྦྱངས་འབྲི་ཞིང་། གླེགས་བམ་གྱི་དབུར་བཞག་ན་གདོད་མ་ནི་སྤྲུལ་པའི་མི་རྣམས་ཤིན་དུ་རྗེས་འབྲང་ནས། ཐག་ཉེ་རིང་བ་རྣམས་ཏ་ལས་བསམ། དཔེ་ན་ཐང་དུས་ཀྱི་ཐའི་ཙུང་གི་དུས་སུ་ཅེན་ཀྭན་གྱི་ལོ་ཉེར་གཉིས་རྒྱ་བན་ཡུན་ཡུང་རྣམས་བོད་ཆོས་པོ་ཏི་དྲུག་བརྒྱ

页上三

ལྔ་བཅུ་ང་བདུན་བསྒྱུར་ནས། བསྒྲུབ་པའི་རྗེས་སུ་རྒྱལ་པོ་རང་གིས་སྡེ་སྣོད་གསུམ་དང་ལྷག་པའི་བསླབ་པས་མཛད་སྦྱངས་འབྲི་ཞིང་རྗེ་ལ་བཀོ་བའི་དོན། ད་ལྟའི་བར་དུ་རིམ་པར་བརྒྱུད། མིང་དུས་ཀྱི་ཐའི་ཙུང་རང་གིས་བརྩམས་པའི་ཡི་གེར་སྤྲོལ་མར་བསྟོད་པའི་ཡི་གེ ཡང་ཤེར་སྙིང་གི་མཛད་སྦྱངས། པདྨ་སདྷ། འཇིག་རྟེན་མེ་ཏོག་སྙིང་པོའི་རིམ་གྱིས་བསྟོད་ནས་འབྲི་བའི་ཡི་གེ་ཡོད། མིང་དུས་ཀྱི་ཆེང་ཙུ་བཀའ་འགྱུར་ཆེན་པོ་ཞུ་དག་ནན་ཏུ་བྱས་ནས་པར་དུ་བཀོས། བཀའ་འགྱུར་གྱི་བསྟོད་ཚིགས་དང་མཁྱེན་རབ་གཞུང་ལུགས་དམ་པའི་ཆོས་གསུང་རབ་གླེགས་བམ་བཞི། ཕལ་པོ་ཆེ། མཚན་བརྗོད་རིམ་པའི་མཛད་སྦྱང་གི་ཡི་གེ་རྣམས་ཆོས་ཀྱི་དབུར་འབྲི་ནས་བཀའ་འགྱུར་གྱི་པོ་ཏིར་བཞག་ཡོད། ཡང་དཔེ་ན་ཐང་དུས་ཀྱི་ཁིའན་ཙུང་། སྙིང་གནས་བསྒོམ་པའི་ཆོས་ཀྱི་མཛད་སྦྱང་གི་ཡི་གེ་འབྲི་ལུགས། སུང་དུས་ཀྱི་ཐའི་ཙུང་རང་མཁྱེན་རབ་ཤེས་བྱ་བའི་ཡི་གེ་པོ་ཏི་ལྔ་བརྩམས་ནས་འབྲི་ལུགས། ཅེན་ཙུང་ཞི་ཏིའན་ཞུས་ཅི་ཞེས་བྱ་བ་ཡི་གེ་པོ་ཏི་གཅིག་འབྲི་ལུགས། འདི་རྣམས་གཙུག་ལག་ཁང་དུ་ཚགས་བྱས་ནས་དཔག་ཏུ་མེད་པ་རིམ་པར་བརྒྱུད། ནན་ཏུ་བསམ་ན། གོང་མའི་ཡོན་ཏན་གནམ་ས་

དང་འགྲན་ཟླ་བ། ལུགས་ནི་ལྷ་དང་མི་ལ་རྫོགས་པར་མཁྱེན། ཟབ་ཅིང་ཞིབ་པ་ཕྲ་བ་ནན་ཏན་བདེན་པར་གསང་བ་རྣམ་མ་གསལ་པའང་མེད་མ་འོངས་པ་ཡང་མཁྱེན། འདས་པ་ཡང་བཟུང་ཕྲ་མོའི་སྤྱོལ་མི་བཙོན་པ་ཅི་ཡང་མེད། གོང་མའི་སླབ་བྱ་ཟབ་ཅིང་ཕྲ་བ། ལྷའི་ཡི་གེར་འོས་པ་ངེས་པར་མཛོས་པ་སྔོན་གྱི་རིང་གི་མི་དབང་རྣམས་ཇི་སྙེད་གཅིག་ཡོད་ཀྱང་འགྲན་ཟླ་མེད། ད་ལྟར་གནམ་ས་སྤེལ་བའི་ཐུགས་ལ་རེ་བ་མི་བསླུན་ཅིང་། གོང་མའི་སྤྱི་ཞུར་ཐུགས་ལ་རྒྱས་པར། གོང་མ་ཐའི་ཧྭང་ཐའི་ཏུ་ཧྭང་ཐའི་ཏུ་རྣམས་ལ་

页下三

བཀྲ་ཤིས་པར་ཕྱུར་ཅིག། འོག་མ་བློན་འབངས་ཁྲི་ཕྲག་རྣམས་ཀྱང་སྐུ་བསོད་དང་ལེན་བགྱིས་ཅེས། བཀའ་འགྱུར་གྱི་བར་བཀོས་ནས། ས་སྙིང་ལ་རིམ་པར་བརྒྱུད་པའི་ཕྱིར་ཆེད་དུ་བཀའ་ཕབ་སྟེ། ཤོ་ལོ་ཀ་གཅིག་གི་སླབ་བྱ་རྫོགས་པར་དཀའ། བོད་ཀྱི་ཆོས་གཏོལ་ནས་དར་བར་བྱ་བ་ཐེ་ཚོམ་མེད། ལྷའི་ལུང་གིས་བསྡུགས་པར་བསྟོད་ན་ད་ལྟར་ཉི་ཟླ་བཞིན་དངས་ཤིང་གསལ་བར་འབྱུང་སོད། འདིའི་ཕྱིར་དུ་དབང་དག་གི་ཞུ་བ་ཕུལ་བ་ལྟར། བདག་པོ་རང་གི་མཛད་སྦྱངས་ཡི་གེར་བཀོད་ནས་ཆོས་ཀྱི་དབྱར་བཞག་ནས། ཤེལ་གྱི་པོ་ཏི་རིན་ཆེན་ཡི་གེར་ངོ་མཚར་བའི་འོད་གསལ་བར། ས་སྙིང་རྣམས་ལ་ཁྱབ་པར་བསྟན། དཔག་མེད་ཡུན་རིང་རིམ་པར་བརྒྱུད་ན་ཅི་གནང་། འདི་ལྟར་ན་ངེས་པར་བདེ་བར་ལེགས་པའི་དུས་ཀྱི་དོན། གོང་མའི་རིམ་གྱི་སྲོལ་ཆེན་པོ་འབྱུང་སོད། དེད་བློན་པོ་རྣམས་ཀྱི་བསམ་པ་ལྟར་མ་ཡིན་པའི་སྟབས་ཀྱིས་ནན་དུ་ཞུ་བ་ལགས། ལུང་ཞུས་ལགས། གཞུང་གི་ཁྲིམས་རའི་བློན་པོའི་གཙོ་བོ་བློན་པོ་བཅས་སན། བློན་པོའི་གཙོ་བོ་བློན་པོ་ཤ་ཆང་། གཡོན་ དུའི་བློན་པོ་གཉིས་པ་བློན་པོ་ཨེ་ཤིང་གེ། ཕལ་ཆེར་ལབས་པའི་བློན་པོ་གཡོན་དུའི་བློན་པོ་གཉིས་པ་ཡི་གེའི་ཁྲིམས་རའི་བློན་པོ་གཉིས་པ་ཡིན་ཅིང་ཡི་གེའི་བློན་པོ་གཏོགས་པ་བློན་པོ་ཡང་ཅིང་ཕུང་། གཡས་དུའི་བློན་པོ་གཉིས་པ་རིམ་པ་གཉིས་བསྣན་པའི་བློན་པོ་ས་དས། ཕལ་ཆེར་ལབས་པའི་བློན་པོ་གཡས་དུའི་ཡི་གེའི་ཁྲིམས་རའི་བློན་པོ་ཡི་གེའི་གཉིས་པ་ལ་གཏོགས་པ་ཁྲིན་ཐིང་གིང་། ཟེ་ཅི་ཆིང་ལི་ཟེའི་དབྱེ་བར་བྱེད་པའི་བློན་པོ་ཧོ་བིང་ཕན་པར་བྱེད་པའི་བློན་པོ་རིམ་པ་གཉིས་བསྣན་པའི་ཆང་ཅའི། ཕན་པར་བྱེད་པའི་བློན་པོ་སང་ག ཕན་པར་བྱེད་པའི་བློན་པོ་རིམ་པ་གཅིག་བསྣན་

页上四

པའི་ས་ཡིན་ཏ། ཕན་པར་བྱེད་པའི་བློན་པོ་རིམ་པ་གཉིས་ཕབ་ནས་སླར་བློན་པོ་སྔར་ལུགས་ལྟར་ཀོ་ཞི་ལུང་། ཕན་པར་བྱེད་པའི་བློན་པོ་ཤིའུ་ཡུང་སོའུ། བརྗེད་ཐོ་འཛིན་པའི་བློན་པོ་ཕང་གིན་ཆེན། བརྗེད་ཐོ་འཛིན་པའི་བློན་པོ་རིམ་པ་གཅིག་བསྣན་པའི་བློན་པོ་ཐིའང་ཀྲུ། བརྗེད་ཐོ་འཛིན་པའི་བློན་པོ་བློན་པོ་ཞུས་བཞིན་ཕུང་། བདེ་སྐྱིད་ཀྱི་ལོ་ཉེར་གཉིས། སྟོན་ཟླ་ཐ་ཆུང་ཚེས་གཅིག། ཞུས་ལགས། ཟླ་བ་འདི་ཁའི་ཚེས་བཞི་ལ། ལུང་ལབས་པ་ལྟར་བགྱི་ཟེར།

页下四

职名

༄། །གོང་མའི་ལུང་གིས་བསྣན་ནས་པར་བཞེངས་ཟེར་བའི་བཀའ་འགྱུར་དོ་དམ་བྱེད་དུ་བཙུག་པ། བཅའ་ཁྲིམས་ཀྱི་བློན་པོ་ཕུ་རྫོན་ཨེལ་གིན་ཆེན་ཕང་། ལས་པར་བྱེད་པའི་བློན་པོ་རྣམས། བོད་ཡིག་གི་སློབ་དཔོན་བློན་པོ་ཨར་པོད་ཏུ། ནང་གི་ཁྲིམས་རའི་ཡི་གེའི་བློན་པོ་ཤུ་ལུ། གཞུང་གི་ཁོ་ཡི་ཁྲིམས་རའི་ཐེ་འཛིན་པའི་སྨྲ་མཁན་བློན་པོ་ཨ་ཤི་ཐན། བཅའ་བའི་ཁོ་ཡི་ཁྲིམས་རའི་ཐེ་འཛིན་པའི་སྨྲ་མཁན་བློན་པོ་ཧེ་ཤིའུ། ཐམས་ཅད་དབྱེ་བའི་ཁྲིམས་རའི་དབྱེས་པར་བལྟ་བའི་བློན་པོ་སེ་ཏེ་རི། དབྱེས་པར་བལྟ་བའི་བློན་པོ་མ་སེ། དབྱེས་པར་བལྟ་བའི་བློན་པོ་ས་ཡིམ་ཕུ། བཅའ་བའི་ཁྲིམས་རའི་དོན་དབྱེས་པའི་

བློན་པོ་ཨུན་ཆ། ལས་བྱེད་ཀྱི་ཁྲིམས་རའི་དོན་དཔྱེས་པའི་བློན་པོ་ལིའུ་ཧིའང་། བློན་པོའི་ཁྲིམས་རའི་ཕན་པར་བྱེད་པའི་བློན་པོ་ཨེང་ཀའི། དམག་གི་ཁྲིམས་རའི་ཕན་པར་བྱེད་པའི་བློན་པོ་ལྷ་ཆའུ་ཙན། ཀོང་ཤན་ཁུ་ཞེས་བྱ་བ་མཛོད་ཀྱི་ཕན་པར་བྱེད་པའི་བློན་པོ་སུ་ཐའི་ཕན་པར་བྱེད་པའི་བློན་པོ་ཏེ་ཆེང་ཀེ། བརྗེད་ཐོ་འཛིན་པའི་བློན་པོ་ཡུང་ཕུ། བརྗེད་ཐོ་འཛིན་པའི་བློན་པོ་ཐུང་ཀི་ཐུ། བློན་པོའི་ཁྲིམས་རའི་ཡི་གེ་པ་བློན་པོ་པེ་པའུ་ཀྲུ། གཞུང་གི་ཁྲིམས་རའི་ཡི་གེ་པ་བློན་པོ་ཕུ་ལུ། དམག་གི་ཁྲིམས་རའི་ཡི་གེ་པ་བློན་པོ་ཀིར་ཟའི། བཅའ་བའི་ཁྲིམས་རའི་ཡི་གེ་པ་བློན་པོ་ཨེལ་གེ ཡི་གེ་པ་བློན་པོ་སུལ་ཐུ། ཡི་གེ་པ་བློན་པོ་ཐང་ཀའི།

页上一

ལས་བྱེད་ཀྱི་ཁྲིམས་རའི་ཡི་གེ་པ་བློན་པོ་ཆ་ཕུ་ཀྲུ། ཐམས་ཅད་དབྱེ་བའི་ཁྲིམས་རའི་ཡི་གེ་པ་བློན་པོ་ནེང་ཀེ། ཡི་གེ་པ་བློན་པོ་ཤལ་ཏ། ཡི་གེ་པ་བློན་པོ་ལིའུ་ཀྲུ། ཡི་གེ་པ་བློན་པོ་ལིའུ་ཟི། ཡི་གེ་པ་བློན་པོ་ལིའུ་ཡི་ཡུ་ཤན། མཛོད་ཀྱི་ཁོ་ཡི་ཁྲིམས་རའི་ཡི་གེ་པ་བློན་པོ་ཧིང་ཐུ། གཞུང་གི་ཁོ་ཡི་ཁྲིམས་རའི་ཡི་གེ་པ་བློན་པོ་ཕ་ཧུན་ཏའི། བཅའ་བའི་ཁོ་ཡི་ཁྲིམས་རའི་ཡི་གེ་པ་བློན་པོ་ཐེང་ཀེ གསར་བཅད་ཞུ་དག་བྱས་མཁན་བླ་མ་རྣམས། ཅང་སྐྱ་ཞབས་དྲུང་། མགོ་པ་བླ་མ་དཔང་ཕྱུག་སྦྱིན་པ། མགོ་པ་བླ་མ་བློ་བཟང་དཔལ་འབྱོར་། ཉིམ་ཆི་དགེ་སློང་བློ་བཟང་རྣམ་རྒྱལ། རབ་འབྱམས་པ་དོན་གྲུབ་རབ་བརྟན། རབ་འབྱམས་པ་ཚུལ་ཁྲིམས་བཟང་པོ།།དགེ་སློང་བསྟན་པ་གསལ་བྱེད། རྒྱལ་པོ་བདེ་སྐྱིད་ཀྱི་ལོ་སུམ་ཅུ་སོ་དགུ་ཟླ་བ་བཞི་པའི་ཚེས་བཟང་པོར་པར་བཞེངས་བསྒྲུབས་པའོ།། དགེའོ། ཞིགས་སྟོ།།

页下一

总理监修

༄།།བཀའ་འགྱུར་རྣམས་དོ་དམ་བྱེད་དུ་བཅུག་པ།། བཅའ་ཁྲིམས་ཀྱི་བློན་པོ་ཕུ་རྟོན་ཨེལ་གེན་མཁྱེན་དབང་། ལྟས་པར་བྱེད་པའི་བློན་པོ་རྣམས། ནང་གི་ཁྲིམས་རིའ་ཡི་གེའི་བློན་པོ།། རིམ་པ་གཉིས་པ་ཡིན་ཞིང་། རིམ་པ་གཉིས་པའི་ཕོག་ཟ་བའི། རིམ་པ་བཞི་བསྣན་པའི་བློན་པོ་ཨུ་ལ་ཏའི། ཚུང་ཤེན་ཕུ་ཁྲིམས་རའི་གཡས་ཕྱོགས་ཀྱི་ཟེའི་དོན་དཔྱེས་པའི་ཐེ་འཛིན་གྱི་བློན་པོ་རིམ་པ་གཅིག་བསྣན་པའི་བློན་པོ་ཀྱི་རོ་ཤེམ་པེའི། དོན་དཔྱེས་པའི་བློན་པོ་རིམ་པ་གཅིག་བསྣན་པ། བློན་པོ་ཀྱོ་རོ་ལི་ལི་མ། ལས་བྱེད་ཀྱི་ཁྲིམས་རའི་ཁོ་ཡི་ཐེ་འཛིན་པའི་སྒྲ་མཁན་བློན་པོ།། རིམ་པ་གཉིས་བསྣན་པའི། བློན་པོ་ཡ་ཆི་ན། ཐམས་ཅད་དཔྱེས་པར་བལྟ་བའི་ཁྲིམས་རའི་བློན་པོ།། རིམ་པ་གཉིས་བསྣན་པའི། བློན་པོ་ཨི་ལ་ཏ། དཔྱེས་པར་བལྟ་བའི་བློན་པོ།། རིམ་པ་གསུམ་བསྣན་པའི། བློན་པོ་ཀེང་གེའི། དམག་གི་ཁྲིམས་རའི་དོན་དཔྱེས་པའི་བློན་པོ། བློན་པོ་ཐུབ་པ་སྐྱབས། ནང་གི་ཁྲིམས་རའི་ཙུན་ཤེན་ཚུང་ཞུ་རིམ་པ་གཅིག་བསྣན་པའི་བློན་པོ་དྷ་ས། ཚུང་ཤེན་ཕུ་ཁྲིམས་རའི་རིམ་པ་བདུན་པའི་ཡི་གེ་པ་ནི། རིམ་པ་གཅིག་བསྣན་པའི་བློན་པོ་ཕྱོན་ཅེ། རིམ་པ་བདུན་པའི་ཡི་གེ་པ་ནི། རིམ་པ་གཉིས་བསྣན་པའི་བློན་པོ་ཆང་རྦའུ། ཐམས་ཅད་དབྱེ་བར་བྱེད་པའི་ཁྲིམས་རའི་རིམ་པ་བདུན་པའི་ཡི་གེ་པ་ནི། རིམ་པ་གཉིས་བསྣན་པའི་བློན་པོ་ཕ་མི་ཏ། ཡི་གེ་པ་ནི། བློན་པོ་ན་ཡན་ཏའི།དམག་གི་ཁྲིམས་རའི་རིམ་པ་བདུན་པའི་ཡི་གེ་པ་ནི། རིམ་པ་གཉིས་བསྣན་པའི་བློན་པོ་ཨུ་ལན།།

页上一

校阅经字喇嘛

༄༅།།བཀའ་འགྱུར་གྱི་ཡི་གེ་རྣམས་ལྷུས་ནས་ཞུ་དག་བཅོས་པར་བྱེད་པ། ཕོ་བྲང་གི་བླ་མ་ཐམས་ཅད་ཀྱི་ཁྲིམས་འཛིན་པའི་བླ་མ་མེར་གེན་ཆོས་རྗེ། ཕོ་བྲང་གི་བླ་མ་ཐམས་ཅད་ཀྱི་ཁྲིམས་འཛིན་པའི་བླ་མ་ཡིན་པ་ལ་བོད་ཡིག་གི་སློབ་དཔོན་པ་བསོད་ནམས་ཆོས་རྗེ། བོད་ཡིག་གི་སློབ་དཔོན་པ་གཉིས་པ་ཡིན་པ་ལ། རིམ་པ་བཞི་པའི་ཕོགས་ཟ་བའི་བློན་པོ་ཞི་ཐེའུ། བཀའ་འགྱུར་གྱི་ཡི་གེ་ཞུ་དག་བྱས་མཁན། དགེ་སློང་དགེ་འདུན་དར་རྒྱས། དགེ་སློང་བློ་བཟང་དཔལ་རྒྱས། དགེ་སློང་བསོད་ནམས་རིན་ཆེན། དགེ་སློང་བློ་བཟང་བློ་གྲུབ།དགེ་སློང་ངག་དབང་སེང་གེ། དགེ་སློང་བློ་བཟང་ཀུན་དགའ། དགེ་སློང་བློ་བཟང་དཔལ་འབྱོར། དགེ་སློང་ཚུལ་ཁྲིམས་བཟང་པོ། དགེ་སློང་བསྟན་པ་བཀྲ་ཤིས། དགེ་སློང་བློ་བཟང་ཤེས་རབ། དགེ་སློང་བསམ་གཏན་རིན་ཆེན། དགེ་སློང་སྦྱིན་པ་དཔལ་འབྱོར། དགེ་སློང་བློ་བཟང་ཆོས་རྒྱལ། དགེ་སློང་རིན་ཆེན་བསོད་ནམས། དགེ་སློང་ཚུལ་ཁྲིམས་དཔལ་འབར། དགེ་སློང་ཚུལ་ཁྲིམས་ཡོན་ཏན། དགེ་སློང་ཚུལ་ཁྲིམས་བཀྲ་ཤིས། དགེ་སློང་དགེ་ལེགས་རིན་ཆེན། དགེ་སློང་བཀྲ་ཤིས་རིན་ཆེན། དགེ་སློང་ངག་དབང་སྦྱིན་པ། དགེ་སློང་བསྟན་པ་རབ་བརྟན། དགེ་སློང་ངག་དབང་སྦྱིན་པ། དགེ་སློང་བཟང་པོ་ཚུལ་ཁྲིམས། དགེ་སློང་བློ་བཟང་བཟོད་པ། དགེ་སློང་ཡོན་ཏན་རིན་ཆེན། དགེ་སློང་ཕུན་ཚོགས་རིན་ཆེན། དགེ་སློང་བློ་བཟང་བསྟན་དར། དགེ་སློང་སྦྱིན་པ་བསོད་ནམས། དགེ་སློང་ཡེ་ཤེས་དཔལ་འབྱོར། དགེ་སློང་ཆོས་འཕེལ་བཟང་པོ། དགེ་སློང་བཀྲ་ཤིས་དར་རྒྱས། དགེ་སློང་བསོད་ནམས་རྒྱལ་མཚན། དགེ་སློང་ཆོས་འཕེལ་བཟང་པོ། དགེ་སློང་བློ་བཟང་དར་རྒྱས། དགེ་སློང་བཟང་པོ་རྒྱལ་མཚན། དགེ་སློང་བློ་བཟང་ཉི་མ། དགེ་སློང་བསོད་ནམས་བརྩོན་འགྲུས། དགེ་སློང་བཀྲ་ཤིས་བཟང་པོ། དགེ་སློང་བརྩོན་འགྲུས་རིན་ཆེན། དགེ་སློང་བློ་བཟང་འཕྲིན་ལས། བོད་ཡིག་གི་སློབ་མ་རྡོ་རྗེ།

页下一

校阅序目录官

༄༅།།འབྲི་སྦྱངས་དང་ཀར་ཆག་ནན་ཏན་དུ་ཞུ་དག་བྱས་པའི་བློན་པོ། ནང་གི་ཁྲིམས་རའི་ཡི་གེའི་བློན་པོ་རིམ་པ་གསུམ་བསྣན་པའི་བློན་པོ་དན་ཏའི། ནང་གི་ཁྲིམས་རའི་ཡི་གེའི་བློན་པོ། རིམ་པ་གསུམ་པའི་ཕོགས་ཟ་བའི། རིམ་པ་གཉིས་བསྣན་པའི་བློན་པོ་ཐུས་རི། ནང་གི་ཁྲིམས་རའི་ཡི་གེའི་བློན་པོ་རིམ་པ་གསུམ་པའི་ཕོགས་ཟ་བའི། རིམ་པ་དྲུག་བསྣན་པའི་བློན་པོ་ཨུང་གིན། བོད་ཡིག་གི་འབྲི་སྦྱངས་ཀར་ཆག་བསྒྱུར་བའི་བློན་པོ། བོད་ཡིག་གི་སློབ་དཔོན་པ་གཉིས་པའི་བློན་པོ། རིམ་པ་བཞི་པའི་ཕོགས་ཟ་བའི་བློན་པོ་ཞི་ཐེའུ། རྒྱ་ཡིག་གི་ཀར་ཆག་བསྒྱུར་བའི་བློན་པོ། ནང་གི་ཁྲིམས་རའི་ཐུན་ལྷེན་ཙུང་ཞུ་བློན་པོ་ཨུ་ཤི་བུ། ནང་གི་ཁྲིམས་རའི་ཐུན་ལྷེན་ཙུང་ཞུ་བློན་པོ་སྙེང་ཏའི། སོག་ཡིག་གི་འབྲི་སྦྱངས་ཀར་ཆག་བསྒྱུར་བའི་བློན་པོ། ནང་གི་ཁྲིམས་རའི་པན་ཞི་ཙུང་ཞུ་རིམ་པ་གཉིས་བསྣན་པ་རིམ་པ་དྲུག་གི་ཕོགས་ཟ་བའི་བློན་པོ་ལམ་སྦྱངས། ནང་གི་ཁྲིམས་རའི་པན་ཞི་ཙུང་ཞུ་རིམ་པ་གཅིག་བསྣན་པ་རིམ་པ་དྲུག་གི་ཕོགས་ཟ་བའི་བློན་པོ་དེ་གེའུ། མན་ཇུ་ཡི་གེ་ནན་ཏན་དུ་འབྲི་བའི་བློན་པོ། ནང་གི་ཁྲིམས་རའི་པན་ཞི་ཙུང་ཞུ་རིམ་པ་བཞི་བསྣན་པ་རིམ་པ་ལྔ་བའི་ཕོགས་ཟ་བའི་བློན་པོ་ཨི་ཧྲ་རི། ནང་གི་ཁྲིམས་རའི་ཐུན་ལྷེན་ཙུང་ཞུ་བློན་པོ་ཅིང་ཤེའུ། ནང་གི་ཁྲིམས་རའི་ཐུན་ལྷེན་ཙུང་ཞུ་བློན་པོ་ཆམ་སྤུ། སོག་ཡིག་ནན་ཏན་དུ་འབྲི་བའི་བློན་པོ། ནང་གི་ཁྲིམས་རའི་པན་ཞི་ཙུང་ཞུ་བློན་པོ་ཤའུ་གེའུ། རྒྱ་ཡིག་ནན་ཏན་དུ་འབྲི་བའི་བློན་པོ། ནང་གི་ཁྲིམས་རའི་པན་ཞི་ཙུང་ཞུ་རིམ་པ་གཅིག་བསྣན་པའི་ཀྲོའུ་ཅེན་ཁི། ནང་གི་ཁྲིམས་རའི་པན་ཞི་ཙུང་ཞུ་བློན་པོ་ཡང་ཁི་ཀྲུ། བོད་ཡིག་ནན་ཏན་དུ་འབྲི་བའི་བླ་མ། དགེ་སློང་བློ་བཟང་བློ་གྲུབ། དགེ་སློང་བློ་བཟང་དཔལ་རྒྱས། དགེ་སློང་བསོད་ནམས་རིན་ཆེན།

（二）藏文录文转写

御制序文

/ / rgyal povi mdzad pavi bod kyi bkav vgyur gyi vbri sbyangs / nged thos na / mang bkur gyi / ri movi rgyas par byed pa la / mdo dang gsung rab kyi kyi dbu vgyang ring nas phye bavo / / yuvi hung phan dar ba la / yi gevi dbyibs chen po brtsam pa mngon par byed pavo / / sngon gyi vdzangs srol shin du rtsad chod de / / vjig rten bar bar pa la snang srid phye bavi don / / lugs chen po gsang tshig / nyi ma skar ma dang bcas gshib par lhan cig du gsal / ngo mtshar can gyi levu yi gevi gtso ri dang rgya mtsho la vgran zla lhan cig yar vphags so / / yang mngav zhabs bsdoms pa vbangs rnams bskyabs pa yin kyang / gsol vdebs pavi blon povi smon lam vdebs pavi yi ge yod / char chu legs par mthun par byas nas / gnam savi bab rnams lta mkhan yang vdug / ji ltar navang yod pa gnyer bavi don thams cad gcig tu bya bavi phyir / de rnams so sovi gsang ba gsal bar brjod pavi bris so / / gang zhig phyogs bcu / vphags pavi bden pa bzhi / snang ba gsum / mngon shes drug yin na / han dus kyi ming te / gser gyi mi rmi ba la / rta dkar thog la bkal te khyer nas vong / / thang dus kyi thavi tsung vphags pavi bslab byavi mdzad sbyangs bris pa yis / pad+ma sngon po rgyas par vbyung / g.yang drevu yi po ti shar phyogs la sleb cing / g.yang drevi sngon povi gleb movi dkyil vkhor la gtso bor byas so / / gser gyi glegs bam lho phyogs su bsgyur nas / seng ge dang vbrug gi tshogs kyang bzhengs / cu lan gyi bslab byas rim pa brgyud de / thog mar levu bzhi bcu zhe gnyis skyangs so / / y+wana tsang gi khyer vong nas / vjags par bkod pavang po ti drug brgyal lhag par

页上一

gyur pa grags pa / vjig rten rnams rtog par / shar phyogs la rtag tu bzhugs so / / devi rim par brgyud nas / che bar grags pavi mdor bsdus pa nan tu byas nas / bsam pa ni snyigs dus slar ldog pa yod / de khavi drang por sri zhu bya ste / tshig rnams phyin ci log pa bsal te bden pa la vjog go / de khavi byams dang snying brtse yod pavi stabs / bsam re bzhin du log vkhu thams cad bcom par gsod pa yang bzhag / sems kyi mar me mtshan mor bsal na / lam nag po thal ste bsal / sems gyi rgyu nang bar bskyed na / mevi ra ba nas bsil bar gyur / lam ji snyed mi vdra navang don gcig yin / nges par yal ga gzhan yin kyang rtse mo ni gcig yin / yang vphags pavi chos kyi rnam par smin pa bshad do / / gong ma rnams la yun ring du vbyung bavi srol la gsol vdebs shing / bslab byar bsgrags / vog ma rnams la phan par sgral bavi grur thob par bgyid / nges par phyogs nas brtson pavi phyir / phan pa snon pa med pa ci / vdi la lhavi mdor bsdus bzung ste / ji tsam bkod pa sangs rgyas kyi dung gi sgra las btsal bavi spyod pavi med na yang / sa gzhi rnams kyi spyir bde ba la brda sprod kyi phyir /

yang ngo mtshar ni spos kyi ngad la shes navang vgyur ro / / ngas sngon dang da lta rnams brtson par phyung ste / mdo dang dpe nan tan zhib tu byas / hwang gsum dang / ti lngavi yi ge dus rnams la dbye nas ltas kyang / ming can ri la sbas te bzhag pavi mdo yang blovi bshad mod / tho rang gi dus bzhengs snga zhing vchad rtsod rtsom pavi gnas sar rgyas par byed pavi dran pa btsal / mtshan mar me sbar nas yi gevi khang par rgyun du btsal nas zhib par rdzogs / bcav khrims lugs srol la vbrel ba

页下一

yin navang / mdo dang dang yi ger rim par brgyud pa nan tan du btsal / yi gevi lugs la gtso bo yin na / rang bzhin gyi lugs kyi bslab bya rim par brgyud nas gsal mod / da lta shing rta dang yi ge gcig du bsdus pavi phyir / ji ltar na dpe dang dbyibs la kun kyang vbrang / yang blo yi shing sems kyi me tog / ta lavi lo mavi chos la ma mthong navang / khrung gi tshal sha bavi ra ba / phar phyin gyi stegs bu la re shig vdeg te ltos pavi don / g.yang drel bskor movi me long gi gzugs mthong mthong nas / ngo mtshar can gyi gser thag gi spyod pa nan tu byas / nan tu bsam na / thavi hwang thavi huvi sku tshe bsod nams yun ring du vphel nas / grong khyer mnyan yod du thugs dag go / hwang thavi huvi bsod nams chen po khyad du dar nas / rgyal bu rgyal byed kyi tshal du tshul bzhin du drin bzab po / sngon las byed kyi khrims ravi blon po rnams lugs bzhin du mthun par byas pa ni / thams cad guvi shes bya bavi shing gi phog / mes shes bya bavi shing gi gdung yin kyang / da ltar sgrub pavi chos la yod pa ni / kun la ya mtshan gtam pavi gsang tshig / skye bo dman pa rnams sdug par ma byas te / vbangs rnams kyi rdzas ma vgul bar las byed rnams la nang gi mdzod nas bstan cing / phyivi mdzod nas / vgul cag btang bavang med / yang dag bslab byavi ngo mtshar can gyi srol grags par byed pa vos pa bsam nas / chos vdon pa dang / gtso bo sgra dbyangs che bar ma byung navang / de rnams sngon nas tshun chad bslab bya rim par brgyud pavi yi ge nan tu byas nas / yang

页上二

sangs rgyas stong rtsa stong phun tshun rim par brgyud pavi levu la bsdus shing shing bod chos rnying pavi par brkos so / / gos chen snum ljang sgrigs par byas nas / bkra shis rtags brgyad ldan pavi thon thi ser povi bzav phud par byas / me tog sna bdun gyi ri mo can khyad vphags byas so so / / nang gi pho brang la yang dag ngo mtshar can gyi vod zer khyab cing / shin tu mdzes pa ni / kun la bsgrags par bya ste / vgrel pavi tshig la bsnan nas rgyas par byed cing / bkav vgyur dar byed pa gtso byas nas / thavi hwang thavi huvi dang hwang thavi hu gnyis la ya mtshan bkra shis gsol ba vdebs pa rigs rus khri phrag rnams la bsod nams chen po gnas par bgyivo zhes / de rnams chos kyi dbur vbri zhing / bsngags par bstod pa bstan yod / bde skyid kyi lo nyer gsum / ston zla vbring povi nyi shu gnyis la /

页下二

请序疏

/ / mdzad byang zhu bavi yi ge bcav khrims kyi blon po phu na el gen mkhyen dbang dag gi zhu ba ni / lung gi rjes vbrang nas / bkav vgyur par bzhengs pavi don / rgyal povi mdzad pavi bris sbyangs bkod nas yun ring brgyud par bya bavi phyir nan du zhu ba ni / bltas nas / rgya gar yul du las kyi dbang gi ngo mtshar sprul pavi rnam vphrul thog mar byung la / vphags lam yan lag brgyad / theg pa rim pa lnga rnams yangs pa can dang mu k+Shavi yul dbu btsugs nas gtad pa dang du blangs pa shin tu / ring mod / rgya nag gi han dang ming zhes bya bavi / / rgyal povi dus su / vphags pa gser gyi mdog can rmi ba las / rgya gar yul la pho nya mngags nas / bstan pavi lugs srol gyi yig tshogs mang po dang tshigs bcad rnams rim par yul dbus su brgyud nas / lo nyi stong nye ba byung zhing / vdi yi vtshams su thang dang sung gi rgyal skabs gsal bar bsngags par bstod pa ji tsam mang yang / sangs rgyas kyi bstan pa dar zhing rgyas pa gcig buvi don duvang min cing / ched du vdis kyang rnam pa khri phrag mang po spel bavi don yin la / gong ma skye tsam nyid ni thugs mkhyen pa mkhas pavi rang bzhin yin pa la / rtul phod yon tan ngo mtshar che ba ni / gnam sa dang vgran zla bavi / bcav khrims / slab ston legs par vbyor bavi / dpal gyi snyan grags chen po mngon par mtho bavi / nyi zla khyab pavi sa steng du gnang sbyin gyi khyab par dang du blangs / lo dang zla bavi dus kyi rjes vbrangs nas / khral gyi rig mi vdzin pavang med / vdi ltar navang / gong mavi thugs bdag gir med pas / nyin re bzhin shin tu nyen nas / gzhengs snga zhing gsol phyi ba / gzhungs don ched du gnyer zhing vbangs la brtse skyongs che / yang khri phrag

页上一

mang povi don dbye bavi / dal skabs suvang / vjig rten bstan chos drug dang bstan chos mang po bstun nas nan tu gzigs pas / yig ris su ma ma thon pavi gsang ba phra mo phye ba yin / gzhung dang srid pa phan tshun rim par brgyud pavi lugs kyi rnam grangs ma mkhyen pavang med / yang gnam savi lugs dang / rgya nag zi ming can gyi yi ge / khyim brgyavi yi ge shes rdzogs shing / spyivi don rgyu skar gyi gnas / vphags pavi chos shing ta lavi lo mavi yi ge sogs / srod dang tho rang dus su nan tan zhib tu byas nas / slab pavi thabs shes rdzogs shing / zab pavi ma phye bavang med / sngon dang dang da lta rnams rdzogs par mkhyen / bdag povi thugs brtson bir reg pa tsam gyi brgya phrag bcuvi tshigs sogs vbyung ba / gnam gyi dgu tshig bzhin du dngas shing lta bavi chog mi shes / nges par ti yan mu yi dpe phung mi yi lugs rdzogs par byas pa ni / vphags pa stong gcig tu vdus pavi bdag nyid chen po mngon sum gsal gsal bar sgrubs pavang yin zhing / yon tan gsum gzhi gcig tu gzhengs pas so / / de ltar navang / g.yang drel myu guvi rin chen yi ge vbrug vphar zhing / ka lan da kavi gar ltar / mang bkur rgyal povi btab pavi ya mtshan thig / han gyi rgyal pos brtsam nas bris pavi / dpe yang mog por mdzad mod don vdi yang dal skabs su byas pa yin la / da lta yang brtse ba chen povi sgo nas khyab cing / ched du bsam na bkav vgyur gyis par brkos pas phan yon chen povi / gong ma thavi hwang thavi havu hwang thavi havu rnams lo khri thub pavi bkra shis dpag med yun ring du vbyung bar gyur cig / sa steng gi blon vbangs vog ma rnams la yang / lo vbum gyi bar du vbyung bavi bkra shis thob par gyur cig / ched du vbras gnas

页下一

bzhi / phar phyin drug gi zab don rtogs par dkav / lhavi lung gi gsal bar ma bstan na / ma rig pavi vkhyam bzhin blun povi skye bo dman pa rnams rdzogs lam ji ltar rnyed / sngon thang gi dus kyi thavi tsung gis ho shang ming can la lung phab ste / glegs bam drug brgya lhag par bsgyur nas / bris sbyangs ched du byas pa yin la / ming dus kyi thavi tsus / vphags mavi thang ka la bstod tshigvang dug / yung lovi dus su vdi thams cad mngav vbangs rgyas pavi yar tshes la bkav vgyur zhu dag byas nas par du brkos / bod kyi lugs srol gyi brtags mngon par byas so so / / gong mavi sri zhu bkur sti byams dang dang spyin pa thang dang ming gi rgyal po gsum gyis cha khris kyang / cha gcig vdra bar ga la nus / gong mavi mdzad pavi bris sbyangs gnang na nam mkhav thams cad vod khyab cing / sa gzhi thams cad la phan bde vbyung mod / zhu ba ni / gong mavi sangs rgyas kyi bstan pa dgongs nas / ched du rgyal povi mdzad pavi bris sbyangs gnang la chos kyi dbur bzhag nas / ma rig pavi blun po rnams la rgyas par bstan / lo khrivi bar du rim par brgyud na ji ltar lags / vdi ltar na dngas pavi nyi mas / bdag povi yi ge vbav zhig la brtson par brtse bavi sprin gyis / gong mavi sku bsod dang mnyam por yun ring du vbyung mod / vdivi don du zhu yig bris nas nan tan du zhu ba ni / lung gi zhu ba yin la / bde skyid kyi lo nyer gnyis / ston zla vbring povi bcu drug nyin / bcav khrims kyi blon po phu na el gen mkhyen dbang / nang gi khrims ravi yi gevi blon po rim pa gnyis pa yin zhing / rim pa gnyis

页上二

pavi phogs za bavi rim pa bzhi bsnan pavi u la tavi / tsung shin phu khrims ravi g.yas phyogs kyi zivi don dbyes pavi thil vdzin gyi blon po rim pa gcig bsnan pavi blon po gyo ro shom dpevi / las byed kyi khrims ravi thil vdzin smra mkhan blon po rim pa gnyis bsnan pavi blon ya chi na / dbyes par blta bavi blon po rim pa gnyis bsnan pavi i la ha / dbyes par blta bavi blon po rim pa gsum bsnan pavi keng gevi / dmag gi khrims ravi don dbyes pavi blon po thub pa skyabs dag gis zhu ba / zhus ma thag pavi zla bavi bco brgyad la lung / gzhung gi khrims rar srol gsal bar byas nas nan tan du gros kyi kyi la zhus gsungs byung / /

页下二

覆请序疏

/ / mdzad byang slar zhu bavi yi ge / gzhung gi khrims ravi blon povi gtso bo / / blon po bcas san dag gi nan gyi / / zhu ba ni / lung gi rjas vbrang nas bkav vgyur gyi par bzhengs pavi don / rgyal povi mdzad pavi vbri sbyangs yun ring brgyud par bya bavi phyir / / nan du zhu ba ni / gzhung gi khrims ravi kho ya mun nas dpe bris nas vbyung / bcav khrims blon po phu na el gen mkhyen dbang dag gi / don vdivi phyir du zhu ba ni / bltas na / rgya gar yul du las kyi dbang gi ngo mtshar sprul pavi rnam vphrul thog mar vbyung la / vphags pavi lam yan lag brgyad / theg pa rim pa lnga rnams yangs pa can dang mu k+Shavi yul du dbu btsugs nas / gtad pa dang du blangs pa shin tu ring mod / rgya nag gi han ming zhes bya bavi rgyal povi dus su / vphags pa gser gyi mdog can rmi ba las / rgya gar yul la pho nya mngags nas bstan pavi lugs srol gyi yig tshogs mang po dang tshigs bcad rnams rim par yul dbus su su brgyud nas / lo nyi stong nye vbyung zhing / vdi yi mtshams su thang dang sung gi rgyal skabs gsal bar bsngags par bstod pa ji tsam mang yang / sangs rgyas kyi bstan pa dar zhing rgyas pa gcig buvi don duvang min cing / ched du vdis kyang rnam pa khri phrag mang povi don yin la / gong ma skye tsam nyid ni thugs mkhyen pa mkhas pavi rang bzhin yin pa la / rtul phod yon tan ngo mtshar che ba ni / gnam dang vgran zla bavi / bcav khrims slab ston legs par vbyor bavi / dpal gyi snyan grags chen po mngon par mtho ba sa steng du khyab pavi gnang sbyin dang du blangs / lo dang zla bavi dus kyi rjes vbrang nas / khral gyi rig mi vdzin pavang med / vdi

页上一

ltar navang / gong mavi thugs bdag gir med pas / nyin re bzhin shin tu nyen nas / gzhengs snga zhing gsol phyi ba / gzhungs don ched du gnyer zhing vbangs la brtse skyongs che / yang khri phrag mang povi don dbye bavi dal skabs suvang vjig rten bstan chos drug dang bstan chos mang po bstun nas nan du gzigs pas / yig ris su ma thon pavi gsang ba phra mo yang phye ba yin gzhung dang srid pa phan tshun rim par brgyud pavi lugs kyi rnam grangs ma mkhyen pavang med / yang gnam savi lugs dang rgya nag zi ming can gyi yi ge / khyim brgyavi yi ge spyivi don dang rgyu skar gnas / vphags pavi chos shing ta lavi lo mavi yi ge sogs / srod dang tho dang tho rang dus su nan tan zhib tu byas nas / slab pavi thabs shes rdzogs shing / zab pavi ma phye bavang med pas / sngon dang da lta rnams rdzogs shing mkhyen / re revi skabs su / bdag povi thugs brtsom bir reg pa tsam gyi brgya phrag bcuvi tshig sogs vbyung ba ni / gnam gyi dgu tshigs bzhin du dngas shing blta bavi chog mi shes / nges par ti yan mu yi dpe phung mi yi lugs rdzogs par byas pa ni / vphags pa stong gcig tu vdus pavi bdag nyid chen po mngon sum gsal bar bsgrubs pavang yin zhing / yon tan gsum gzhi gcig tu bzhengs pas so / / de ltar navang / g.yang drel myu guvi rin chen yi ge vbrug vphar zhing / ka lan da kavi gar ltar / mang bkur rgyal povi btab pavi ya mtshan thig / han gyi rgyal pos brtsam nas bris pavi dpe yang mog por mdzad mod / don vdi yang dal skabs su byas pa yin la / da lta yang brtse ba chen povi sgo nas khyab cing / ched du bsam na slar bkav vgyur gyi par brkos

页下一

pas phan yon chen po / gong ma thavi hwang thavi hu hwang thavi hu rnams lo khri thub pavi bkra shis dpag med yun ring du vbyung bar gyur cig / sa steng gi blon vbangs vog ma rnams la yang / lo vbum gyi bar du vbyung bavi bkra shis thob par gyur cig / ces so / / spyir vbras gnas bzhi / phar phyin drug gi zab don rtog par dkav / lhavi lung gi gsal bar ma bstan / ma rig pavi vkhyam bzhin blon po skye bo dman pa rnams rdzogs lam ji ltar rnyed / sngon thang gi dus kyi thavi tsung gis ho shang ming can la lung phab ste ste / glegs bam drug brgya lhag par bsgyur nas / vbri sbyangs ched du byas pa yin la / ming dus kyi thavi tsuvi vphags mavi thang ka la bstod tshig byas pavang vdug / yung lovi dus su bkav vgyur chen po zhu dag zhib par byas nas brkos pa vdi thams cad mngav vbangs rgyas pavi yar tshes la / bod kyi lugs srol gyi rtags mngon par byas so / gong mavi sri zhu bkur sti byams dang sbyin pa ni shin tu khyad par vphags / thang dang / ming gi rgyal po gsum gyis / cha khris kyang cha gcig vdra bar ga la nus / gong mavi mdzad pavi bris sbyangs gnang na nam mkhav thams cad vod khyab cing / sa gzhi thams cad la phan bde vbyung mod / zhu ba ni / gong mavang sangs rgyas kyi bstan pa dgongs nas / ched du rgyal povi mdzad pavi bris sbyangs gnang la / chos kyi dbur bzhag nas / ma rig pavi blun po rnams la rgyas par bstan / lo khrivi bar du rim par brgyud na ji ltar lags / vdi ltar na dngas pavi nyi mas bdag povi yi ge la vbav zhig gsal nas / brtse bavi sprin gyis gong mavi sku bsod dang mnyam por yun ring du vbyung mod / vdivi

页上二

don du zhu yig vbri nas nan tan du zhu ba ni / lung zhus lags / zhes bde skyid kyi lo nyer gnyis / ston zla vbring povi bcu drug la zhus lags / zla ba vdi khavi bcwa brgyad la / lung gzhung gi khrims ravi srol gsal bar dbye nas nan du gros byas nas zhus zer / vdivi rjes vbrang nan gyis / zla ba vdi khavi bcu dgur gzhung gi khrims ra la phab byung / blon po bdag cag gi gros byas pa nas / bcav khrims kyi phu na el gen chen wang dag gi zhu bavi yi ge la / slab bya / sho lo ka yul dbus su brgyud nas lo nyis stong nye ba song / thang dang / sung gi rgyal skabs gsal bar bsngags par bstod pa ni / sangs rgyas kyi bstan pa dar zhing rgyas pa gcig buvi don duvang min / ched du vdis kyang rnam pa khri phrag mang po spel bavi don yin la / gong ma skye tsam nyid ni mkhyen pa mkhas pavi rang bzhin yin pa la / rtul phod yon tan che ba ni / gnam sa dang vgran zla bavi / khri phrag mang povi don dbye bavi dal skabs suvang vjig rten bstan chos drug dang bstan chos mang po bstun nas nan du gzigs pas / zi mang povi yi ge / khyim brgyavi yi ge vphags pavi chos / shing ta la lo mavi yi ge sogs / srod dang tho dang tho rang dus nan tan zhib tu byas nas / zab pavi bsam pa ma phye ba cig yang med / da ltar / ched du brtse ba chen povi sgo nas khyab cing / bkav vgyur gyis par yang slar brkos pavi phan yon chen po ni / gong ma thavi hwang thavi hu / hwang thavi huvi lo khri thub pavi bkra shis dpag med yun ring du vbyung bar gyur cig / sa steng gi blon vbangs vbangs vog ma la yang / lo vbum gyi bar du byung bavi bkra shis thob par gyur cig / sngon thang gi dus kyi thavi tsung gis / ho shang ming can

页下二

la bkav phab ste / glegs bam drug brgya lhag bsgyur nas / bris sbyangs ched du byas pa yin la / ming dus kyi thavi tsu / vphags mavi thang ka la bstod tshig byas pavang vdug / yung lovi dus su bkav vgyur chen po zhu dag zhib par byas nas brkos pa / vdi thams cad mngav vbangs rgyas pavi yar tshes la / bod kyi lugs srol gyi brtags mngon par byas so / gong mavi sri zhu bkur sti byams dang sbyin pa ni shin tu khyad par vphags / thang dang ming gi rgyal po gsum gyi cha khri yang cha cig vdra bar ga la nus / zhu ba ni / gong ma sangs rgyas kyi bstan pa dgongs nas / ched du rgyal povi mdzad pavi bris sbyangs gnang la chos kyi dbur bzhag nas / ma rig pavi blun po rnams la rgyas par bstan / lo khrivi bar du rim par brgyud nas ji ltar lags / bdag cag blon po rnams kyis bltas na / tshigs bcad dang slab byavi yi ge mang po / bkav vgyur la ma tshang ba ci yang med / slab byar / gsal bar / gsang ba / dbye bar bya bavi srol rang bzhin rnam par spyod pa ni gzhan navang devi bsam pavi tshad khri phrag gi bya bavi don du vgro rnams rnams smin par byas nas vkhrid yod / skabs kyi gong ma rnams kyi rgyun du rgyas par khyab ste / kha cig gi ni bsgyur ba dang / kha cig gi par du brkos nas de rnams slab bya chad pa med par byas / phyir yang slab byavi lugs lhag par grags srol rnams dar ba la / the tshom med par rang gi mdzad sbyangs vbri zhing / glegs bam gyi dbur bzhag na gdod ma ni sprul pavi mi rnams shin tu rjes vbrang nas / thag nye ring ba rnams ha las bsam / dbyen thang dus kyi thavi tsung gi dus su cen kwan gyi lo nyer gnyis kyi rgya ban y+wana y+wanga rnams bod chos po ti drug brgya

页上三

lnga bcu nga nga bdun bsgyur nas / bsgrub pavi rjes su rgyal po rang gis sde snod gsum dang lhag pavi bslab pas mdzad sbyangs vbri zhing rdo la brko bavi don / da ltavi bar du rim par brgyud / ming dus kyi thavi tsung rang gis brtsams pavi yi ger sgrol mar bstod pavi yi ge / yang sher snying gi mdzad sbyangs / pad+ma satwa / vjig rten me tog snying povi rim gyis bstod nas vbri bavi yi ge yod / ming dus kyi cheng tsu bkav vgyur chen po zhu dag nan tu byas nas par du brkos / bkav vgyur gyi bstod tshigs dang mkhyen rab gzhung lugs dam pavi chos gsung rab glegs bam bzhi / phal po che / mtshan brjod rim pavi mdzad sbyang gi yi ge rnams chos kyi dbur vbri nas bkav vgyur gyi po tir bzhag yod / yang dbye na thang dus kyi khivana tsung / snying gnas bsgom pavi chos kyi mdzad sbyang gi yi ge vbri lags / sung dus kyi thavi tsung rang mkhyen rab shes bya bavi yi ge po ti lnga brtsams nas vbri lags / cen tsung zhi tivana zhus ci zhes zhes bya ba yi ge po ti gcig vbri lags / vdi rnams gtsug lag khang du tshags byas nas dpag tu med pa rim par brgyud / nan du bsam na / / gong mavi yon tan gnam sa dang vgran zla ba / lugs ni lha dang mi la rdzogs par mkhyen / zab cing zhib pa phra ba nan tan bden par gsang ba rnam ma gsal bavang med ma vongs pa yang mkhyen / vdas pa yang bzung phra movi srol mi brtson pa ci yang med / gong mavi slab bya zab cing phra ba / lhavi yi ger vos pa nges par mdzes pa sngon gyi ring gi mi dbang rnams ji snyed gcig yod kyang vgran zla min / da ltar gnam sa spel bavi thugs la re ba mi bstun cing / gong mavi sri zhur thugs la rgyas par / gong ma thavi hwang thavi hu hwang thavi hu rnams la

页下三

bkra shis par gyur cig / vog ma blon vbangs khri phrag rnams kyang sku bsod dang len bgyis ces / bkav vgyur gyi par brkos nas / sa steng la rim par brgyud pavi phyir ched du bkav phab ste / sho lo ka gcig gi slab bya rtogs par dkav / bod kyi chos kyi chos gtol nas dar bar bya ba the tshom med / lhavi lung gis gis bsngags par bstod na da ltar nyi zla bzhin dngas shing gsal bar vbyung mod / vdivi phyir du dbang dag gi zhu ba phul ba ltar / bdag po rang gi mdzad sbyangs yi ger bkod nas chos kyi dbur bzhag nas / shel gyi po ti rin chen yi ger ngo mtshar bavi vod gsal bar / sa steng rnams la khyab par bstan / dpag med yun ring rim par brgyud na ci gnang / vdi ltar na nges nges par bde bar legs pavi dus kyi don / gong mavi rim gyi srol chen po chen po vbyung mod / nged blon po rnams kyi bsam pa ltar ma yin pavi stabs kyis nan du zhu ba lags / / lung zhus lags / gzhung gi khrims ravi blon povi gtso bo blon po bcas san / blon povi gtso bo blon po sha chang / g.yon ruvi blon po gnyis pa blon po e shing ge / phal cher labs pavi blon po g.yon ruvi blon po gnyis pa yi gevi khrims ravi blon po gnyis pa yin cing yi gevi blon po gtogs pa yang ceng phung / g.yas ruvi blon po gnyis pa rim pa gnyis bsnan pavi blon po sa has / phal cher labs pavi blon pavi g.yas ruvi yi gevi khrims ravi blon po yi gevi gnyis pa la gtogs pa khrin thing ging / zi ci ching li zivi dbye bar byed pavi blon po ho bing phan par byed pavi blon po gnyis bsnan bsnan pavi chang tsavi / phan par byed pavi blon po sang ga / phan par byed pavi blon po rim pa gcig bsnan pavi sa yin ta / phan par byed pavi blon po rim pa gnyis phab nas slar blon po sngar lugs lugs ltar ko zhi lung / phan par byed pavi blon po shivu yung sovu / brjed tho vdzin pavi blon po wang gin chen / brjed tho vdzin pavi blon po rim pa gcig bsnan

页上四

pavi blon po phivang ku / brjed tho vdzin pavi blon po zhus bzhin phung / bde skyid kyi lo nyer gnyis / ston zla tha chung gi tshes gcig / zhus lags / zla ba vdi khavi tshes bzhi la / lung la bas pa ltar bgyi zer /

页下四

职名

/ / gong mavi lung gis bsnan nas par bzhengs zer bavi bkav vgyur do dam byed du bcug pa / bcav khrims kyi blon po phu na el gin chin wang / ltas par byed pavi blon po rnams / bod yig gi slob dpon blon po ar pid hu / nang gi khrims ravi yi gevi blon po shu lu / gzhung gi kho yi khrims ravi the vdzin pavi smra mkhan blon po a shi than / bcav bavi kho yi khrims ravi vdzin pavi smra mkhan blon po he shevu / thams cad dbye bavi khrims ravi dbyes par blta bavi blon po se te ri / dbyes par blta bavi blon po ma se / dbyes par blta bavi blon po sa yim pu / bcav bavi khrims ravi don dbyes pavi blon po un cha / las byed kyi khrims ravi don dbyes pavi blon livu hivang / blon povi khrims ravi phan par byed pavi blon po eng kavi / dmag gi khrims ravi phan par byed pavi blon po mA chavu tsan / kong shan khu zhes bya ba mdzad kyi phan par byed pavi blon po su thavi / phan par byed pavi blon po te cheng ke / brjed tho vdzin pavi blon po yung pu / brjed tho vdzin pavi blon po thung ki thu / blon povi khrims ravi yi ge pa blon po pe pavu cu / gzhung gi khrims ravi yi ge pa blon po phu lu / dmag gi khrims ravi yi ge pa blon po kir zavi / bcav bavi khrims ravi yi ge pa blon po el ge / yi ge ba blon po sul thu / yi ge pa blon po thang kavi

页上一

las byed kyi khrims ravi yi ge pa blon po cha pu ku / thams cad dbye bavi khrims ravi yi ge pa blon neng ke / yi ge pa blon po wal ta / yi ge pa blon po livu cu / yi ge pa blon po livu zi / yi ge pa blon po livu yi yu wan / mdzad kyi kho yi khrims ravi yi ge pa blon po hing thu / gzhung gi kho yi khrims ravi yi ge pa blon po wa hun tavi / bcav bavi kho yi khrims ravi yi ge pa blon po theng ke / gsar bcad zhu dag byas mkhan bla ma rnams / cang skya zhabs drung / mgo pa bla ma dbang phyug sbyin sbyin pa / mgo pa bla ma blo bzang dpal vbyor / tem chi dge slong blo bzang rnam rgyal / rab vbyams pa don grub rab brtan / rab vbyams pa tshul khrims bzang po / dge slong bstan pa gsal byed / rgyal po bde skyid kyi lo sum cu so dgu zla ba bzhi pavi tshes bzang por par bzhengs bsgrubs pavo / / dge vo / legs s+ho / /

页下一

总理监修

/ / bkav vgyur rnams do dam byed du bcug pa / bcav khrims kyi blon po phu na el gen mkhyen dbang / ltas par byed pavi blon po rnams / nang gi khrims ravi yi gevi blon po / rim pa gnyis pa yin zhing / rim pa gnyis pavi phog za bavi / rim pa bzhi bsnan pavi blon po u la tavi / tsung shin phu khrims ravi g.yas phyogs kyi zivi don dbyes pavi the vdzin gyi blon po rim pa gcig bsnan pavi blon po gyo ro shom pevi / don dbyes pavi blon po rim pa gcig bsnan pa / blon po gyo ro li ma / las byed kyi khrims rivi kho yi the vdzin pavi smra mkhan blon po / rim pa gnyis bsnan pavi / blon po ya chi na / thams cad dbyes par blta bavi khrims rivi blon po / rim pa gnyis bsnan pavi / blon po i la ha / dbyes par blta bavi blon po / rim pa gsum bsnan pavi / blon po keng gevi / dmag gi khrims ravi don dbyes pavi blon po / blon po thub pa skyabs / nang gi khrims rivi cwan wen tsung zhu rim pa gcig bsnan pavi blon po hwas / tsung shin phu khrims ravi rim pa bdun pavi yi ge pa ni / rim pa gcig bsnan pavi blon po khwon ce / rim pa bdun pavi yi ge pa ni / rim pa gnyis bsnan pavi blon po chang b+havu / thams cad dbye bar byed pavi khrims ravi rim pa bdun pavi yi ge pa ni / rim pa gnyis bsnan pavi blon po wa mi ta / yi ge pa ni blon po na yan tavi dmag gi khrims ravi rim pa bdun pavi yi ge pa ni / rim pa gnyis bsnan pavi blon po u lan /

页上一

校阅经字喇嘛

/ / bkav vgyur gyi yi ge rnams ltas nas zhu dag bcos par byed pa / pho brang gi bla ma thams cad kyi khrims vdzin pavi bla ma mer gen chos rje / pho brang gi bla ma thams cad kyi khrims vdzin pavi bla ma yin pa la bod yig gi slob dpon bsod nams chos rje / bod yig gi slob dpon pa gnyis pa yin pa la / rim pa bzhi pavi phogs za bavi blon po zhi thevu / bkav vgyur gyi yi ge zhu dag byas mkhan / dge slong dge vdun dar rgyas / dge slong blo bzang dpal rgyas / dge slong bsod nams rin chen / dge slong blo bzang don grub / dge slong ngag dbang seng ge / dge slong blo bzang kun dgav / dge slong blo bzang dpal vbyor / dge slong tshul khrims bzang po / dge slong bstan pa bkra shis / dge slong blo bzang shes rab / dge slong bsam gtan rin chen / dge slong sbyin pa dpal vbyor / dge slong blo bzang chos rgyal / dge slong rin chen bsod nams / dge slong tshul khrims dpal vbar / dge slong tshul khrims yon tan / dge slong tshul khrims bkra shis / dge slong dge legs rin chen / dge slong bkra shis rin chen / dge slong ngag dbang sbyin pa / dge slong bstan pa rab brtan / dge slong ngag dbang sbyin pa / dge slong bzang po tshul khrims / dge slong blo bzang bzod pa / dge slong yon tan rin chen / dge slong phun tshogs rin chen / dge slong blo bzang bstan dar / dge slong sbyin pa bsod nams / dge slong ye shes dpal vbyor / dge slong chos vphel bzang po / dge slong bkra shis dar dar rgyas / dge slong bsod nams rgyal mtshan / dge slong chos vphel bzang po / dge slong blo bzang dar rgyas / dge slong bzang po rgyal mtshan / dge slong blo bzang nyi ma / dge slong bsod nams brtson vgrus / dge slong bkra shis bzang po / dge slong brtson vgrus rin chen / dge slong blo bzang vphrin las / bod yig gi slob ma rdo rje /

页下一

校阅序目录官

/ / vbri sbyangs dang kar chag nan tan du zhu dag byas pavi blon po / nang gi khrims ravi yi gevi blon po rim pa gsum bsnan pavi blon po dan tavi / nang gi khrims ravi yi gevi blon po / rim pa gsum pavi phogs za bavi / rim pa gnyis bsnan pavi blon po sbas ri / nang gi khrims ravi yi gevi blon po rim pa gsum pavi phogs za bavi / rim pa drug bsnan pavi blon po ung gin / bod yig gi vbri sbyangs kar chag bsgyur pavi blon po / bod yig gi slob dpon pa gnyis pavi blon po / / rim pa bzhi pavi phogs za bavi blon po zhi thevu / rgya yig gi kar chag bsgyur pavi blon po / nang gi khrims ravi cwan wen tsung zhu blon po u shi bu / nang gi khrims ravi cwan wen tsung zhu blon po steng tevi / sog yig gi vbri sbyangs kar chag bsgyur pavi blon po / nang gi khrims ravi ban zhi tsung zhu rim pavi gnyis bsnan bsnan pa rim pa drug gi phogs za bavi blon po lam sbyangs sbyangs / nang gi khrims ravi ban zhi tsung zhu rim pa gcig bsna pa rim pa drug gi phogs za bavi blon po he kevu / man ju yi ge nan tan du vbri bavi blon po / nang gi khrims ravi ban zhi tsung zhu rim pa bzhi bsnan pa rim pa lnga bavi phogs za bavi blon po i b+ha ri / nang gi khrims ravi cwan tsung zhu blon po tseng shevu / nang gi khrims ravi cwan wen tsung zhu blon po cham pu / sog yig nan tan du vbri bavi blon po / nang gi khrims ravi ban zhi tsung zhu blon po shavu kevu / rgya yig nan tan du vbri bavi blon po / nang gi khrims ravi ban zhi tsung zhu rim pa gcig bsnan pavi tshivu cen khi / nang gi khrims ravi ban zhi tsung zhu blon po wang khi u / bod yig nan tan du vbri bavi bla ma / dge slong blo bzang klu grub / dge slong blo bzang dpal rgyas / dge slong bsod nams rin chen /

三、蒙古文录文转写

御制序文

qaγan-u bičigsen töbed g'anǰur-un orosil. bi sonosbasu. fo ki. ǰiruqai-yi badaraγuluγsan-dur. nom sudur-un eki qoladača negegdeǰüküi. ioi. qüng fan-i delgeregülügsen-dür. bičig-un düri egüskel yekede iledǰüküi. masi erten-ü siluγun qauli-yi nengǰiǰü. dumdadu yirtinčü-dür gegen orčilang-i nekegsen-ü tula. yeke yoson niγuča üge. naran ba odon-luγ-a ǰergečen qamtu geyibei. γayiqamsiγ-tu bülüg erkin bičig aγula ba dalai-dur tenggečeǰü qamtu-bar übedegsi bolba. basa ulus-i ǰongkilaqu irgen-i ibegeküi-dür bolbasu. ǰalbariqu tüsimel. qutuγ γuyuqu bičig bui.. ǰokiraγuluγči kei sayin qur-a-dur bolbasu. tngri γaǰar-un čaγ-i üǰegčid-ber bui. kerkibesü-ber čöm bükü-yi erkilekü-yi nigen udq-a-du bolγaqu-yin tula. teyin öber-e öber-e niγuča-yi todorqayilaqu ögülel-i bičiǰükui. kerber arban ǰüg. qutuγ-tan-u dörben ünen. γurban gegen. ǰirγuγan ǰöng bilig bolbasu. qan ulus-un ming di. altan kömün-yi ǰegüdülegsen-dür. čaγan morin-dur ačiǰu abču ireǰüküi. tang ulus-un tayisung boγdas-un surγaγuli-yin orosil-i bičigsen-iyer. köke linqu-a delgeren γarǰuqui. qas bodi doron-a γaǰar-tur kürčü ireged. qabtaγai köke qas mandal-dur erkilegdebei.

页上一

altan debter-i emün-e-dü g'anǰur-tur orčiγulǰu.arslan luus-un čiγulγan-yi bayiγulbai.. ǰu lan surγaγuli-yi ulamǰilaǰu. eng uridaki döčin qoyar bölög-i manduγulbai.. yuwan dzang abču ireged. toγtaγaγsan ǰokiyal-i-bar ǰirγuγan ǰaγun ilegü bodi bolγaǰu aldarsiγulbai.. bükü yirtinčü-yi uqaγul-un. doron-a-du ǰüg-dür egenegte orosiγulba.. tegün-i ulamǰilaǰu aldarsiγuluγsan yeke tobčiy-a-yi kinabasu. sanaγan anu čöb-ün čaγ-i ǰiči egegülküi-dür bui mön kü sidurγu takimdaγu bolǰu. üge büri čöm buruγu alǰiyas i arilγaǰu ünen-i aquγulǰuqui. mön kü örösiyel asaral bükü-yin tula. sedkikü büri bügüde γačiqu-yi ilaγun ilaqui-yi bailγaǰuqui.. sedkil-ün ǰula söni gegen bolbasu. qarangγui mör-i nebte geyigülümü.. sedkil-ün edügülbüri-yi erte manaγar egüskebesü. γal-un küriyen-eče serigün bolumui.. kedüi mör adali busu bolbasu-bar udq-a anu nigen.. maγad-iyar salaγ-a öber-e bolbaču-bar eki anu nigen bui.basa qutuγ-tan-u nom-i bolbasuraγul-un nomlaǰu. degedüs-tür öni qola bolqu yoson-i ǰalbariγad. soyon surγal-i tunqaγlan γarγaǰu. dooradus-tu rtusalaǰu getülgekü onggoča-yi kürtegülbei. maγad-iyar qalayiǰu kičiyekü-yin tula. tusa kiged nemeges-ün ügei yaγun-y-a. egün-dür

页下一

takir-yin tobčiy-a-yi bariǰu. kedüi ǰokiyal-i burqan-u labai-yin daγun-dur eriküi yabudal ügei bolbasu-bar. delekei-dakin yerü engke-dür tokiyalduγsan-u tula. basa γayiqamsiγ.. küǰis-ün aγar-tur medebesü bolqu bolai.. bi. erte ba edüge dakin-i kičiyen γarγaǰu sudur üliger-i kinan niγtalaǰu. γurban quwang. tabun di-yin bičig-i tutum-a ilγaǰu üǰen bögetel-e neretü aγulan-dur niγuǰu qadaγalaγsan sudur-i basa ergičegülümüi.. ür geyikü-yin urida bosču ögüleldüküi γaǰar-tur. badaraγulqu ba duradqu tusa-yi erimüi.. söni düli kürtel-e ǰula sitaγaǰu bičig-ün gerte ürgülǰide erin kinaqu-yi tegüskemüi.. čaγaǰa qauli-dur qolbaγdaγsan bolbasu. bičig sudur-tur ulamǰilaγsan-i kinan erimüi.. bičig-ün yoson-dur erkilekü inü bolabasu. mön činar-un yoson-un surγal-i ulamǰilan todorqayilamui.. edüge tergen ba bičig nigen bolon quriyaγdaγsan-u tula. kerkibesü üliger keb-dür čöm daγaǰuqui.. basa oyun-u modon sedkil-ün čečeg-i. tala modon-u nabčin-u nom-dur üǰege edüi bolbaču-bar. toγoruun-u oi. buγu-yin küriyen. baramid-un tabsang-dur tür ǰaγur-a önggeyigsen-ü tulada. qas tolin-un tögörig gerel-i üǰeǰü. altan siǰim-ün γayiqamsiγ-tu yabudal-i kinamui.. kündüde sedkibesü.

页上二

(+)tai quwang tayikeü-yin nasun kiged buyan egüride nemegdeǰü. sirwasta balγasun-dur sedkil-iyen ariγulabai.. (+)quwang tayikeü-yin yeke qutuγ ülemǰi badaraǰu. zidawan-u γaǰar-tur yosolan ačilabai.. urida üyile-yin yabudal-un yamun-u tüsimed keb-dür ǰokilduγul-un üiledügsen anu čöm güi kemekü modon-u köndelen niruγun. mai kemekü modon-u niruγun bögetel-e. edüge tegüsügsen nom-dur büküi anu bügüde γayiqamsiγ ögülel niγuča üge. bükü kereg-ten-dür dooradus arad-i ǰobaγaγsan ügei boluγad. irgen-ü ed-i kereglegsen ügei.. egüdküi üiledküi-dür bügüde ordon-u dotor-a-ača γarγaγsan-iyar küü-yin ed-i köndegsen-ber ügei. üneker surγaγuli-yin γayiqamsiγ-tu yoson-i aldarsiγulqu ǰokistu-yi sedkiǰü. nom ungsiqu kiged erkin ayalqu yekede boluγ-a edüi bolbasu-bar. tein erten-eče inaγsi surγaγuli ulamǰilaγsan bičig-i kinaǰu. basa mingγan burqan-u inaγsi činaγsi ündüsülegsen bülüg-i quriyaγad. töbed nom-un qaγučin bičig-i seyilgegülbei.. noγobtor torγan-yi neilegül-ün kiǰü. naiman ölǰei-tü belges tegüsügsen sir-a ǰuwangγuwan-u qubčasun-i tailun. doloγan ǰüil čečeg-ün ar ilangquy-a übedegsi bolbai.. üneker γayiqamsiγ-tu gerel-i dotoγ-a-du ordon-dur kürtegülüged. masi

页下二

sayiqan anu. qotal-a bükün-e tungqaγlaγulǰu .tailburi ügen-dür nemeǰü delgeregülüged. g’anǰur-i badaraγulul-un erkileǰü.(+) qoyar ordon-u γayiqamsiγ qutuγ-i ǰalbarin. tümen oboγ tan-dur yeke qutuγ orosituγai kememü.. tein nom-un ekin-dür bičiged. saisiyan maγtaqui-yi γarγabai..engke amuγulang-un qorin γurbaduγar on.namur-un dumdadu sar-a-yin qorin qoyar-a..

页上三

请序疏

orosil γuyun ayiladqaγsan bičig.. ǰasaγ-un elbeg čin wang tüsimel fuciowan tan-u kündüde (+)ayiladqaqu anu (++)ǰarliγ-i daγan g'anǰur nom-i seyilküi-yin tula.(++)qaγan-u orosil bičig ǰokiyaqu-yi kičiyen γuyuγad. öni qolada ulamǰilaγulqu-yin učir. üǰebesü. enedkeg-ün γaǰar-a γayiqamsiγ ǰayaγaγdaǰu qubilγan düri tulγur γarbai.. naiman töbtabun kölgen. waisali mogš-a γaǰar-ača egüskeged. qatangγadqaγsan ba küliyeǰü abuγsan anu masi qola buyu. qan ulus-un ming di. altan önggetü qubilγan-i ǰegüdüleged. enedkeg ulus-tur elči ilegegsen-dür. egünče silüg šaǰin-u surγaγuli-yin olan bičig. dumdadu ulus-tur ulamǰilaǰu. qoyar mingγan ǰil siqam bolba. ene ǰabsar-a tang ulus sung ulus-un manduγsan učir-a todorqay-a γarγaγsan saisiyan maγtaγsan anu kedüi olan bolbasu-bar. γaγča kü burqan-u surγaγuli-yi delgeregül-ün tarqaγasuγai kemegsen busu. čuqum egüber tümen ǰüil yaγum-a-yi kümüǰigülsügei kemegsen bolai.(++)quwangdi sečen gegegen uqaγa-tu mergen törölki ǰayaγ-a-tai bögetel-e yeke erdem kiged γayiqamsiγ-tu güng-ber. tngri γaǰar-luγ-a tenggečeǰüküi.. ǰasaγ surγaγuli sayitur

页上一

büridüged. čoγ aldar yekede ileddügsen-iyer naran saran-u geigüldegsen γaǰar dakin (++) tügemel kesig-i küliyeged. on sar-a-yi daγaǰu ǰisiya alba ülü bariγčid-bar ügei bolai. eimü bögetel-e.(++)boγda-yin sedkil barimtalal ügei-yin tula. imaγta edür büri kinan emiyeǰü. erte boson. oroiǰoγoγlan. törö-yi kičiyebei. ulus-i örösiyebei. basa (++) tümen kereg-i ilγaγsan čilögen-dür-iyen ǰirγuγan ging-i simdan kičiyeǰü. olan sudur-i qabsurču üǰen ǰiruγ ǰuil-dur ese γarγaγsan narin niγuča-yi nekebei.. törö ba orčilang-i qarilčan ǰalγamǰilaγsan yoson tuq-a-yi inu ailadbai.. basa tngri γaǰar-un yoson ba olan dzy bičig kiged ǰaγun ger-ün bičig ba. yerü-yin kereg kiged odon-u oron-ba. qubilγad-un nom kiged. tala modon-u nabčin-u bičig. terigüten-i-ber üdesi manaγar kičiyen niγtalan gün sanaγan-i ese γarγaγsan anu ügei-yin tula suruγsan anu arγa bilig-i tuγuluγad.uqaγsan anu erte ba edügeki tegüskeǰüküi nigen nigen učir-a.(++)eǰen-ü sedkil kürülčeǰü (++)gegegen-iyaran ǰokiyaǰu bičin. bir kürüged sača mingγan üges-i γarγaqui anu tngri-yin mören

页下一

metü gegegen üǰesküleng-dü sayiqan bolai. üneker diyan. mo-yin üliger. ǰung ya-yinyoson-i tegüskeǰüküi. toda ilete mingγan boγdas-i quriyangγuilan yekede bütügebei. γurban erdem-i nigedken törö-i baiγulbai.teyin atal-a (+)erdeni bičig. qas üsüg. luu degdekü k'alandaka böǰiglekü i metü. fo ki-yin ǰiruqai-yin γayiqamsiγ-i ǰirumlaγsan-iyar qan ulus-une güskeǰü bičigsen üliger daruγdaǰuqui.ene basa kü čilöge γaruγsan učir-un kereg buyu.. tuqai (++) tuslaǰu yeke örösiyel-i tarqaγan. g'anǰur nom-i dakiǰu seyilgeged. ači tusa-yi badaraγulqu anu kingnabasu degedüs-e bolbasu. (+++) tai quwang tayikeü. (+++) quwang tayikeü-yin tümen nasun-u čaγlasi ugei ölǰei qutuγ-i egüride boltuγai. dooradus-tur bolbasu. delekei dakin-u tüsimel irgen-i tüg tümen od-tur kürtel-e bolquiqudtuγ-i oltuγai kemegsen buyu. yerü dörben urusqal. ǰirγuγan baramid-un gün činar-i dailaquy-a berke. (++)tngri-yin ǰarliγ-iyar ilerkey-e ese γarγabasu door-a-du tögerigsen metü arad. kerkiǰü čöm tuγulqu mör-i olomu. erte tang ulus-un tayisung-bar. neretü quwašang-dur

页上二

ǰarliγ baγulγaǰu. ǰirγuγan ǰaγun ilekü bodi nom-i orčiγuluγad. tuslaǰu orosil-i ǰokiyaǰuqui.. ming ulus-un tayisu-yin bey-e burqan-u eke-yin körög-dür maγtaγal üges-i ǰokiyaǰuqui.. yong lo-yin čaγ-tur. yeke g'anǰur nom-i kinaǰu nairaγuluγad seyilǰüküi.. ene čöm ulus-i delgeregülügsen übedegsi čaγ-tur.töbed-ün surγaγuli-yi iledken temdeglegsen bolai.. (++) quwangdi-yin örösiyel kičiyenggüi takimdaγu öglige anu masi silγaraγad. tang ulus.ming ulus-un γurban qaγan-bar. tümen qubi-yin nigen qubi-dur adalidqaǰu ülü bolumu.. (++)eǰen bičig ǰokiyaǰu baγulγabasu. oγtarγui bükün-e gilbelüged. qotal-a γaǰar dakin-a tusa bolomu.. γuyuqu anu.(++)quwangdi. burqan-u surγaγuli-yi sedkiǰü tuslan qaγan-u ǰokiyaγsan orosil bičig-i soyorqaǰu. nom-un ekin-dür talbiγuluγad mungqaγ γani arad-tur delgeregül-ün üǰegülüged tümen od-dur kürtel-e ulamǰilaγulqu aǰiyamu. eyimü bolbasu gegegen naran-bar (++)eǰen-ü bičig-dür imaγta geyiǰü. örösiyel-tü egülen-ber (++)boγda-yin kesig-lug-e qamtu egüride bolumu.. egün-ü tula ayiladqaqu bičig bičiǰü kündüde ayiladqaba.. (++)ǰarliγ-i γuyumu..

页下二

ǰasaγ-un elbeg čin wang tüsimel fučiowan. dotoγ-a-du yamun-u bičig-ün dedlegsen tüsimel böged. ded ǰerge-yin funglu idekü dörben ǰerge-yin tüsimel uladai sung žin fu yamun-u baraγun eteged-ün sy-yin tamγa bariγsan ilγaγči tüsimel böged. nigen ǰerge nemegsen tüsimel gioro-yin sumbai. üile-yin yabudal-un k'o yamun-u tamγa bariγsan ögülegči tüsimel böged. qoyar ǰerge nemegsen tüsimel yačina. ilγan üǰegči tüsimel böged qoyar ǰerge nemegsen tüsimel ilaqa ilγan üǰegči tüsimel böged. γurban ǰerge nemegsen tüsimel genggei. čerig-ün yabudal-un yamun-u ilγaγči tüsimel tüsimel tubasiki. engke amuγulang-un qorin qoyaduγar on. namur-un dumdadu sar-a-yin arban ǰirγuγan-a (+) ayiladqaba. mön kü sar-a-yin arban naiman-a (++) ǰarliγ törö-yin yabudal-un yamun qauli-yi todorqayilan ilγaǰu kinan kelelčeged ayiladq-a kemebe..

页上三

覆请序疏

orosil γuyun ayiladqaγsan-yi dakiǰu ayiladqaγsan bičig törö-yin yabudal-un yamun-u erkin tüsimel. tüsimel ǰaisan tan-u kündüde (+) ayiladqaqu anu (++) ǰarliγ-i daγan g'anǰur nom-i seyilkü-yin tula. (++) qaγan-u orosil bičig ǰokiyaqu-yi kičiyen γuyuγad. öni qolada ulamǰilaγulqu-yin učir. törö-yin yabudal-un yamun-u k'o yamun-ača sudurlan bičiǰü γarγaba. ǰasaγ-un elbeg čin wang fučiowan tan ene kereg-ün tula ayiladqaγsan anu. üǰebesü. enedkeg-ün γaǰar-a γayiqamsiγ ǰayaγaγdaǰu. qubilγan düri tulγur γarbai. naiman töb. tabun kölgen. waislai mongš-a γaǰar-ača egüskeged. qatangγadqaγsan ba küliyeǰü abuγsan anu. masi qola buyu. qan ulus-un ming di. altan önggetü qubilγan-i ǰegüdüleged. enedkeg ulus-tur elči ilegegsen-dür egünče silüg šaǰin-un surγaγuli-yin olan bičig. dumdadu ulus-tur ulamǰilaǰu. qoyar mingγan ǰil siqam bolba.. ene ǰabsar-a tang ulus. sung ulus-un manduγsan učir-a todorqay-a γarγaγsan saisiyan maγtaγsan anu kedüi olan bolbasu-bar. γaγča kü burqan-un surγaγuli-yi delgeregül-ün tarqaγasuγai kemegsen busu. čuqum egüber tümen ǰüil yaγuma-yi kümüǰilsügei kemegsen bolai..

页上一

(++) quwangdi sečen gegegen uqaγ-a-tu mergen törölki ǰayaγ-a-tai bögetel-e yeke erdem kiged γayiqamsiγ-tu güng-ber. tngri γaǰar-luγ-a tenggečeǰüküi. ǰasaγ surγaγuli sayitur büridüged. čoγ aldar yekede iledtügsen-iyer naran saran-u geigüldegsen γaǰar dakin (++) tügemel kesig-i küliyeged. on sar-a-yi daγaǰu ǰisiya alba ülü bariγčid-bar ügei bolai. eimü bögetel-e (++)boγda-yin sedkil barimtalal ügei-yin tula. imaγta edür büri kinan emiyeǰü. erte boson oroi ǰoγoγlan. törö-yi kičiyebei. ulus-yi örösiyebei. basa (++) tümen kereg-i ilγaγsan čilögen-dür-iyen ǰirγuγan ging-i simdan kičiyeǰü. olan sudur-i qabsurču üǰen ǰiruγ ǰuil-dur ese γarγaγsan narin niγuča-yi nekebei.. törö ba orčilang-i qarilčan ǰalγamǰilaγsan yoson tuq-a-yi inu ayiladbai. basa tngri γaǰar-un yoson ba olan dzy bičig kiged. ǰaγun ger-ün bičig ba. yerü-yin kereg kiged. odon-u oron ba. qubilaγad-un nom kiged. tala modon-u nabčin-un bičig terigüten-i-ber. üdesi manaγar kičiyen niγtalan gün sanaγan-i ese γarγaγsan anu ügei-yin tula. suruγsan anu arγa bilig-i tuγuluγad. uqaγsan anu erte ba edügeki tegüskeǰüküi nigen nigen učir-a

页下一

(++) eǰen-ü sedkil kürülčeǰü (++) gegegen-iyaran ǰokiyaǰu bičin. bir kürüged sača mingγan üges-i γarγaqui anu. tngri-yin mören metü gegegen üǰesküleng-dü sayiqan bolai.. üneker diyan. mo-yin üliger. fung. ya-yin yoson-i tegüskeǰükü.. toda ilete mingγan boγdas-i quriyangγuilan yekede bütügebei. γurban erdem-i nigedken töb-i bayiγulbai. teyin atal-a (+) erdeni bičig. qas üsüg. luu degdekü. k'alandaka böǰiglekü̈i metü. fo ki-yin ǰiruqai-yin γayiqamsiγ-i ǰirumlaγsan-iyar qan ulus-un egüskeǰü bičigsen üliger daruγdaǰuqui. ene basa küčilöge γaruγsan učir-un kereg buyu.. tuqai (++) tuslaǰu yeke örösiyel-i tarqaγan g'anǰur nom-i dakiǰu seyilgeged. ači tusa-yi badaraγulqu anu kingnabasu degedün-e bolbasu. (+++) tai quwang tayikeü (+++) quwang tayikeü-yin tümen nasun-u čaγlasi ügei ölǰei qutuγ-i egüride boltuγai. dooradus-dur bolbasu. delekei dakin-u tüsimel irgen-i tüg tümen od-tur kürtel-e bolqui qutuγ-i oltuγai kemegsen buyu. yerü dörben urusqal. ǰirγuγan baramid-un gün činar-i dailaquy-a berke. (++) tngri-yin ǰarliγ-iyar ilerkey-e ese γarγabasu door-a-du tögerigsen metü arad. kerkiǰü čöm tuγulqu mör-i olomu. erte tang ulus-un tayisung-bar. neretü quwasang-dur

页上二

ǰarliγ baγulγaǰu. ǰirγuγan ǰaγun ilekü bodi nom-i orčiγuluγad. tuslaǰu orosil-i ǰokiyaǰuqui. ming ulus-un tayisu-yin bey-e burqan-u eke-yin körög-dür maγtaγal üges-i ǰokiyaǰuqui. yong lo-yin čaγ-tur. yeke g'anǰur nom-i kinaǰu nayiraγuluγad seyilǰükü̈i.ene čöm ulus-i delgeregülügsen übedegsi čaγ-tur. töbed-ün surγaγuli-yi iledken temdeglegsen bolai. (++) quwangdi-yin örösiyel kičiyenggüi takimdaγu öglige anu masi silγaraγad. tang ulus.ming ulus-un γurban qaγan-bar. tumen qubi-yin nigen qubi-dur adalidqaǰu ülü bolumu..(++)eǰen bičig ǰokiyaǰu baγulγabasu. oγtarγui bükün-e gilbelüged. qotal-a γaǰar dakin-a tusa bolumu.. γuyuqu anu(++)quwangdi burqan-u surγaγuli-yi sedkiǰü (++)tuslan qaγan-u ǰokiyaγsan orosil bičig-i soyorqaǰu. nom-un ekin-dür talbiγuluγad mungqaγ γani arad-tur delgeregül-ün üǰegülüged tümen od-tur kürtel-e ulamǰilaγulqu aǰiyamu. eyimü bolbasu gegegen naran-ber (++)eǰen-ü bičig-dür imaγta geyiǰü. örösiyel-tü egülen-ber (++)boγda-yin kesig-lug-e qamtu egüride bolumu.. egün-ü tula ayiladqaqu bičig bičiǰü kündüde ayiladqaba.(++)ǰarliγ-i γuyumu kemen engke amuγulang-un qorin

页下二

qoyaduγar on. namur-un dumdadu sar-a-yin arban ǰirγuγan-a ayiladqaba. mön kü sar-a-yin arban naiman-a (++)ǰarliγ. törö-yin yabudal-un yamun qauli-yi todurqailan ilγaǰu kinan kelelčeged ayiladq-a kemebe.egün-i kündüde daγaǰu. mön kü sar-a-yin arban yisün-e yabudal-un yamun-dur kürčü iregsen-i. tüsimel man-u kelelčegsen anu. ǰasaγun elbeg čin wang fuciowan tan-u ayiladqaγsan bičig-dür. silüg surγal. dumdadu ulus-tur ulamǰilaǰu qoyar mingγan ǰil siqam bolba. tang ulus. sung ulus-un manduγsan učir-a todorqay-a γarγaγsan saisiyan maγtaγsan anu. γaγča kü burqan-u surγaγuli-yi delgeregül-ün tarqaγasuγai kemegsen busu. čoqom egüber tümen ǰüil yaγum-a-yi kümüǰilsügei kemegsen bolai.(++)quwangdi sečen gegegen uqaγ-a-tu mergen törölki ǰayaγ-a-tai bögetel-e. yeke erdem kiged.γayiqamsiγ-tu güng-ber. tngri γaǰar-luγ-a tenggečeǰüküi. (++)tümen kereg-i ilγaγsan čilögen-dür-iyen. ǰirγuγan ging-i simdan kičiyeǰü. olan sudur-i qabsurču üǰen. olan dzy. ǰaγun ger. qubilγad-un nom kiged. tala modon-u nabčin-u bičig terigüten-i-ber üdesi manaγar kičiyen niγtalan gün sanaγan-i ese γarγaγsan-bar ügei. tuqai (++)tuslaǰu yeke örösiyel-i tarqaγan. g'anǰur nom-i

页上三

dakiǰu seyilgeged. ači tusa-yi badaraγuluγči anu degedüs-e bolbasu. (+++)tai quwang tayikeü. (+++)quwang taikeü-yin tümen nasun-u čaγlasi ügei ölǰei qutuγ-i egüride boltuγai.. dooradus-tur bolbasu delekei dakin-u tüsimel irgen-i tügtümen od-tur kürtel-e bolqui qutuγ-i oltuγai kemegsen buyu.. erten-ün tang ulus-un tayisung-bar ner-e-tü quwašang-dur ǰarliγ baγulγaǰu ǰirγuγan ǰaγun ilekü bodi nom-i orčiγuluγad tuslaǰu orosil ǰokiyaǰuqui.. ming ulus-un tayisu-yin bey-e burqan-u eke-yin körög-dür mataγal üges-i ǰokiyaǰuqui. yong lo-yin čaγ-tur. yeke g'anǰur nom-i kinaǰu nayiraγuluγad seyilǰüküi.. ene čöm ulus-i delgeregülügsen übedegsi čaγ-tur. töbed-ün surγaγuli-yi iledken temdeglegsen bolai.(++) quwangdi-yin örösiyel kičiyenggüi takimdaγu öglige anu masi silγaraγad. tang ulus.ming ulus-un γurban qaγan-bar tümen qubi-yin nigen qubi-dur adalidqaǰu ülü bolumu.γuγuqu anu (++) quwangdi burqan-u surγaγuli-yi sedkiǰü (++) tuslan qaγan-u ǰokiyaγsan orosil bičig-i soyorqaǰu nom-un ekin-dür talbiγuluγad. munγqaγ γaniarad-tur delgeregülün üǰegülüged tümen od-tur kürtel-e ulamǰilaγulqu aǰiyamu kemeǰüküi..

页下三

tüsimel bide üǰebesü. silüg ba surγaγuli-yin olan bičig. g'anǰur nom-dur ese büriddügsen anu ügei.. kedüi surγaγuli-dur. ilerkei.niγuča. ilγaγdaγsan. yoson-dur törölki ba düri anu öber-e yabudal bolbasu-bar tegün-ü sanaγan-i kinabasu tümen yaγum-a-dur tusalaǰu.eldeb amitan-i bolbasuraγul-un uduridqui-dur bui.. üy-e üy-e-yin di wang-ud ürgülǰi badaraγul-un tarqaγaǰu. nigen nigen inu orčiγuluγsan ba. nigen nigen inu seyilgegülügsen-dür. teyin surγaγuli ese tasuraǰuqui.. nögögede surγal yoson-u aldarsiγul-un übedegsi qauli-yi badaraγulqui-dur. saγar ügei bey-e-ber bičig ǰokiyan bičiged. debter-ün ekin-dür talbiqu bolbasu. edüge sayi qubilγan.kömün kündüde daγaǰu. qola ba oyira dakin inu γayiqalčan üǰemü.. ilγabasu tang ulus-un tayisung-un ǰen guwan-u qorin qoyaduγar on quwašang yuwan juwang tan ǰirγuγan ǰaγun tabin doloγan bodi töbed nom-i orčiγulǰu tegüskegsen-ü qoyin-a. qaγan-un bey-e. γurban sang kiged ülemǰi medeküi-yin orosil bičig bičiged čilaγun-dur čabčiγsan-u tula.edüge boltal-a ulamlaǰuqui.. ming ulus-un tayisu-yin bey-e-ber ǰokiyaǰu bičigsen bičig-ün dotor-a burqan-u eke-yi

页上四

maγtaγsan bičig. basa bilig baramid-un orosil. badm-a saduwa. čečeg-ün ǰirüken yirtinčü-yin ǰerge-yi maγtaǰu bičigsen bičig bui.. ming ulus-un čengsü. yeke g'anǰur nom-i kinan nayiraγuluγad seyilǰüküi.. g'anǰur nom-i maγtaγsan bičig. basa ǰeng sung da giyoo miyao ging.dörben bodi-dur. olangki. namasanggiti ǰerge-yin orosil bičig-i čöm nom-un ekin-dür bičiǰü g'anǰur nom-dur oroγulǰuqui.. basa ilγabasu. tang ulus-un kiyan sung . sedkil-dür orosiγul-un bisilγaqui nom-un orosil bičig bičiǰüküi.. sung ulus-un tayisung-un bey-e sayitur medegči kemekü bičig tabun debter ǰokiyan bičiǰüküi.. ǰen sung ši tiyan ioi ǰi kemekü bičig nigen bodi bičiǰüküi.. egün-i čöm burqan-u süm-e-dür qadaγalaǰu čaγlasi ügei ulamǰilaǰu.. kündüde sedkibesü. (++)quwangdi-yin güng. tngri γaǰar-luγ-a tenggečeǰüküi. yoson anu tngri kümün-dür tuγulγaγad. gün-i niγtalan narin-i kinan. maγad niγuča-yin ǰüil-i ese todorqayilaγsan ügei. irege edüi-yi anu meden. nögčigsen-i anu toγtaγan. qauli-yin narin yabudal-i ese kinaγsan anu-bar ügei..(++)boγda-yin surγal gün narin.(++)tngri-yin bičig ǰokistu böged üǰesküleng-dü maγad-iyar uridu üy-e-yin di wang-ud tümen-dür nigeken-ber adalidqaǰu bolqu busu.. tuqai

页下四

tngri. γaǰar-i örgeǰegülküi küsekü sedkil-dür neyilegülüged. boγda kümün-ü takimdaγu-dur anu sedkil-i badaraγul-un. degedüs-e bolbasu.(+++) qoyar güng. ölǰei qutuγ orosituγai. dooradus-tur bolbasu tümen irgen. kesig-i kuliyetügei kemen g'anǰur nom seyilǰü. delekei deger-e ulamǰilaγulqu-yin tula. (++) tuslaǰu ǰarliγ baγulγaǰuqui.. γaγča silüg-ün surγal-i uqakuy-a berke.. töbed-ün nom-i tarqaγaqui anu tulγur-un tula saγar ügei (++) tngri-yin ǰarliγ-iyar saisiyan maγtaqu bolbasu. edüge naran saran metü gegegen toda bolumu. eyimü-yin tula wang tan-u γuyun ayiladqaγsan-u yosoγar (++) eǰen-ü bey-e. orosil bičig bičiǰü. nom-un ekin-dür talbiγad qas bodi. erdini bičig-dür (++) γayiqamsiγ gerel-i geyigülün. delekei dakin-dur üǰügülün tarqaγaǰu. čaγlasi ügei egüride ulamǰilaγulqu aǰiyamu. eyimü bolbasu maγad (++)engke čaγ-un erkin kereg.(++)boγda-yin üye-yin yeke qauli bolumu.. tüsimel man-u ǰoriγ-iyar bolγaqu busu-yin tula kündüde ayiladqaba..(++)ǰarliγ-i γuyumu. törö-yin yabudal-un yamun-u erkin tüsimel tüsimel ǰaisan. erkin tüsimel. tusimel ša čeng.

ǰegün eteged-ün ded tüsimel. tüsimel esingge.

页上五

yekebčilen ögüleldükü tüsimel ǰegün eteged-ün ded tüsimel. bičig-ün yamun-u bičig-ün ded tüsimel qabsuruγsan. tüsimel yang ǰeng ǰung. baraγun eteged-ün ded tüsimel. qoyar ǰerge nemgsen tüsimel saqai. yekebčilen ögüleldükü tusimel. baraγun eteged-ün ded tüsimel bičig-ün yamun-u bičig-ün ded tüsimel qabsuruγsan tüsimel čen ting ging. dzy ǰi čing li sy-yin ilγaγči tüsimel tüsimel qo bing. tusalaγči tüsimel qoyar ǰerge nemegsen.tüsimel čangdzai. tusalaγči tüsimel. tüsimel sangge. tusalaγči tüsimel nigen ǰerge nemegsen.tüsimel sayinda tusalaγči tüsimel. tüsimel g'o ši lung. tusalaγči tüsimel. tüsimel siyao yong soo. temdeglegči tüsimel. tüsimel wang ǰing čen. temdeglegči tüsimel nigen ǰerge nemegsen. tüsimel fiyangγu. temdeglegči tüsimel. tüsimel sioi žin fung. engke amuγulang-un qorin qoyaduγar on. namur-un segül sar-a-yin sin-e-yin nigen-e ayiladqaba. mön kü sar-a-yin sin-e-yin dörben-e (++) ǰarliγ kelelčegsen yosoγar bolγ-a kemebe..

页下五

职名

ǰarliγ-iyar nököǰü seil kemegsen g'anǰur nom-i küliyen üǰeǰü üiledkegülügsen. ǰasaγ-un elbeg čin wang tüsimel fučiowan. üǰeǰü üiledkegsen tüsimel. tangγud bičig surγaγči ded tüsimel tüsimel arbidqu. dotoγ-a-du yamun-u dedlegsen bičig-ün tüsimel tüsimel šulu. törö-yin kü yamun-u tamγ-a bariγsan ögülegči tüsimel tüsimel asitan. ǰasaγ-un kü yamun-u tamγ-a bbariγsan ögülegči tüsimel tüsimel kešeö. bügüde-yi ilγaγči yamun-u ilγan üǰegči tüsimel tüsimel sederi. ilγan üǰegči tüsimel tüsimel mase. ilγan üǰegči tüsimel tüsimel saimbu. ǰasaγ-un yabudal-un yamun-u ilγaγsi tüsimel tüsimel unča. üile-yin yabudal-un yamun-u ilγaγči tüsimel tüsimel liosiyang. said-un yabudal-un yamun-u tusalaγči tüsimel tüsimel angγai. čerig-ün yabudal-un yamun-u tusalaγči tüsimel tüsimel ma čoo zan. guwang šan küü-yin tusalaγči tüsimel tüsimel sutai. tusalaγči tüsimel tüsimel dečengge. temdeglegči tüsimel tüsimel yongfu. temdeglegči t¨simel tüsimel tunggitu.

页上一

said-un yabudal-un yamun-u bičigči tüsimel beböǒǰü. törö-yin yabudal-un yamun-u bičigči tüsimel fulu. čerig-ün yabudal-un yamun-u bičigči tüsimel girsai. ǰasaγ-un yabudal-un yamun-u bičigči tüsimel elge. bičigči tüsimel sultu. bičigči tüsimel tangγai. üile-yin yabudal-un yamun-u bičigči tüsimel čabuukü. bügüde-yi ilγaγči yamun-u bičigči tüsimel nengge. bičigči tüsimel walda. bičigči tüsimel lioǰu. bičigči tüsimel liosy. bičigči tüsimel lio i yuwan. sang-un kü yamun-u bičigči tüsimel kingtü. törö-yin kü yamun-u bičigči tüsimel waqundai. ǰasaγ-un kü yamun-u bičigči tüsimel tengge. nairaγul-un ǰasaγsan lam-a nar. ǰanggiy-a qutuγtu. terigün lam-a wangšuγ ǰimba gelung. terigün lam-a lobzang balǰur gelung. demči lobzang namǰal gelung. donrub rabdan ramǰamba. čholčim zangbo ramǰamba. damba serǰi gelung. engke amuγulang-un γučin yisüdüger-ün ǰun-u terigün sar-a-yin sain edüi seilǰü egüskebe.

页下一

bka-'a 'agyur-un üsüg-ud-i üǰeǰü nairaγul-un ǰasaγsan. ging hotan-u blam-a bandi nar bügüde-yi ǰakiruγči ǰasaγ-un terigün blam-a mergen čoirǰe. ging hotan-u blam-a bandi nar bügüde-yi ǰakiruγči ǰasaγ-un terigün blam-a böged töbed bičig-yi erkilen surγaqu bsod nams čoirǰe. töbed bičig-ün dedlen surγaqu tüsimel böged. dörbedüger ǰerge-yin funglu idekü tüsimel siteö. bka-'a 'agyur-un üsüg-ud-i nairaγuluγsan. dgindun darrgyas dgeslong. dbal rgyas dgeslong. bsod nams rinčen dgeslong. blo bzang klurub dgeslong. nga dvang sengge dgeslong. blo bzang kun dga-'a dgeslong. blo bzang dbal 'abyor dgeslong. bzangbo čhulbrims dgeslong. bstan ba bkrašis dgeslong. blo bzang šisrab dgeslong. bsam gtan rinčen dgeslong. sbya ba dbal 'abyor dgeslong. blo bzang čhos 'abel dgeslong. rinče bsod nams dgeslong.

页上一

čhulbrims dbal 'abar dgeslong. čhulbrims yondan dgeslong. čhulbrims bkrašis dgeslong. dgeleg rinčen dgeslong. bkrašis rinčen dgeslong. nga dvang sbyin ba dgeslong. bstan ba rabtan dgeslong. nga dvang sbyin pa dgeslong. bzangbu čhulbrims dgeslong. blo bzang bzod ba dgeslong. yondan rinčen dgeslong. phu čhogs rinčen dgeslong. blo bzang bstan dar dgeslong. sbyin ba bsod nams dgeslong. yešis dbal 'abyor dgeslong. čhois 'phal bzangbo dgeslong. bkrašis darrgyas dgeslong. bsod nams rgyal mčhan dgeslong. čhois 'abal bzangbo dgeslong. blo bzang dargyas dgeslong. bzangbo rgyalmčhan dgeslong. blo bzang nyim-a dgeslong. bsod nams brčhon 'arois dgeslong. bkrašis bzangbo dgeslong. brčhon 'arois rinčen dgeslong. blo bzang 'aphrin lais dgeslong. töbed bičig suruγči dorǰi.

页下一

orosil garčaγ-i kinaǰu nairaγuluγsan tüsimel. dotoγ-a-du yamun-u dedlegsen tüsimel γurban ǰerge nemegsen. tüsimel dandai. dotoγ-a-du yamun-u dedlegsen tüsimel γurbaduγar ǰerge-yin funglu idekü. qoyar ǰerge nemegsen. tüsimel bairi. dotoγ-a-du yamun-u dedlegsen tüsimel γurbaduγar ǰerge-yin funglu idekü ǰirγuγan ǰerge nemegsen. tüsimel unggin. tangγud bičig-ün orosil garčaγ-i orčiγuluγsan tüsimel. tangγud bičig-i dedlen surγaqu tüsimel. dörbedüger ǰerge-yin funglu idekü. tüsimel siteö. kitad bičig-ün garčaγ-i orčiγuluγsan tüsimel. dotoγ-a-du yamun-u ǰuwan wen ǰungšu tüsimel usibu. dotoγ-a-du yamun-u ǰuwan wen ǰungšu tüsimel dengdei. mongγol bičig-ün orosil garčaγ-i orčiγuluγsan tüsimel. dotoγ-a-du yamun-u banši ǰungšu qoyar ǰerge nemeǰü. ǰirγuduγar ǰerge-yin funglu idekü tüsimel lamǰang. dotoγ-a-du yamun-u banši ǰungšu nigen ǰerge nemeǰü. ǰirγuduγar ǰerge-yin funglu idekü tüsimel kegeo.

页上一

manǰu bičig-i kinaǰu bičigsen tüsimel. dotoγ-a-du yamun-u banši ǰungšu dörben ǰerge nemeǰü tabuduγar ǰerge-yin funglu idekü. tüsimel ibari. dotoγ-a-du yamun-u ǰuwan wen ǰungšu. tüsimel dzangšeö. dotoγ-a-du yamun-u ǰuwan wen ǰungšu. tüsimel čambu. mongγol bičig-i kinaǰu bičigsen tüsimel. dotoγ-a-du yamun-u banši ǰungšu tüsimel šookeo. kitad bičig-i kinaǰu bičigsen tüsimel. dotoγ-a-du yamun-u banši ǰungšu nigen ǰerge nemegsen. tüsimel tsoo ǰan gi. dotoγ-a-du yamun-u banši ǰungšu. tüsimel wang ki o. tangγud bičig-i kinaǰu bičigsen blam-a. lobdzang lorob gelung. lobdzang bailǰi gelung. sonom rinčin gelung.

页下一

γanǰur nom-i üǰeǰü üiledkegülügsen. ǰasaγ-un elbeg čin wang tüsimel fučiowan. üǰeǰü üiledkegsen tüsimel. dotoγ-a-du yamun-u dedlegsen tüsimel böged ded ǰerge-yin funglu idekü dörben ǰerge nemegsen tüsimel ulatai. dzung žin fu yamun-u baraγun eteged-ün sy-yin tamγ-a bariγsan ilγaγči tüsimel böged nigen ǰerge nemegsen tüsimel gioroi šombai. ilγaγči tüsimel böged [ni]gen ǰerge nemegsen tüsimel gioroi lilima. üile-yin yabudal-un kü yamun-u tamγ-a bariγsan ögülegči tüsimel böged qoyar ǰerge nemegsen tüsimel yačina. bügüde-yi ilγaγči yamun-u ilγan üǰegči tüsimel böged qoyar ǰerge nemegsen tüsimel ilaγa. ilγan üǰegči tüsimel böged γurban ǰerge nemegsen tüsimel genggei. čerig-ün yabudal-un yamun-u ilγaγči tüsimel tüsimel tobasiki. dotoγ-a-du yamun-u ǰuwan wen ǰungšu böged nigen ǰerge nemegsen tüsimel quwase. dzung žin fu yamun-u ǰirγuduγar ǰerge-yin bičigči böged nigen ǰerge nemegsen tüsimel küwenǰe. doloduγar ǰerge-yin bičigči böged

页上一

qoyar ǰerge nemegsen tüsimel čangboo. bügüde-yi ilγaγči yamun-u doloduγar ǰerge-yin bičigči böged qoyar ǰerge nemegsen tüsimel wamida. bičigči tüsimel nayantai. čerig-ün yabudal-un yamun-u doloduγar ǰerge-yin bičigči böged qoyar ǰerge nemegsen tüsimel ulan.

页下一

四、满文录文转写

御制番藏经序

han i araha fan dzang ging ni sioi. bi donjici. fu hi. jijun be badarambure jakade. ging suduri i sekiyen gorokici neibuhebi. ioi. hūng fan be fisembure jakade. šu yangse i deribun ambarame iletulehebi. umesi julgei gulu kooli be feteme. dulimbai jalan de genggiyen forgon be neihe be dahame. amba jurgan somishūn gisun. šun usiha de jergilefi sasa eldeke. ferguwecuke fiyelen oyonggo bithe. yo bilten de teherefi uhei wesihun oho. jai gurun be karmara irgen be dalire de oci. jalbarire hafan. hūturi baire bithe bi. hūwaliyasun edun sain aga de oci. in yang ni erin be tuwara urse bi. eiterecibe gemu bisire be wesihulere be tuhen obume ofi. tuttu meni meni somishūn be getukelere leolen be arahabi. aikabade juwan ergi. duin jurgan i duka. ilan genggiyen. ninggun hafu i doro oci. han gurun i ming di aisin i niyalma be tolgire jakade. suru morin de acifi gajihabi. tang gurun i taidzung enduringge tacihiyan i sioi arara jakade. niowanggiyan šu

页上一

ilga jolhome tucikebi. gu i dobton dergi bade isinjifi. suwayan fiyahan. niowanggiyan gu i tan de wesihulebuhe. aisin i debtelin be julergi bade ubaliyambufi. arsalan. muduri i hūi be ilibuha. ju lan tacihiyan be ulafi. da sekiyen i dehi juwe fiyelen be yendebuhe. yuwan dzang gajime jifi. toktoho acabun i ninggun tanggū funcere yohi obume badarambuha. gubci jalan be ulhibume. dergi ergi bade enteheme bibuhe. terei ulame badarambuha amba hešen be kimcici. gūnin. dubei jalan be amasi maribure de bi. kemuni tondo hiyoošun ofi. gisun tome gemu balai be geterembume unenggi be bibuhebi. inu gosin jilan ofi. gūnin tome yooni oshon be eteme wara be nakabuhabi. mujilen i dengjan dobori genggiyan oci. farhūn jugūn de šuwe eldembi. gūnin i fulhuren erde deribuci. tuwa i kūwaran ci šahūrun banjinambi. udu jugūn adali akū bicibe. tuhen emu. yargiyan i gargan encu seme sekiyen uhe. geli enduri ging be urebume hūlame. dergi de goro goidara doro be jalbariha. tacihiyan jorin be selgiyeme

页下一

tucibume. fejergi de tusa arame doobure cuwan be isibuha. yargiyan i hargašame ginggulere be dahame. tusa niyececun akū ainaha. ede kiyan i hešen be jafafi. udu acabun be fucihi i buren i jilgan de baire ba akū bicibe abkai fejergi jing taifin de teisulehe be dahame. geli ferguwecun be hiyan i arbun de saci ombikai. bi. julge te be kimcime feteme. mo. diyan be sibkime mohobume. ilan hūwang. sunja di i bithe be erindari ilgame tuwambime. gebungge alin de somime asaraha suduri be geli fuhašambi. farhūn suwaliyame erde ilifi. giyangnara bade neilere jombore tusa be baimbi. dobori dulin de dengjan dabufi. bithei boode fetereme kimcire be akūmbumbi. fafun kooli de holbobuhangge oci. dangse suduri de tutahangge be sibkime baimbi. bithei doro de wesihulerengge oci. banin giyan i tacin be sirame getukelembi. te sejen bithe. emu ome šošobuha be dahame. ainci durun kemun de yooni dahahabi. jai gūnin i moo. mujilen i ilga be. bei do abdaha i ging de tuwara unde

页上二

bicibe. bulehen i bujan. buhū i kūwaran i bo že i tai de dartai enggelehe be dahame. gu i buleku i muheliyen elden be tuwame. aisin futa i ferguwecuke jurgan be kimcimbi. gingguleme gūnici. (+) tai hūwang taiheo. se jalafun enteheme nonggibufi. še wei gurun de mujilen be bolhomiha. (+) hūwang taiheo. amba hūturi ambarame badarafi. ki wan i bade dorolome karulaha. neneme weilere jurgan i hafasai kemun de acabume weilehengge. gemu gui moo taibu. mei moo i mulu bime. te šanggaha ging de bisirengge. yooni ferguwecuke leolen somishūn gisun. geren baitangga de fejergi urse be šuilabuhakū ofi. irgen i ulin be dambuhakū. weilere arara de yooni gung ni dorgici tucibure jakade. kuingge be acinggiyaha ba akū. unenggi tacihiyan i ferguwecuke doro be algimbuci acara be gūnime. ging hūlara wesihun mudan ambula ojoro unde seme. tuttu julgeci ebsi tacihiyan ulaha bithe be kimcifi. geli minggan fucihi i ishunde siranduha fiyelen be isabufi.

页下二

fan dzang ging ni fe bithe be folobuha. nioboro suje be acabume weilefi. jakūn hacin i ukcarangge colhorome tucike. haksan gecuheri wadan be neime. nadan hacin i ilga lakcame wesihun oho. yargiyan i ferguwecuke elden be dorgi gung de isibufi. umesi saikan gubci bade selgiyebume. suhe gisun de nonggime fisembufi. amba dzang ging be badarambume wesihuleme (+) juwe gung ni ferguwecuke hūturi be jalbarime. tumen hala de amba kesi isinakini sembi. tuttu bithei uju de arafi. saišame maktara be tucibuhe. elhe taifin i orin ilaci aniya jakūn biyai orin juwe de.

页上三

请序疏

(+) sioi baime wesimbuhe bithe. hošoi elgiyen cin wang. amban fuciowan sei gingguleme (+) wesimburengge. (++) hese be dahame. g'anjur ging be foloro be dahame. (++) han i sioi bithe arara be gingguleme baifi. goro goidame tutabure jalin. tuwaci. giya wei ba ci ferguwecun salgabufi. arbun fa tuktan tucinjihe. jakūn tob. sunja tangkan. pi siyei. mo giyei ba ci deribufi. afabuha alime gaihangge umesi goro. han gurun i ming di. aisin i enduri be tolgifi. tiyan ju gurun de elcin takūrara jakade. ereci ši tacihiyan i geren bithe dulimbai gurun de ulafi. juwe minggan aniya hamika. ere sidende tang gurun. sung gurun i mukdeke fon i getukeleme tucibuhe. saišame maktahangge udu ambula bicibe. fucihi tacihiyan be teile badarmbume selgiyeki sehengge waka. cohome ede tumen jaka be hūwašabuki sehengge. (++) hūwangdi sure genggiyen ulhisu mergen. banitai hesebuhe bime. amba erdemu ferguwecuke gung. elbehe aliha de teherehebi. dasan wen umesi akūnara. horon algin ambula iletulere jakade. šun biyai eldekele baingge.

页上一

(++) desereke kesi be alifi. aniya biya be dahafi alban i jaka benjirakūngge akū. uttu bime. (++) enduringge mujilen kumdu ofi. ele inenggidari gingguleme ulgošome erde ilime goidafi jeme dasan ba kicehe. irgen be gosiha. geli (++) tumen baita be icihiyaha šolo de. ninggun ging be sithūfi kimcime. geren suduri be kamcifi tuwame. nirugan hacin de tucibuhekū arhūn somishūn be neihe. dasan forgon i ishunde siraha giyan. ton be bulekušehe. jai abkai šu. na i gina. geren dzi. tanggū boo. geturi baita. usiha oron. eduri ging. bei abdaha i bithe be seme yamji cimari kiceme sibkime. šumin gūnin be tucibukekūngge akū ofi. tacin. in yang be hafufi. sahangge. julge te be akūmbuhabi. ememu fonde. (++) ejen gūnin isinjifi. (++) genggiyen i banjibume arame. fi nikebume minggan gisun be tuciburengge. abkai birai adali eldengge saikan. yargiyan i diyan. mo i durun. fung. ya i jurgan be yongkiyahabi. gehun iletu minggan enduingge be šošofi. ambajame mutebuhe. ilan erdemu be uherilefi. ten ilibuha. tere dade

页下一

(+)boobai bithe. gu i hergen. muduri deyere. funghūwang maksire gese. fu hi i jijun i ferguwecuke be songkololofi. han gurun i deribume araha durun gidabuhabi.. ere geli šolo tucike ucuri i baita.. jakan (++)cohome amba gosin be selgiyeme. g'anjur ging be dasame folobufi. aisi tusa be badaramburengge ainci dergi de oci. (+++)tai hūwang taiheo. (+++)hūwang taiheo i tumen sei mohon akū hūturi be enteheme okini. fejergi de oci. duin mederi i hafan irgen be tumen tumen aniya de isitala ojoro fengšen be bahakini sehengge.. damu duin eyen. ninggun kicen i somishūn giyan be sure de mangga.. (++)abkai gisun i getukeleme tuciburakū oci. fejergi fambuha adali urse adarame gemu hafure jugūn be bahambi.. julge tang gurun i taidzung. gebungge hūwašan de hese wasimbufi. ninggun tanggū yohi funcere ging ni bithe be ubaliyambufi. cohome sioi arahabi.. ming gurun i taidzu i beye. fucihi i eme i nirugan de maktara gisun arahabi.. yung lo i fonde. da dzang jen ging ni bithe be kimcime acabufi folohobi.. ere gemu gurun be neihe wesihun

页上二

forgon de. fan i tacihiyan be iletuleme temgetulehengge.. (++)hūwangdi i gosin ginggun hiyoošun fulehun umesi lakcafi. tang gurun. ming gurun i ilan han. tumen ubu de emu ubu hono duibuleci ojorongge waka.. (++)ejen i bithe be arafi wasimbure ohode. geren abka de jerkišeme. gubci bade tusa ombi.. bairengge. (++)hūwangdi. fucihi jorin be gūnime. (++) cohome han i araha sioi bithe be bufi. ging ni uju de sindabufi. mentuhun ulhirakū urse de neileme tuwabume. tumen aniya de tutabureo.. uttu ohode. genggiyen šun. (++)ejen i bithe de ele eldefi. gosingga tugi. (++)enduringge kesi i sasa enteheme ombi.. erei jalin wesimbure bithe arafi ginggulеme (+)wesimbuhe. (++)hese be baimbi.. hošoi elgiyen cin wang. amban fuciowan.. dorgi yamun i adaha bithei da bime. jai jergi funglu jetere. duin jergi nonggiha. amban uladai.. dzung žin fu yamun i ici ergi sy i doron jafaha icihiyara hafan bime. emu jergi nonggiha. amban gioroi šombai

页下二

weilere k'o yamun i doron jafaha gisurere hafan bime juwe jergi nonggiha. amban yacina.. baicame tuwara hafan bime. juwe jergi nonggiha. amban ilaka.. baicame tuwara hafan bime. ilan jergi nonggiha. amban genggei.. coohai jurgan i icihiyara hafan. amban tubasihi.. elhe taifin i orin juweci aniya. jakūn biyai juwan ninggun de (+)wesimbuhe.. ineku biyai juwan jakūn de. (++)hese. dorolon i jurgan. kooli be getukeleme baicafi kimcime gisurefi wesimbu sehe..

页上三

覆请序疏

sioi baime wesimbuhe be dahūme wesimbuhe bithe.. dorolon i jurgan i aliha amban. amban jaisan sei ginggulеme (+)wesimburengge.. (++)hese be dahame. g'anjur ging be foloro be dahame. (++)han i sioi bithe arara be ginggulеme baifi. goro goidame tutabure jalin.. dorolon i jurgan i k'o yamun ci doolame arafi tucibuhe.. hošoi elgiyen cin wang fuciowan sei ere baitai jalin wesimbuhengge. tuwaci. giya wei ba ci ferguwecun salgabufi. arbun fa tuktan tucinjihe. jakūn tob. sunja tangkan. pi siyei. mo giyei ba ci deribufi. afabuha alime gaihangge umesi goro.. han gurun i ming di. aisin i enduri be tolgifi. tiyan ju gurun de elcin takūrara jakade. ereci ši tacihiyan i geren bithe. dulimbai gurun de ulafi. juwe minggan aniya hamika.. ere sidende tang gurun. song gurun i mukdeke fon i getukeleme tucibuhe. saišame maktahangge udu ambula bicibe. fucihi tacihiyan be teile badarambume selgiyeki sehengge waka. cohome ede tumen jaka be hūwašabuki

页上一

sehengge.. (++)hūwangdi sure genggiyen ulhisu mergen. banitai hesebuhe bime. amba erdemu. ferguwecuke gung. elbehe aliha de teherehebi.. dasan wen umesi akūnara. horon algin ambula iletulere jakade. šun biyhai eldekele baingge. (++)desereke kesi be alifi. aniya biya be dahafi alban i jaka benjirakūngge akū.. uttu bime. (++)enduringge mujilen kumdu ofi. ele inenggidari gingguleme olhošome erde ilime goidafi jeme. dasan be kicehe. irgen be gosiha.. geli (++)tumen baita be icihiyaha šolo de. ninggun ging be sithūfi kimcime. geren suduri be kamcifi tuwame. nirugan hacin de tucibuhekū narhūn somishūn be neihe.. dasan forgon i ishunde siraha giyan ton be bulekušehe.. jai abkai šu. na i giyan. geren dzy. tanggū boo. heturi baita. usiha oron. enduri ging. bei abdaha i bithe be seme. yamji cimari kiceme sibkime. šumin gūnin be tucibuhekūngge akū ofi. tacin. in yang be hafufi. sahangge. julge te be akūmbuhabi.. ememu fonde

页下一

(++)ejen gūnin isinjifi. (+)genggiyen i banjibume arame. fi nikebume minggan gisun be tuciburengge. abkai birai adali eldengge saikan.. yargiyan i diyan. mo i durun. fung ya i jurgan be yongkiyahabi.. gehun iletu minggan enduringge be šošofi ambarame mutebuhe.. ilan erdemu be uherilefi. ten ilibuha. tere dade (+)boobai bithe. gu i hergen. muduri deyere funghūwang maksire gese.. fu hi i jijun i ferguwecuke be songkolofi. han gurun i deribume araha durun gidabuhabi.. ere geli šolo tucike ucuri i baita.. jakan (++)cohome amba gosin be selgiyeme. g'anjur ging be dasame folobufi aisi tusa be badaramburengge. ainci dergi de oci (+++)tai hūwang taiheo. (+++)hūwang taiheo i tumen sei mohon akū. hūturi be enteheme okini.. fejergi de oci. duin mederi i hafan irgen be tumen tumen aniya de isitala ojoro fengšen be bahakini sehengge.. damu duin eyen. ninggun kicen i somishūn giyan be sure de mangga.

页上二

(++)abkai gisun i getukeleme tuciburakū oci fejergi fambuha adali urse adarame gemu hafure jugūn be bahambi.. julge tang gurun i taidzung. gebungge hūwašan de hese wasimbufi. ninggun tanggū yohi funcere ging ni bithe be ubaliyambufi cohome sioi arahabi.. ming gurun i taidzu i beye. fucihi i eme i nirugan de maktara gisun arahabi. yong lo i fonde da dzang jen ging ni bithe be kimcime acabufi folohobi.. ere gemu gurun be neihe wesihun forgon de fan i tacihiyan be iletuleme temgetulehengge.. (++)hūwangdi i gosin ginggun hiyoošun fulehun umesi lakcafi. tang gurun. ming gurun i ilan han. tumen ubu de. emu ubu hono duibuleci ojorongge waka.. (++)ejen i bithe be arafi wasimbure ohode. geren abka de jerkišeme. gubci bade tusa ombi.. bairengge. (++)hūwangdi fucihi jorin be gūnime.

(++)cohome han i araha sioi bithe be bufi. ging ni uju de sindabufi. mentuhun ulhirakū urse de neileme tuwabume. tumen aniya de tutabureo.. uttu ohode genggiyen šun (++)ejen i bithe de ele eldefi. gosingga tugi

页下二

(++)enduringge kesi i sasa enteheme ombi.. erei jalin wesimbure bithe arafi gingguleme wesimbuhe.. (++)hese be baimbi seme elhe taifin i orin juweci aniya. jakūn biyai juwan ninggun de wesimbuhe. ineku biyai juwan jakūn de (++)hese. dorolon i jurgan kooli ba getukeleme (+)baicafi. kimcime gisurefi wesimbu sehe.. erebe gingguleme dahafi. ineku biyai juwan uyun de jurgan de isinjihabi.. amban meni gisurehengge hošoi elgiyen ci wang fuciowan sei wesimbuhe bithede. ši i tacihiyan. dulimbai gurun de ulafi.. juwe mingga aniya hamika.. tang gurun sung gurun i mukdeke fon i getukeleme tucibuhe. saišame maktahangge. fucihi tacihiyan be teile badarambume selgiyeki. sehengge waka. cohome ede tumen jaka be hūwašabuki sehengge.. (++)hūwangdi. sure genggiyen ulhisu mergen banitai hesebuhe bime. amba erdemu. ferguwecuke gung. elbehe aliha de teherehebi.. (++) tumen baita be icihiyaha šolo de ninggun ging be sithūfi kimcime. geren suduri be kamcifi tuwame. geren dzy. tanggu boo. enduri ging. bei abdaha i bithe be seme yamji cimari kiceme sibkime. šumin

页上三

gūnin be tucibuhekūngge akū. jakan (++)cohome amba gosin be selgiyeme g'anjur ging be dasame folobufi. aisi tusa be badaramburengge dergi de oci. (+++)tai hūwang taiheo. (+++) hūwang taiheo i tumen sei mohon akū hūturi be enteheme okini. fejergi de oci duin mederi i hafan irgen be tumen tumen aniya de isitala ojoro fengšen be bahakini sehengge.. julgei tang gurun i taidzung. gebungge hūwašan de hese wasimbufi ninggun tanggū yohi funcere ging ni bithe be ubaliyambufi cohome sioi arahabi.. ming gurun i taidzu i beye. fucihi i eme i nirugan de maktara gisun arahabi.. yung lo i fonde. da dzang jen ging ni bithe be kimcime acabufi folohobi.. ere gemu gurun be neihe wesihun forgon de. fan i tacihiyan be iletuleme temgetulehengge.. (++)hūwangdi i gosin ginggun hiyoošun fulehun umesi lakcafi. tang gurun.ming gurun i ilan han. tumen ubu de. emu ubu hono duibuleci ojorongge waka.. bairengge. (++)hūwangdi fucihi jorin be gūnime. (++)cohome han i arhan sioi bithe ba bufi. ging ni uju de sindabufi. mentuhun

页下三

ulhirakū urse de neileme tuwabume. tumen aniya de tutabureo sehebi.. amban be tuwaci. ši i tacihiyan i geren bithe. dzang ging de jalukabi.. udu tacihiyan de. iletu somishūn ilgabuha. doro de banin arbun i encu ba bicibe. terei gūnin be kimcici. tumen jaka de tusa arame. ergengge be wembume yarhūdara de bi.. jalan jalan i di wang se kemuni badarambume selgiyeme. ememungge ubaliyambure folobure jakade. tuttu tacihiyan lakcahakūbi.. jai doroi tacin be algimbume. wesihun kooli be badarambure de. urunakū beye bithe banjibume arafi. debtelin i uju de sindara ohode. teni enduri niyalama gingguleme dahame. goroki hancikingge harhašame tuwambi.. baicaci. tang gurun i taidzung ni jen guwan i orin juweci aniya. hūwašan yuwan juwang se ninggun tanggū susai nadan yohi fan i ging be ubaliyambume wajiha manggi. han i beye. san dzang šeng giyoo sioi bithe arafi wehe de foloro jakade. tetele tutahabi.. ming guron i taidzu i beye i banjibume araha bithei dolo fucihi i eme be maktaha bithe. jai sin ging sioi.

页上四

liyan hūwa pusa. hūwa dzang ši giyai i jergi maktame araha bithe bi.. ming gurun i cengdzu. da dzang jen ging be kimcime acabufi folohobi. dzang ging be maktaha bithe. jai jeng dzung da giyoo miyoo ging. sy bu ging. hūwa yan ging. jen ši ming ging ni jergi sioi bithe be gemu ging ni uju de arafi dzang ging de dosimbuhabi.. geli baicaci. tang gurun i hiyan dzung sin di guwan ging sioi bithe arahabi.. sung gurun i taidzung ni beye miyoo giyo ji sere bithe sunja debtelin banjibume arahabi.. jen dzung. ši diyan ioi ji sere bithe emu yohi arahabi.. erebe gemu fucihi miyoo de asarafi mohan akū ulahabi. gingguleme gūnici. (++) hūwangdi i gung. elbehe aliha de teherehe. doro abka niyalma de hafunaha. šumin be sibkime narhūn be kimcime. giyan i somishūn babe getukelehekūngge akū. jiderengge be same. dulekengge be ejeme. kooli i narhūn babe kimcihakūngge akū. (++) enduringge tacin šumin narhūn. (++) abkai bithe fujurungga yangsangga.. yargiyan i nenehe jalan i di wang sei tumen de emgeri duibuleci ojorongge waka.. jakan. abka. na i banjibure de amuran

页下四

mujilen de acabume. enduringge niyalmai hiyoošun de ilinara gūnin be badarambume. dergi de oci. (+++)juwe gung. hūturi be bahakini fejergi de oci. tumen irgen. kesi be alikini seme g'ajur ging folofi mederi dorgide tutabure jalin (++)cohome hese wasimbuhabi.. damu ši tacihiyan be ulhirengge mangga. fan i ging be selgiyerengge tuktan be dahame. urunakū (++)abkai gisun i saišame maktara ohode. teni šun biyai gese gehun iletu ombi.. uttu be dahame. wang sei baime wesimbuhe songkoi (++)ejen i beye. sioi bithe arafi. ging ni uju de sindafi. gu i dobton. boobai bithe de. (++)ferguwecuke elden be eldembume. abkai fejerigi de tuwabume selgiyefi. mohon akū enteheme tutabureo.. uttu ohode yargiyan i (++)

taifin forgon i wesihun baita. (++)enduringge jalan i amba kooli ombi.. amban meni cisui gamara ba waka ofi. gingguleme wesimbuhe.. (++)hese be baimbi.. dorolon i jurgan i aliha amban. amban jaisan..

页上五

aliha amban. amban ša ceng. hashū ergi ashan i amban. amban esingge.. ambarame giyangnara hafan hashū ergi ashan i amban. bithei yamun i ashan i bithei da kamciha. amban yang jeng jung.. ici ergi ashan amban juwe jergi nonggiha. amban sahai.. ambarame giyangnara hafan. ici ergi ashan i amban. bithei yamun i ashan i bithei da kamciha. amban cen ting geng.. dzy ji cing li sy i icihiyara hafan. amban ho bing. aisilakū hafan juwe jergi nonggiha.. amban cangdzai.. aisilakū hafan. amban sangge. aisilakū hafan emu jergi nonggiha. amban sainda.. aisilakū hafan. amban g'u ši lung. aisilakū hafan. amban sioo yung dzoo ejeku hafan. amban wang ging cen.. ejeku hafan emu jergi nonggiha. amban fiyanggū. ejekū hafan. amban sioi žin fung elhe taifin i orin juweci aniya. uyun biyai ice de wesimbuhe. ineku biyai ice duin de

页下五

(++) hese.gisurenhe songkoi obu sehe..

页上六

职名

hesei niyeceme folo sehe g'anjur ging be alifi tuwame weilebuhengge. hošoi elgiyen cin wang fuciowan. tuwame weilehe hafan. tanggūt bithe tacibure ilhi hafan amban arbithū. dorgi yamun i adaha bithei da amban šulu. dorolon i k'u yamun i doron jafaha gisurere hafan amban asitan. beidere k'u yamun i doron jafaha gisurere hafan amban hešeo. uheri be baicara yamun i baicame tuwara hafan amban sederi. baicame tuwara hafan amban mase. baicame tuwara hafan amban saimbu. beidere jurgan i icihiyara hafan amban unca. weilere jurgan i icihiyara hafan amban liosiyang. hafan i jurgan i aisilakū hafan amban anggai. coohai jurgan i aisilakū hafan amban ma coo dzan. guwang šan ku i aisilakū hafan amban sutai. aisilakū hafan amban decengge. ejeku hafan amban yungfu. ejeku hafan tunggitu. hafan i jurgan i bithesi amban beibooju. dorolon i jurgan i bithesi amban fulu. coohai jurgan i bithesi amban girsai. beidere jurgan i bithesi amban elge. bithesi amban sultu.

页上一

bithesi amban tanggai. weilere jurgan i bithesi amban cabuhu. uheri be baicara yamun i bithesi amban nengge. bithesi amban walda. bithesi amban lioju. bithesi amban liosy. bithesi amban lio i yuwan. boigon i k'u yamun i bithesi amban hingtu. dorolon i k'u yamun i bithesi amban wahūndai. beidere k'u i yamun i bithesi amban tengge. acabume dasaha lamasa. janggiya kūtuktu. da lama wangšuk jimba gelung. da lama lobdzang baljur gelung. demci lobdzang namjal gelung. donrub rabdan ramjamba. tsulcim dzangbu ramjamba. damba serji gelung. elhe taifin i gūsin uyuci aniya. duin biyai sain inenggi folome šanggabuha.

页下一

ging ni hergen be tuwame acabume dasatahangge. ging hecen i lama bandi be uheri kadalara jasak i da lama mergen corji. ging hecen i lama bandi be uheri kadalara jasak i da lama bime tanggūt bithe be alifi tacibure sonom corji. tanggūt bithei ilhi tacibure hafan bime duici jergi funglu jedere amban siteo. ging ni hergen be acabuhangge. gendun darji gelung. lobdzang balji gelung. sonom rincen gelung. lobdzang lonrub gelung. awang sengge gelung. lobdzang gungge gelung. lobdzang baljur gelung. tsulcim dzangbu gelung. damba rasi gelung. lobdzang sirab gelung. samdan rincen gelung. jimba baljur gelung. lobdzang coijal gelung. rinjen sonom gelung. tsulcim balbar gelung.

页上一

tsulcim yondan gelung. tsulcim rasi gelung gelek rincen gelung. rasi rincen gelung. awang jimba gelung. damba rabdan gelung. awang jinba gelung. dzangbu tsulcim gelung. lobdzang tsoomba gelung. yondan rincen gelung. punsuk rincen gelung. lobdzang dandir gelung. jimba sonom gelung. yeši baljur gelung. coimpel dzangbu gelung. rasi darja gelung. sonom jiyamsan gelung. coimpel dzangbu gelung. lobdzang darji gelung. dzangbu jiyalsan gelung. lobdzang nima gelung. sonom dzunrui gelung. rasi dzangbu gelung. dzunrui rincen gelung. lobdzang parlai gelung. tanggūt bithei tacikūi dorji.

页下一

sio mulu be gingguleme acabuha hafan. dorgi yamun i adaha bithei da ilan jergi nonggiha amban dandai. dorgi yamun i adaha bithei da. ilaci jergi funglu jedere. juwe jergi nonggiha. amban bairi. dorgi yamun i adaha bithei da. ilaci jergi funglu jedere ninggun jergi nonggiha amban unggin. tanggūt bithei sioi mulu be ubaliyambume araha hafan. tanggūt bithei ilhi tacibure hafan. duici jergi funglu jedere. amban siteo. nikan bithei mulu be ubaliyambuha hafan. dorgi yamun i juwan wen jungšu. amban usibu. dorgi yamun i juwan wen jungšu.

amban dengdei. monggo bithei sioi mulu be ubaliyambuha hafan. dorgi yamun i banši jungšu. juwe jergi nonggifi. ningguci jergi funglu jedere amban lamjang. dorgi yamun i banši jungšu. emu jergi nonggifi. ningguci jergi funglu jedere amban hegeo. manju bithe be gingguleme araha hafan. dorgi yamun i banši jungšu. duin jergi nonggifi. sunjaci jergi funglu

页上一

jedere amban ibari. dorgi yamun i juwan wen jungšu. amban dzangšeo. dorgi yamun i juwan wen jungšu. amban cambu. monggo bithe be gingguleme araha hafan. dorgi yamun i banši jungšu. amban šookeo. nikan bithe be gingguleme araha hafan. dorgi yamun i banši jungšu. emu jergi nonggiha. amban tsoo jan gi. dorgi yamun i bansi jungšu. amban wang ki o. tanggūt bithe be gingguleme araha lama. lobdzang lurub gelung. lobdzang bailji gelung. sonom rinca gelung.

页下一

g'anjur ging be alifi tuwame weilebuhengge. hošoi elgiyen cin wang amban fuciowan. tuwame weilehe hafan. dorgi yamun i adaha bithei da bime jai jergi funglu jedere. duin jergi nonggiha. amban uladai. dzung žin fu yamun i ici ergi sy i doron jafaha icihiyara hafan bime emu jergi nonggiha amban gioroi šombai. icihiyara hafan bime emu jergi nonggiha. amban gioroi lilima. weilere k'u yamun i doron jafaha gisurere hafan bime juwe jergi nonggiha amban yacina. uheri be baicara yamun i baicame tuwara hafan bime juwe jergi nonggiha amban ilaka. baicame tuwara hafan bime ilan jergi nonggiha. amban genggei. coohai jurgan i icihiyara hafan amban tubasihi. dorgi yamun i juwan wen jungšu emu jergi nonggiha amban hūwase. dzung žin fu yamun i ningguci jergi bithesi emu jergi nonggiha amban huwenje. nadaci jergi bithesi juwe jergi

页上一

nonggiha amban cangboo. uheri be baicara yamun i nadaci jergi bithesi juwe jergi nonggiha. amban wamida. bithesi amban nayantai. coohai jurgan i nadaci jergi bithesi juwe jergi nonggiha amban ulan.

页下一

梵文尊名检索

Index of Sanskrit Names

Cf= 参见

藏文尊名检索

Index of Tibetan Names

Cf= 参见

（一）藏文尊名

མ

ཙ

ཚ

ཟ

འ

ཡ

ར

ཤ

ས

ཧ

（二）藏文尊名转写

汉文尊名检索

Index of Chinese Names

G

H

J

N

P

R

S

T

W

X

Y

Z

蒙古文尊名检索

Index of Mogalian Names

Cf= 参见

满文尊名检索

Index of Manchu Names

Cf= 参见

图书在版编目（CIP）数据

尊像集成：清康熙北京版藏文《甘珠尔》初印本插图 / 民族文化宫图书馆版本提供；杨鸿蛟，魏文导读 . -- 北京：中国藏学出版社，2024. 9. --（藏传佛教图像学丛书）. -- ISBN 978-7-5211-0538-4

Ⅰ. B941

中国国家版本馆 CIP 数据核字第 2024GR8904 号

尊像集成：清康熙北京版藏文《甘珠尔》初印本插图 · 藏传佛教图像学丛书

民族文化宫图书馆版本提供

责任编辑 张荣德
装帧设计 翟跃飞
责任印制 马建军
制　　版 海龙视觉
出版发行 中国藏学出版社
社　　址 北京市朝阳区北四环东路 131 号
印　　刷 北京隆昌伟业印刷有限公司
开　　本 787 毫米 × 1194 毫米　1/16
图　　幅 243 幅
印　　张 22.75
字　　数 250 千字
版　　次 2024 年 9 月第 1 版
印　　次 2024 年 9 月第 1 次印刷
书　　号 ISBN 978-7-5211-0538-4
印　　数 3000 册
定　　价 138.00 元

图书如有质量问题，请与本社联系

E-mail: dfhw@zzcb.com 电话: 010-64892902